Intellectuals in the public sphere in Britain and Norway after World War II

JAN EIVIND MYHRE (ed.)

Unipub 2008

© Unipub 2008

ISBN 978-82-7477-291-5

Contact info Unipub:
T: + 47 22 85 33 00
F: + 47 22 85 30 39
E-mail: post@unipub.no
www.unipub.no

Publisher: Oslo Academic Press, Unipub Norway
Printed in Norway: AIT e-dit AS, Oslo 2008

All rights reserved. No part of this publication may be reproduced or transmitted, in any form or by any means, without permission.

Series preface

ISSUES IN CONTEMPORARY HISTORY is a series of publications from the Forum for Contemporary History (FCH) at the University of Oslo, whose main focus is the study of changes in political culture as a means towards understanding broader social transformations in the post-World War II period. Our aim is to identify and analyse specific features and patterns of change in the field of consumer culture, the public sphere, feminism, collective social movements, the welfare state, and foreign and security policies in Scandinavian and other Western societies during the last three decades of the 20th century.

The essays in this volume are revised versions of papers given at an English-Norwegian workshop in Oxford 6 May, 2006. The exception is the first essay, which is included in the anthology because the editor felt the need for an overarching introduction on intellectuals in Britain and Norway after World War II.

The organizers were Jose Harris on behalf of the Modern European History Research Centre at the University of Oxford and Jan Eivind Myhre from the FCH. We would like to thank the organisers as well as all participants and helpful administrators on both side of the North Sea.

Even Lange and Helge Pharo

Contents

Introduction: Intellectuals in the public sphere
Jan Eivind Myhre 7

Professionalism and populism in British intellectual
life since 1945
Brian Harrison 35

On the expert system of popular journalism
Martin Eide 79

The intellectuals' ideal: British views of Scandinavia
in the 1950s and 1960s
Glen O'Hara 91

Norwegian academics as public intellectuals after
World War II
Ragnvald Kalleberg 123

Equality or meritocracy?
Ben Jackson 155

Academics as intellectuals: Studying Norwegian
academics and intellectuals in the public sphere
Jan Eivind Myhre 183

Contributors 209

Introduction: Intellectuals in the public sphere

Jan Eivind Myhre

Examples from Britain and Norway

Writing about intellectuals is not like writing about, say, professionals or certain occupations. Though value judgements may certainly occur when writing academically about medical doctors or craftsmen, with intellectuals, value judgments often seem to be at the fore; for while doctors and plumbers are necessary specimens in society, intellectuals, according to quite a few writers, are not. They are public commentators characterized by superficial and sloppy thinking (according to Steve Fuller), or they are authors harbouring questionable motives and despicable personal traits (in the words of Paul Johnson).[1] These two men, like many others, seem to select people whom they dislike in the public sphere, and name them intellectuals; neither is this practice uncommon in Norway. To Nils-Fredrik Nielsen, celebrities with predictably leftist political viewpoints, even without any identifiable intellectual content, were the typical intellectuals.[2] But even when one is more detached about intellectuals, there is astonishing disagreement as to whom we ought to call intellectuals, both *in* the past and the present, and *about* the past and the present.

---

[1] S. Fuller, *The intellectual*, Cambridge 2005; P. Johnson, *Intellectuals*, New York 1990 (1988).
[2] N.-F. Nielsen, 'Hva er galt med de intellektuelle?', *Aftenposten* 23 December 2001.

The usual approach to studying intellectuals, however, is more open, both in Britain and Norway. Stefan Collini's recent monumental study of intellectuals in Britain mainly looks at the uses of the term and the attitudes towards intellectuals, and a major point is the widespread denial that such people exist, especially among people most likely to be called intellectuals.[3] The British and Norwegian contributors to the present volume have a more pragmatic attitude towards defining intellectuals (*intellektuelle*), in that they write about people presenting reasoned thought in public. For example, such people may, in Benjamin Jackson's words, be 'intellectually inclined politicians' or 'politically inclined intellectuals', who participated in the British debate on the political left about the concept and content of equality.

However, the examples above of negative attitudes to intellectuals do not represent all attitudes. The Norwegian liberal daily newspaper *Dagbladet* in January 2005 presented whom they considered to be the ten most prominent intellectuals in the country. An intellectual in this case was a person to admire and listen to, underscored by the fact that quite a few of the ten were regular contributors to the paper itself.[4] One of the ten, the Polish emigré and scholar of cultural studies, Nina Witoszek, was shocked by the low standing of intellectuals in Norway.[5] But who thinks lowly of intellectuals? Not Witoszek, evidently, and surely not many of the people who are often thought of as intellectuals. A recent survey, however, has demonstrated that a large portion of the educated Norwegian middle class lends the word 'intellectual' rather negative associations.[6] Britain seems to be no different in this respect. *Denying* being classified as an intellectual, Stefan Collini has shown, is a persistent trait, not only among British intellectuals, but also among their counterparts in many other countries, with the possible exception of France.[7]

---

[3] S. Collini, *Absent Minds. Intellectuals in Britain* (Oxford 2006).
[4] *Dagbladet*, January 2005
[5] *Aftenposten*, 25 August 2002
[6] O. Skarpenes, 'Den "legitime kulturens" moralske forankring', *Tidsskrift for samfunnsforskning*, 4, 2007.
[7] Collini, *Absent Minds*.

In this article, I shall attempt to approach the phenomenon of intellectuals analytically and empirically, emphasizing Britain and Norway. Initially, the two countries may seem too different to warrant a comparison, as we would be pitting a large, central (although sometimes insular) European country with a wide-ranging political, economic and cultural influence against a small country on Europe's outskirts, peripheral at best in terms of historical influence. No wonder the question of *size* may prove an element in the analysis. However, these two countries have traipsed a similar and almost parallel road to modern societies, Britain usually (but not always) a little ahead in time. Both countries possessed liberal societies at a very early date. Britain was the model for the evolution of a public sphere in the eighteenth century. The Danish-Norwegian monarchy showed tendencies in that direction in the last half century before Norwegian (semi-) independence in 1814. The historian Jens Arup Seip has coined the phrase 'absolutism governed by public opinion' to characterize the vision of some contemporary intellectuals.[8] In addition, both Britain and Norway have enjoyed nearly uninterrupted democracy and unusually extensive freedom of expression for the past two hundred years.

Over the past two hundred years, influence has flowed mainly north-eastwards, from Britain to Norway, resulting in British politics, culture and scholarship being much admired in Norway. However, German, French, American and Soviet influences have at times also bequeathed important legacies for Norwegian culture. That said, less attention has been paid to influences at times taking the opposite direction, from Norway to Britain. This has been the case with some literature, especially Ibsen, and with the politics of 1905 and of Nansen in the 1920s. Here, however, we shall look into the admiration of British intellectuals for the Scandinavian welfare state, particularly in the 1960s. Although their attention was mainly on Sweden, as Glen O'Hara's essay in this volume shows, Norway and Denmark also received their share of positive recognition.

---

[8] J. A. Seip, *Teorien om det opinionsstyrte enevelde* (Oslo 1958).

Who are the intellectuals?

Who, then, in the Norwegian or British tradition, are the intellectuals? Norwegian dictionaries or encyclopaedias, old or new, are very short on this point. Intellectuals are people engaged in intellectual work, defined as work of the mind or spiritual work (*åndelig arbeid*)[9]. This is sometimes specified as 'writers and researchers (scholars, *forskere*), people with high theoretical education'.[10] The entry in the British Wikipedia, which in this case seems trustworthy, opens with the following definition: 'An intellectual is one who tries to use his or her intellect to work, study, reflect, speculate on, or ask and answer questions with regard to a variety of different ideas.'[11] Wikipedia goes on to distinguish between three meanings of the term: the first corresponds to the Norwegian definition above; the second refers to the educated occupations, whether professors, lawyers or engineers; the third points to people speaking publicly based on cultural authority often stemming from literary or other humanist studies about many social matters beyond their field of authority.

It is mainly within this third meaning – undoubtedly the most common – that the term intellectual has acquired a mixed reputation, as the quotations above show. In English unfavourable uses of the term may even be said to have been dominant up to the middle of the twentieth century, which may account for why some of the obvious candidates for the label, such as Georg Orwell or Bertrand Russell, often refute it.[12] A pejorative meaning of the word 'intellectual' is prevalent in a number of countries, such as Germany, Russia, the Netherlands, Hungary or the Czech Republic. The term sometimes has ironic connotations, associations with a condescending attitude towards others, or may signal that such a person is cut of from the real world.[13] Sweden and Norway have, respectively, the parallel concepts of the *tyckare* or *synser*, denoting a person who has views voiced in public

---

[9] *Tanums store rettskrivningsordbok*, Oslo 2005. The Norwegian term *åndelig* is somewhat less otherworldly than the English word spiritual.
[10] *Store norske leksikon*, vol. 7, 1997.
[11] http://www.wikipedia.org/wiki/intellectual
[12] Collini, *Absent Minds;* R.. Williams, 'Intellectual', *Keywords* (London 1988 (1976)).
[13] Collini, *Absent Minds*, p. 205.

about everything.¹⁴ Such negativity may also stem from a rejection of cultural authority, from political disagreements or from a rejection of an implied social superiority.

Who did *Dagbladet* pick in 2005 as the ten most important intellectuals in Norway? Six were university academics in the fields of philosophy, sociology and social anthropology. There was one philosopher/writer, one newspaper editor, one lawyer (solicitor), and one writer (mainly novelist). Only the editor did not have a higher university degree. The top ten were unequivocally academic (see my essay later in the volume). In the 2005 Global Intellectuals Poll, compiled by *Prospect Magazine* in the UK, seven of the top ten were world-class scholars, while the remaining three were also university educated. These ten are in this respect fairly representative of the 100 names on the list.¹⁵ The names on both lists not only have an academic reputation, but also other interesting characteristics: very few are scientists (none of the Norwegian ten); they speak on a variety of matters and not only as experts; many of them seem to be relatively independent, at least in that they seldom serve organized interests; most definitely possess cultural authority. Other characteristics are more open to discussion. Are the intellectuals in any sense a social group, except for the fact they have been lumped together with a common designation? Do they speak top-down, with self-appointed social authority? Do they take any special political position? Has the role of intellectuals changed over time and in what respects? These themes will be dealt with below. Only one trait seems to be wholly common to Norwegian, British and world intellectuals, one which fascinatingly deviates from the simplest and most general of the definitions of an intellectual. The intellectual is – and was – a public person, needing a public sphere.

---

[14] A *synser* is derived from *synes*, to think or mean. In English, something like 'I think that...'
[15] http:/en.wikipedia.org/wiki/The_2005_Global_Intellectuals_Poll; http://www.infoplease.com/spot/topintellectuals.html

A public voice

The concept of 'the ivory tower' (German *Elfenbeinturm*, Norwegian *elfenbenstårn*) is old, but rather recent as a polemical concept, dating back to when students in the 1960s criticized the remoteness of the role of professors and universities in society.[16] Although many intellectuals are academics, they cannot be ivory-tower professors. I think it is safe to say that one main characteristic of an intellectual is that he or she is a person who has a voice in the public sphere. People who in theory have something to say to the public, but keep their mouth shut, or only communicate with a small circle of colleagues, can hardly, by any definition, be intellectuals. Such people may be academics, scholars or researchers, but not intellectuals. Therefore, the expression *The Public Intellectual* is, of course, a pleonasm, as the editor of a book by that name willingly admits.[17]

The public sphere is not an unambiguous term. It does necessarily, however, refer to a kind of sphere of communication, a common ground or communication market where people can make their views known to other people. Or, put another way, the public sphere is an arena for the creation of the mutual exchange of opinions. The concept of the public sphere and a discussion of its characteristics are intimately connected to at least four elements. First, there is the *size* of the public sphere: is everybody, at least in principle, reached by it? Second, there is the question of *openness*: is there a freedom of expression? Third, is there not one, but *several* public spheres in a society? If so, is there one general public sphere? Lastly, through which communication *channels* does the public sphere work?

'The public' in 'the public sphere' is not necessarily a large audience. At a time when the means of communication were simple, relatively few people played a public role.[18] This was also due to the fact that a majority of the population were denied political rights, like in Britain and Norway

---

[16] M. Schalenberg, 'Geschichte des "Elfenbeinturms". Eine erstaunliche Karriere', *Forschung & Lehre*, 8, 2000, p. 402.
[17] H. Small (ed.), *The Public Intellectual* (Oxford 2002), p. 1.
[18] A. Briggs and P. Burke, *A Social History of the Media From Gutenberg to Internet* (Oxford 2002).

throughout the nineteenth century. However, a certain, although not necessarily extensive, freedom of expression was important for the rise of a group of contemporary commentators. Although freedom of expression was better taken care of in Britain and Norway than in almost all other countries during the nineteenth century, one should not underestimate the helpful role of its restrictions for the rise of intellectuals, since such tend to thrive in opposition and when (mildly) persecuted. A case in point might be the Russian *intelligentsia*, a group between the major occupational and social groups in nineteenth-century Russia (the nobility, the peasantry, the tsarist bureaucracy and the rising urban economic bourgeoisie), and from which oppositional political groups were drawn, such as the *narodniks* (populists).

Although the term 'intellectual' dates from early nineteenth century in Britain[19], widespread use of the word in Europe did not occur until the Dreyfus case in France between 1894 and 1906. Many French men of letters and their foreign peers rushed to Dreyfus' defence.[20] At that time literacy had become widespread in the West, and newspapers reached much of the population. In the sense that most of the population had access to a public sphere, this sphere existed from around the turn of the century 1900.

In the course of the twentieth century, parallel and partly separate public spheres have developed in most Western countries, even in small nation-states like Norway. In one sense this is a contradiction in terms; if something is public, it is in principle public to everybody. In practice however, different people concentrate on different public channels, and so there are sub-spheres. There are several reasons for this: when there are important social and political cleavages, each group tends to establish its own sphere, displaying its own culture. An example that easily comes to mind is the labour movement, which created its own cultural organizations (even sporting ones), had its own press, its own meeting

---

[19] Williams, 'Intellectual'.
[20] B. Hagtvet, *'Hvor gjerne vilde jeg have været I Deres sted...'. Bjørnstjerne Bjørnson, de intellektuelle og Dreyfus-saken* (Oslo 1998); R. Sennett, *The Fall of Public Man* (N. Y. 1977), chapter 10. One ought to mention that many of Dreyfus' public opponents musty be classified as intellectuals.

places, indoors as well as outdoors. In Oslo, for many decades certain districts and parks were regarded as the public sphere of the workers, whereas other spheres where dominated by the bourgeoisie or wider middle classes. In certain areas of the urban centre, regarded as particularly important to civic prowess, prostitutes were forbidden, according to the police ordinances of the late nineteenth century.[21]

While the emergence of public broadcasting in the first half of the twentieth century and the television mainly in the latter half contributed to making *one* large public sphere, in Britain as well as in Norway, in the last decades of the twentieth century one has clearly witnessed a new disintegration into many separate spheres. The reason this time is not mainly political in the narrow sense of the word; rather it is due to the rise of a number of subcultures associated with the emergence of youth culture, the feminist movement, gay and lesbian activism and multicultural societies, where ethnic and religious minorities create their own public spheres. This has been facilitated by the revolution in public media; although the written press still plays a certain role, the flourishing of radio and TV channels and the rise of the internet are of utmost importance. In Norway around 1980 the state radio and television monopoly was broken and at the same time the press ceased to be attached to political parties. This development had taken place earlier in Britain, but the introduction of the Internet occurred fairly simultaneously in the two countries, from the late 1990s onwards.

The main question when we speak of public spheres in the plural, is whether there is one public sphere, *the* public sphere, which takes precedence over the others. I believe most scholars think there is such a general public sphere within one political unit (state) or one language area. One good reason for this is simply that there is only one government, and while its aptness may be discussed in a number of spheres, arenas and sub-cultures, we need one place where all viewpoints, in principle, might meet. In a recent book, an Australian scholar, Alan McKee, argues that the various

---

[21] A. Schiøtz, 'Prostitusjon og samfunn I 1870-årenes Christiania', in J. E. Myhre and J. S. Østberg (eds), *Mennesker i Christiania. Sosialhistorisk søkelys på 1800-tallet* (Oslo 1979).

local public spheres ought to have equal standing (his main examples are black, feminist and youth movements).[22] The idea of one main public sphere, in his eyes, reflects *modern*, Habermasian thinking, which he strongly disapproves of. Such a sphere, he argues, only cares about high politics, and is shaped and dominated by heterosexual white men, in particular academics, whose idea the public sphere was in the first place. One also gets the strong feeling, although he does not say so explicitly, that quite a few of his targets are public intellectuals, of whom quite a few are white, heterosexual, male, middle-class and middle-age. Nevertheless, the element of females is becoming stronger, as is that of gays and lesbians, non-whites and young people. We will return to class shortly.

The character of the public sphere is shaped by the means, or channels, of communication. The sphere has moved from face-to-face meetings at political institutions, marketplaces or salons, via meeting places through the written word – newspapers probably being the most influential – and the ether media of the radio and television, to the internet. Within these broad categories, there are major turning points, such as the invention of the rotation press (*rotasjonspressen*) in the printing business. In the last decades of the nineteenth century, a virtual revolution in the West European postal services was also witnessed.[23] At this time, the majority of the population in the West were also taking on reading and writing. It is thus no coincidence that the breakthrough of the European intellectual occurred in the 1890s, with the Dreyfus scandal.[24] 'I would very much have liked to be in your place', a prominent Norwegian author and intellectual, Bjørnstjerne Bjørnson, wrote to Zola in an open letter published in a Norwegian newspaper and later in *L'Aurore*, in which Zola published his famous 'J'accuse'[25] Bjørnson's role as an intellectual also points to another prerequisite for the rise of the modern intellectual, namely the possibility to be

---

[22] A. McKee, *The Public Sphere* (Cambridge 2005).
[23] See examples in Hagtvet, *'Hvor gjerne...'*, p. 132ff.
[24] See Collini, *Absent Minds*; Sennett, *The Fall of Public Man*.
[25] Hagtvet, *'Hvor gjerne...'*, p. 17; *Verdens Gang* 21 January 1898; *L'Aurore* 19 January 1898.

able to make a living from writing. In Norway, this occurred around 1870, in Britain considerably earlier.

In many respects, the written word has remained the intellectuals' arena par excellence, since their influence largely rests on verbal reasoning and rationality, and is therefore often rather space-demanding. This is why the asserted decline (or even death) of the intellectual is often linked to the rise of television and the tabloid press, discussed below. The concept of the 'mass media' is, by the way, in some respects misleading. The mass media reaches the masses, to be sure, but mainly as individuals, often in isolation.

It would be erroneous to claim that the public sphere and the intellectuals arose simultaneously, and thereby imply that the one created the other. The public sphere was a bourgeois phenomenon which arose in Britain in the eighteenth century. Intellectuals as a discernable group did not emerge until rather later. In that sense the public sphere contributed to their rise. In Denmark-Norway something resembling a public sphere was present in the latter stages of the absolute monarchy, during which for shortish periods of time there was considerable freedom of speech. Although the Constitution of 1814 laid down the principle of freedom of expression, public debates did not begin to flourish until the 1830s. At that time voluntary organizations, newspapers and journals grew more numerous, the Parliament (*Stortinget*) opened its gallery to the public so newspapers could report from its meetings and local government was introduced. The participants in this public sphere were usually well educated, but may be described more as civil servants rather than intellectuals in the sense which we are about to describe.

On the other hand, intellectuals have also been instrumental in upholding the *rules of conduct* in the public sphere, the ideals or principles that were shaping the public sphere in the first place.[26] These ideals are, roughly, three in number, laying out the who, how and what of public debates. First,

---

[26] J. Habermas, *The structural transformation of the public sphere : an inquiry into a category of Bourgeois society* (Cambridge 1989); Norwegian translation *Borgerlig offentlighet* (Oslo 1971); German original 1962; J. van Horn Melton, *The Rise of the Public in Enlightenment Europe* (Cambridge 2001).

everybody is entitled to participate in the exchange of ideas. Second, it is the arguments that count, not who presents them. Finally, everything may in principle be discussed and criticized, even the head of state and religion.

As is immediately evident, these principles raise a number of questions pertaining to democracy, freedom of expression (or freedom of utterance, as one usually puts it in Norwegian: *ytringsfrihet*). Even though everybody is free to speak his or her mind, some are more easily heard than others, for example the ones who own their own newspapers or television stations. Many are prone to listen more carefully to older male professors than younger female students, even when the latter have better argument. And lastly, should there be a limit to freedom of expression, for example vis-à-vis blasphemy and pornography? Intellectuals tend to push this limit as far as possible, both out of conviction and self-interest. After all, they live on 'uttering themselves'. The 16-strong Norwegian governmental commission scrutinizing freedom of expression, which consisted of no less than seven university professors, advised Parliament to include only two principal limits to freedom of utterance: privacy was not to be invaded, and children were to be left alone.[27] The politically pragmatist *Storting*, however, chose to make only minor adjustments to § 100 of the Constitution, and retained restrictions on blasphemy and pornography.[28]

Religion, and thereby blasphemy, have been recurrent issues in public debates generally, and in debates about freedom of expression specifically. In his article in this volume, Brian Harrison lists religion (the decline of religion) as one of the four broad influences acting upon British intellectuals since World War Two, the others being internationalism, professionalism and populism.

---

[27] NOS 1999:27 *Ytringsfrihed bør finde sted*. The commission was chaired by the historian Francis Sejersted.
[28] Since the ban on blasphemy had been out of work for a couple of generation, the decision to keep it must be regarded as a concession to immigrant groups, especially Muslims, who had actually voiced their intention to strengthen the ban.

Universal views

While intellectuals need a public sphere, not everything that appears there is produced by intellectuals. Ordinary journalistic activity, expressions made by politicians and information from e.g. organizations can hardly be called intellectual activities. What then is the intellectuals' contribution to the public sphere?

Journalists often bring to the fore experts commenting on politics, culture or science: these are often academics of various kinds, scholars, researchers and scientists. These are not infrequently referred to as intellectuals, because the term is sometimes taken to mean people doing intellectual work. However, probably few people would contend that supplying an expert commentary within a restricted field makes an intellectual. Since the 1960s the Norwegian Broadcasting Corporation has repeatedly turned to the engineer Erik Tandberg when something new happens in space, whether it be satellites orbiting the earth or people walking on the moon. Tandberg always restricted himself to commenting on the scientific side; this would clearly make him an expert, but no intellectual.

Intellectuals must have opinions or information of general interest to the public. General interest often means politics, but cultural and all other sorts of matters may also come into play here. Although experts talking publicly about a limited field of knowledge within their expertise are not intellectuals, this limit may easily be breached, as one crosses over into matters of general interest; but the information an intellectual conveys must be of consequence to the public. Detailed knowledge can be interesting enough to be broadcasted or printed, but does not necessarily possess any wider societal scope. The role of an intellectual, it is often thought, is to communicate knowledge of wider consequence to the society and the public. To do this, expert knowledge in the sense of detailed, perhaps technical knowledge is not required; rather an ability to connect pieces of knowledge into a wider picture is needed. A concept of society, sometimes perhaps even a theory, are thus called for. The boundaries between detailed expert knowledge and reasoned, overarching viewpoints are not often clear-cut.

An intellectual, then, is in practice – or is commonly regarded as – a person who speaks about a diversity of things in society, sometimes from a discernible overarching point of view, sometimes with no distinguishable leitmotif. The latter inspired the definition, attributed to Sartre, of the intellectual as a person who interferes with things with which he has no business. The role of the intellectual as a social generalist is augmented in a society in which the media demand evermore utterances from people who are already public figures. The fine line between intellectual and celebrity has thus become blurred and easier to cross.

Expert knowledge exists in various fields: in science and technology, law, culture or politics. And such knowledge is often the starting point of intellectuals, whether philosophical, literary, historical, theological or legal. Intellectuals do not however often take science as their point of departure. The intellectual public sphere has largely been an arena for people from the humanities, although the status of the English biologist Richard Dawkins is but one exception disproving the rule. However, his standing as a prominent intellectual rests primarily on his unique capacity to show the relevance of biology to human societies in general. His latest contribution, bringing him international fame, is his critique of religion.[29]

Education

Experts in the public sphere are often academics. Despite their often being experts in narrow scholarly fields, their education and training in reasoning, logic, generalizing etc. often allows them to speak in general terms, thus stretching knowledge from one field into another. Academics are often well oriented in political, social, cultural and even economic affairs through extensive reading, although this certainly does not apply to all of them. In a regular column in the Norwegian business newspaper *Dagens Næringsliv*, a journalist regularly asks business people (nowadays usually well educated) about their reading habits ('what's on your

---

[29] R. Dawkins, *The God Delution* (London 2006).

bedside table?'). The answers do not reveal much cultural capital among business people.

The education of people commonly called intellectuals is often humanistic, literary, historical or social scientific, mainly because these are often trained writers and because the topics in question are often cultural or political. However, with ecology, climate change and evolution becoming major topics of public debate, more intellectuals are nowadays prone to be scientists (Richard Dawkins in Britain, Dag O. Hessen in Norway). But with their philosophical, historically and literary bent, intellectuals have traditionally tended to shy away from the physical world, excluding it from the public debate, due often to their hostile attitude to science. 'Intellectuals, particularly literary intellectuals, are natural Luddites,' C.P. Snow said in 1959.[30] The Norwegian professor of science education Svein Sjøberg, trained in both physics and education, has written about science as liberal education (*naturvitenskap som allmenndannelse*), using the word *dannelse* (breeding) which is best known in its German version, *Bildung*, a term having no exact counterpart in English. Sjøberg's point is that having *Bildung* ought to entail a knowledge of science as well as political and cultural competence. Science ought to be a part of a liberal education.[31]

While many acknowledged intellectuals throughout history have been academically educated, most observers would agree that this is no necessity. A few generations back, when very few people had a higher education, quite a few intellectuals were intellectually self-taught (autodidacts), or 'organic intellectuals', as Antonio Gramsci called them. Quite a few of them were to be found in the labour movement in Britain as well as in Norway, where the tradition for keeping records and writing minutes, in addition to the need for counter expertise to that of the political establishment, produced some eminent amateur scholars, as well as essayists and novelists. A 'complete' Norwegian intellectual like Sigurd Evensmo

---

[30] C. P. Snow, *The Two Cultures* (Cambridge 1993, with an Introduction by Stefan Collini), p. 22.
[31] S. Sjøberg, *Naturvitenskap som allmenndannelse: En kritisk fagdidaktikk* (Oslo 1998). Note that Sjøberg before *dannelse* puts the prefix *allmenn* (common or general).

(1912–1978), novelist, political essayist, journalist, editor, cultural historian, biographer, literature critic, playwright and film expert, had little formal education. Significantly, for his and earlier generations, his intellectual training was in the press and politics.[32]

Novelists, who may also be academics, represent a special brand of intellectuals (see my essay below). Up to the 1870s, in Norway the academic (or university) and the literary sphere were one and the same, before parting. The most famous Norwegian historian of his day, Ernst Sars, thinking of the golden era of Norwegian authors in the last two decades of the nineteenth century spoke of a *poetokrati* (poetocracy). Without a doubt, poets, novelists, playwrights and essayists have played an important role in the Norwegian public sphere also in the first half of the twentieth century (S. Hoel, H. Krogh, A. Øverland). Likewise in Britain with authors like George Orwell and T. S. Eliot, despite their denial of having intellectual status. The opportunity to carve out a career as a writer, sometimes combined with journalism, led to a certain separation of the academic and literary fields. Interestingly, a fair share of the most prominent Norwegian novelists of the second third of the twentieth century would seem to be academically well-versed, not that surprisingly in a highly educated society. There are even academies teaching the writing of fiction.[33]

Insofar as the status of being professionals lent weight to one's authority as an intellectual, authors and publishers in Britain were disadvantaged as they 'did not qualify as professionals, because they lacked the professional person's exclusive status, formal entry qualifications and standardized career pattern', Brian Harrison writes.[34] To some degree this applies to Norway as well, although in the last quarter of the 2000s the publishing business became

---

[32] *Dagbladet* 16 January, 2005.
[33] Examples of academically trained novelists in contemporary Norway are Kjartan Fløgstad, Jan Kjærstad, Helene Uri, Henrik Langeland, the last two even with a doctorate. In Britain it suffices to mention the sisters A. S. Byatt and Margareth Drabble and from an older generation, J. R. R. Tolkien and the critic F.R. Leavis.
[34] See B. Harrisons article in this volume.

inundated with well-educated people, many of whom would qualify as public intellectuals.[35]

The advent of mass higher education, the rise of the social sciences and what we may call the return of an atmosphere of *Sachlichkeit* in the 1960s challenged the influence of what some saw as a poetocracy. Higher education was to be basis of an enlightened public debate. As the young philosopher Gunnar Skirbekk proclaimed in 1968: 'The age of poetocracy is over. The rule of the literary realm (*litteratveldet*) has ended. In the course of the last 10–15 years other groups have taken over. Those are the philosophers and the social scientists.'[36] His thoughts were anticipated already during the war, when the philosopher Arne Næss wrote a book to be read by all new students at the university about the logic of argumentation; its wider aim was to make public debate more rational and enlightened.[37] There ought to be little room in a serious public exchange of words for irrational outbursts or purely emotional contributions, and no room for intellectual bluffers. It must be added that Skirbekk felt no animosity towards novelists in general; his critique was aimed at novelists who played the wrong role, characterized by him as 'uncommitted humanistic chit-chat' (*uforpliktende humanisteri*).[38]

Perversions of the public sphere

Some would claim that bluffers, to the extent that they exist, are a consequence of the modern media, which we shall turn to in a moment. However, much evidence points to the fact that bluff and irrationality have long been endemic to the public sphere, irrespective of whether the instigator was called an intellectual or not. Stefan Collini, on his rather strict scale, counts Colin Wilson's rise to fame

---

[35] Most of them would have a *cand. philol.* title, a degree somewhere between a master's and a doctorate.
[36] Preface to *Er ideologiane døde?* (Oslo 1968). Translations by JEM.
[37] A. Næss, *En del logiske emner* (Oslo 1941 and numerous edition). See also Myhre's essay in this collection.
[38] J. I. Sørbø, 'Filosofiske essay i samtida' in E. B. Johnsen and T. B. Eriksen (eds), *Norsk litteraturhistorie. Sakprosa fra 1750 til 1995. Bind II* (Oslo 1998), p. 270.

as such a phenomenon.[39] The best arguments, according to the criteria of reason, logic and the best available scholarly insights, have not always prevailed. And why should they? Adhering to reason in the very strictest manner can only be rather irrational.

Many intellectuals themselves, however, have seen it as their task not only to argue best possible about important societal issues, but also to lay the foundations for a public sphere based on reason, democracy and humanism. This may be regarded as Jürgen Habermas' project from the very beginning. His classic from 1962 was translated relatively early into Norwegian (1971), long before a French or English (1989) version appeared.[40] Some of his Norwegian followers have since worked on questions pertaining to the public sphere, as in Kalleberg's contribution to this volume.

It is Kalleberg's fellow sociologist/anthropologist Ottar Brox who has taken upon himself to write a rather normative, but insightful pamphlet, *Our Collective Folly*, about the conditions of the public debate in Norway. Its subtitle is 'How the Norwegian Public Discussion gets Perverted'.[41] Brox points out a number of perverting mechanisms, such as the tendency to stage discussions like court cases and the related inclination to highlight disagreement and suppress the doxic agreement often present. There is also frequently a propensity for the debaters' self-presentation to overshadow their subject matter, thereby pulling the argument off the track and individualizing problems which ought to be collective. This heightens the tendency to use *ad hominem* arguments.

Participants in public debates, but in particular journalists conveying them, have a habit of bunching arguments which do not belong together. If you are clearly in favour of, say, an arrangement, you must not voice expostulation, because this alone will be noted. Certain terms are used quite misleadingly because of their emotional or ambiguous content. One such word in Norwegian is *valgfrihet* (freedom of choice), not because *valg* (choice) may also mean election, but because

---

[39] Collini, *Absent Minds*, pp. 415–422.
[40] C. Calhoun (ed.), *Habermas and the Public Sphere* (Cambridge, Mass. 1992).
[41] O. Brox, *Vår kollektive dårskap. Hvordan perverteres den norske offentlige samtalen?* (Oslo 2003). Also presented in Myhre's article.

its ideological content, that of economic liberalism, is half hidden. Another ambiguous word is *offentlig* (public) which may mean belonging to the state or municipality, but also something not belonging to the private sphere, like the family. The two are often confused in the public (*sic*) sphere.[42]

There is also a tendency for public debates to concentrate on individual personages and unusual cases to the detriment of general experience and questions that are about principles. One may thus easily lose sight of the more important questions which are at stake. Good intentions are emphasized over the possibility of good outcomes, because proponents of the former appear to be nicer people than proponents of the latter, who risk only appearing realistic or even cynical. Related to this problem is the tendency to favour what is aesthetically appealing, whether we mean physical appearance or models of society.

Mentioning negative aspects of the workings of the public sphere reminds us that is has often been the task of intellectuals, like Brox in Norway and Collini in Britain, not only to fill the sphere with utterances, but also to reflect on how it works.[43]

Independence

One of the reasons that intellectuals are supposed to be worth listening to is their independence, their not being tied to material or organized interests. That is why so many classic intellectuals were simply (freelance) writers, like Sartre. Karl Mannheim spoke of 'Freischwebende Intellektuelle'[44]. The Russian intelligentsia was not tied to any of the major estates; their only power was their pen.

Linked to the concept of the independent intellectual is the notion of the intellectual as 'outsider', the romantic

---

[42] *Dagbladet* 31 March 2003 told its readers that the government wants to publish the private life of judges on the internet ('*Dommernes privatliv legges ut på nett*'), which simply meant that their organisational and economic affiliations should be made public for the purposes of impartiality, not that their family life should be made public, as the title suggests.
[43] Brox, *Vår kollektive dårskap*; Collini, *Absent Minds*.
[44] Collini, *Absent Minds*, p. 62.

air of which could at least in part explain the popularity of Colin Wilson's book by that name in the mid-fifties[45]. Quite a few novelists and other writers have been quite independent in the sense of having no material interests or formal associations. The writers of the twentieth century were seldom under the wings of a Maecenas. They usually had commitments, often very serious ones, of various kinds, but these were normally shouldered voluntarily.

One is even inclined to think that independence is a condition for being called an intellectual. Quite a few journalists have often been regarded as intellectuals and there is certainly a tradition for independent journalism, in Britain and Norway. However, for a century up to around 1980 most of the Norwegian press was heavily partisan, intimately tied to a political party or other ideological groups, like trade unions, the temperance movement, or organizations of a religious or cultural kind. Around 1980, however, newspapers steadily became more independent of political parties. As far as I can see, there were two interrelated reasons for this. Firstly, in order to survive financially, the papers had to orientate themselves more towards the market, especially as the parties could no longer afford to support them. Secondly, the professionalization of journalism, on a par with other professions, required that journalists behave independently. The question is, of course, whether relating oneself to the market is just another kind of dependency. Too much dependence may jeopardize one's standing as an intellectual.

Writing about Norway's best-selling newspaper, *VG*, Martin Eide in an article in this volume points out how modern popular journalism arose as a system meant to be independent, also of external experts and intellectuals, who were profoundly challenged. *VG*, a semi-tabloid, created an expert system of its own, especially in legal and technological matters. An ideology of journalism was created, within which the role of journalists was to act as the independent party in a society consisting of two other party, those in power and ordinary people; it was the interests of the man in the street the newspaper was to serve. This development may also be viewed as an illustration of Harrison's point about populism

---

[45] Collini, *Absent Minds*, p. 413.

influencing intellectuals. Populism is, among other things, a reaction to cultural authority.

Cultural authority and elitism

An intellectual is often regarded as a person who writes and speaks with authority. Edward Shils has identified an intellectual as a person finding it natural to appear with special authority in questions of the politics of ideas (*idépolitiske spørsmål*).[46] Sometimes such authority is (partly) borrowed from titles or university degrees. Whereas in principle the standing of intellectuals rests with the content of what they write, in practice earlier intellectual achievements create a platform from which they speak or write. Whatever the source of their status, the message from intellectuals is commonly interpreted as coming from above, if not quite *ex cathedra*.

There are a number of attitudes and terms stemming from this authority. 'Highbrow' is originally an American term, imported to Britain in the early twentieth century and then to other European countries, including Norway. A contemporary Norwegian dictionary translates it with *intellektuell* or *åndssnobb* (culture snob), and adds that both terms are used pejoratively.[47] Sometimes intellectuals are associated with what Norwegians call *finkultur* (high culture, e.g. classical music etc.), also a word with an elitist and therefore bad ring. The dominant Norwegian culture at the turn of the century, one media scholar holds, is 'middlebrow culture', a fact often overlooked in the debate about high and popular culture.[48]

An air of authority on the part of intellectuals is not infrequently met with accusations of arrogance, condescension and snobbery. It has proven particularly dangerous to question the quality of bestsellers. Two examples from Norway in 2007 illustrate this well, as Myhre shows in his article. When a reviewer characterized a best-selling novel as middlebrow literature of limited literary value, he was immediately

---

[46] According to Hagtvet, '*Hvor gjerne...*', p. 40.
[47] W. Kirkeby, *English-Norwegian Dictionary*, Universitetsforlaget, Oslo 1995.
[48] E. Ytreberg, 'Norge: mektig middelklassekultur', *Samtiden*.

accused of arrogance.⁴⁹ A mass producer of popular paperback novels (*kiosklitteratur*) was denied membership of the Norwegian Authors' Union (*Den norske forfatterforening*) for lacking literary quality, a decision widely criticized in the media.⁵⁰ The reaction was partly in defence of popular taste, but just as much against what is perceived as the intellectual's *Besserwisser* attitude, judging matters of taste. British examples abound: A. S. Byatt's critical article, *Harry Potter and the Childish Adult*, about J. K. Rowling's books, was berated for being intellectually and culturally snobbish.⁵¹

Intellectuals, their critics would say, themselves erect the pedestals or positions of authority from which they speak and are a self-appointed elite of the mind: patronizing, pretentious and self-important.⁵² They have a number of tricks through which they distance themselves from the population at large, such as 'intellectualizing', making simple things difficult or complicated by using exclusive words to exclude the non-intellectual reader, while seemingly addressing a wider audience.

This critique, often populist, also slams time-honoured popular education (*folkeopplysning*), which all political parties use to embrace. After all, the term 'popular education' implies there is somebody who knows and someone who does not (but wants to learn), nowadays conceived as somebody *up there* and somebody *down there*. The populist bent of much of the public sphere from the late twentieth century onwards means that fewer people now put up with being lectured or taught at all, outside of formal education settings.

A social group?

Have intellectuals ever comprised a discernible social group and do they now? This question can be approached three ways. First, by asking whether one can empirically identify intellectuals via external criteria, such as who they are

---

⁴⁹ K.-I. Skjerdingstad on some of Anne B. Ragde's novels. *Dagbladet* 25 August 2007.
⁵⁰ Her name is Frid Ingulstad, the author of about 140 historical novels with a total circulation of several million books.
⁵¹ *New York Times*, 7 July 2003.
⁵² See Collini, *Absent Minds*, 2006, chapter 1.

(gender, age, place of residence) or what they do (occupation, expressions in the public), the Kantian category of *an sich*. Second, by asking whether coherence can be found within a group with a common feeling of being intellectuals (*für sich*). Lastly, is there a group identified by the outside world as intellectuals (a category *für andere*, so to speak).

To classify intellectuals by external sociological variables is to some degree what is attempted in this paper. There is, however, not much agreement as to their characteristics, although they do tend to have higher education, to be male, and to occupy positions in which they write a lot. They express themselves in public, but so do many other people. As to to the third approach, the term 'intellectual' is one that is definitely in use, in Britain, Norway and many other countries. In Norway, people describing intellectuals as a group seem to be vacillating between academic elites, cultural elites and media or entertainment elites, the last of these being a more recent phenomenon. In any case the notion of *elite* carries negative connotations, and all three categories are sometimes lumped together as having elitist viewpoints.

Modern newspapers, freed from the allegiances of party politics, often see themselves as knights of the ordinary man and woman. This has at times in history been the task of many an intellectual. The modern press, however, often treats intellectuals as enemies because they are regarded as part the social elite, and therefore at odds with common people. At times the press even talks about intellectuals as if they were in concerted action, behaving collectively.

Are intellectuals a category *für sich*, behaving in any way collectively? There is no doubt that the intellectuals in the Dreyfus case felt united by a common cause. There are probably other examples associated with important political, social or cultural issues, such as resisting war (e.g. Vietnam) or the threat of climate change. In fact, intellectuals are not infrequently accused of ganging up together. However, intellectuals usually cherish their independent status, not just because originality is an intellectual (and scholarly) value, but because their words will carry more weight if they come from people instructed by no one.

Social position / occupational position

Do intellectuals occupy any specific position in the social structure, for example in terms of class or otherwise? Usually, a person's social position is decided by economic means or by his occupation. Placing an intellectual socially would not be difficult if intellectuals were a distinct class or layer or even profession. It is however, difficult to treat them as such. Although there are definitely people whose activities as intellectuals fill their total working time, an intellectual is usually not seen as a sociological term. It must rather be considered a public social role, used by people of various occupations or professions, some of course far more usual than others, like academic ones.

Lenin contended that the intelligentsia was not a class, just a group, and could obtain influence only by attaching itself to a class, be it the bourgeoisie, the working class or the peasantry. In the twentieth century it would be true to say that most individual intellectuals belong to a large and vague middle class, whose economic circumstances they largely share. If one wants to define a bourgeoisie, a *Bürgertum* or *borgerskap*, intellectuals are to be found in its educated part as opposed to the business side.

Whereas intellectuals are traditionally to be found in the academic world, in the press or as independent authors, since the 1970s, when the tempo of the expansion of the universities slowed, a fairly large intellectual field has emerged in Norway outside of the universities. This field filled an empty space between university scholars and news journalism. As a result of the explosion in university education in the 1960s and 1970s, university graduates filled the ranks of publishing houses, journals, culture bureaucracies, research administration and the growing sector of commissioned research. Some of the cultural hegemony has moved from the university to these milieux.[53] The pattern in not too different from Britain, although this intellectual area between academe and the press is larger in Britain and arose rather earlier. 'Intellectuals in their impact on public life', Harrison writes at the beginning of

---

[53] Ø. Østerud, Maktutredningen og det intellektuelle hegemoniet, *Nytt Norsk Tidsskrift*, 1, 2002.

his paper, 'should be defined broadly to include those in universities who are employed to think, but also those who act as intermediaries between thinkers and the general public: writers, journalists, members of think tanks, and experts on policy'.

Viewpoints

Unless they sided with the working classes, Lenin would probably have regarded the intellectuals as parasites, doing nothing useful (even something harmful) and living off other people's money. Quite a few intellectuals have indeed taken a stand on the side of the working class or other groups in society which they have regarded as disadvantaged, exploited or downtrodden, urgently in need of somebody to rescue them. Throughout the nineteenth and twentieth centuries this means that most intellectuals have leant towards the left, politically and ideologically. 'The ideological divide between Left and Right is all-pervading and overriding,' Collini writes of French intellectuals.[54] That is why they are so despised by an author leaning to the right, like Paul Johnson. This does not mean that there have been no intellectuals on the political right.

On both sides, however, quite a few intellectuals have taken their commitment to ideological extremes and supported various dictatorships. This may, at a first glance, appear strange; one would have thought that the combination of an academic background, a love of freedom, a critical attitude, rationality and a wish to be original and independent, would deter intellectuals from such extremes. Juan Linz suggests that some intellectuals turn to anti-democratic ideologies because democratic societies tend to disappoint with their 'banality of routine political processes', lacking visionary and utopian elements.[55] In other words, democracy was not seen as intellectually challenging enough.

Stefan Collini presents plenty of examples of intellectuals taking leave of their critical faculties when championing a cause. A prominent case is Edward Said, not because

---

[54] Collini, *Absent Minds*, p. 250.
[55] According to Hagtvet, *'Hvor gjerne...'*, p. 34.

the cause he champions is unworthy, siding with the powerless, 'the forgotten and ignored' (thinking specifically of the Palestinians), but because his programme, as an intellectual, is to put criticism before solidarity.[56]

It was against this partisanship that Julien Benda, also in favour of worthy cause, published in 1927 his book on the treason of intellectuals.[57] His ideal was a detached intellectual who saw his task as telling the truth. Most British as well as Norwegian intellectuals, however, have not been detached, but dedicated to one or more causes without dictatorial consequences. Norwegian intellectuals from the late nineteenth century onwards were often champions of the national cause, which in this case meant independence and democracy. The archetypical intellectual between the wars, as well as for a while after World War II, was the so-called 'cultural radical' (*kulturradikaler*), whose leanings were urbane, theoretical, elitist, moralistic and anti-church (but in favour of female priests, as the irony goes).

Although intellectuals often stretch their comments well beyond their original field of knowledge (sometimes regarded as a characteristic of intellectuals), even these comments are usually based on good general qualifications (extensive reading) and well developed abilities for reasoning. There is nevertheless room for bluffers or semi-bluffers. Collini singles out Colin Wilson as one such bluffer[58], or quasi-intellectual. Why was (or is) there room for intellectual bluffers and impostors? In the first place, there is always a good deal of deference, and therefore uncritical attitudes, to intellectuals among certain groups. In the second place, the media likes to make intellectuals out of celebrities and celebrities out of intellectuals.

---

[56] Collini, *Absent Minds*, p. 428, commenting on E. W. Said, *Representations of the Intellectual* (London 1994).
[57] J. Benda, *The Treason of the Intellectuals* (London 2007, originally published 1927). The English translation of the French 'clercs' as 'intellectuals' is disputed. See Roger Kimball's introduction.
[58] Collini, *Absent Minds*, pp. 413ff. One could not call Wilson an impostor on the grounds that he did not deceive people intentionally.

Decline of intellectuals?

Has there been a decline of the intellectual in Britain, Norway or elsewhere in the West in past decades? It is, at least, a favourite pastime of intellectuals to complain about the decline of intellectuals.[59] However, there are good reasons to maintain that intellectuals have an (even) lower standing than they used to, and that they are *relatively* fewer than before in an increasingly crowded public sphere, on which they are totally dependent. Those who think there has been, or will be, a decline, offer three explanations.

Firstly, the specialization of knowledge has contributed. This may also be called professionalization. In particular, scientists stay out of the public eye (the separation of the two cultures remains, although there are exceptions), but also knowledge within law, the social sciences and humanities is often so specialized that even trained intellectuals have problems covering much ground in a trustworthy manner. There is a paradox here: while the specialization of knowledge makes it more difficult to be intellectuals, for the same reason they are more needed than ever. Justification for them lies in the very extreme specialization of modern society. The role of intellectuals is to look beyond narrow expertise and try to grasp the bigger picture.

It is hard to tell which ones are the best equipped for such a task, to take a broad Enlightenment-inspired view of society. It is probably easier for a scientist to acquire some knowledge about society than vice versa. Some humanities or social sciences, like history or sociology, have a reputation for comprehending more broadly than many others.

The second explanation is the rise of celebrity culture. The phenomenon of fame or reputation is of course nothing new.[60] Being a celebrity (Norwegian: *kjendis*)[61] is not the same as being famous or well known, although the media increasingly uses the word that way. It is illustrated by the fact that *kjendis* is a relatively new word, as opposed to *velkjent* (well known), *berømt* (famous) or *beryktet* (notorious). A *kjendis*,

---

[59] J. Habermas in *Morgenbladet* 2–8 June 2006.
[60] L.Braudy, *The Frenzy of Reknown* (Oxford 1986).
[61] *Kjendis* is a Swedish word deriving from *kjenne*, to know. A *kjendis* is somebody known to people.

as this word came to be employed in Sweden and Norway after World War II, is first of all a person who is famous (more or less accidentally) just being in the media spotlight. The media will exploit this position by presenting this person in a number of other settings, preferably in private. The privatization of public personages is a phenomenon which also occurs to people who are justifiably famous for the positions they hold (e.g. the prime minister) or for something they do (writing a bestseller). When these people are exposed extensively (with or without their consent) in areas outside their initial fame, they tend to become celebrities, too.

The cabinet member, the Nobel laureate or even the champion footballer is not by definition a *kjendis* (a celebrity), and neither is the renowned public intellectual. But intellectuals do sometimes cross the border into celebrity status. This, however, may not be the main reason why the role of intellectuals is declining. To many commentators, perhaps most of all intellectuals themselves, they are on the decline because celebrities of all other kinds are taking up too much time, space and attention in the public sphere.

The third, and related, cause of the decline of intellectuals is the change in the structure of the media in general. The tabloidization of much of the press is one aspect, although it is not nearly as new as some would have it. Another aspect is the rise of television, a medium based on pictures. Images do not promote reasoning, and since the intellectuals' performances are based on reasoning, TV is not, to put it mildly, very conducive to enhancing the role of intellectuals. The exception is, of course, when one can make celebrities out of them. Some intellectuals accept the invitation to self-staging (*selviscenesettelse*) inherent to television.[62] It is only fitting that this last aspect comes from the scholar who introduced the concept of the public sphere being the stage of intellectuals; Jürgen Habermas is also one of the most prominent and recognized contemporary intellectuals.

---

[62] J. Habermas in *Morgenbladet* 2–8 June 2006.

Professionalism and populism in British intellectual life since 1945

Brian Harrison

Intellectuals in their impact on public life should be defined broadly to include those in universities who are employed to think, but also those who act as intermediaries between thinkers and the general public: writers, journalists, members of think tanks, and experts on policy. The discussion cannot be confined to people who are self-consciously intellectual by lifestyle, if only because such people have in any case been rare in modern Britain. Among the four broad influences acting upon British intellectuals thus defined after 1945, secularization demands first place, given the prominence of religion in British intellectual life and public debate before 1945 and its marked decline thereafter.

I

The Church of England was in some ways stronger in 1945 than in the Victorian heyday of organized religion, for the nonconformist challenge had for some time been fading fast. The massive decline in nonconformist Sunday-school attendance from the 1940s onwards[1] was ominous. In a historically less literate society, the seventeenth-century traditions so central to nonconformist vigour were fading, the grievances nonconformists felt most strongly had long been removed, and a geographically mobile society subverted the localism

---

[1] See, e.g., the statistics in L.J.Williams, *Digest of Welsh Historical Statistics* (Department of Economics, Cardiff, 1985), ii, p.272.

that had been integral to chapel life. The Roman Catholic Church, by contrast, was still growing[2], fuelled by Irish and European immigrants, but its mood was not aggressive. Nor had the time yet come for immigrants from outside Europe to reinforce the non-Christian religious challenge to the established church. So in the 1950s the Anglicans still dominated the public stage, never more magisterially than at the Queen's coronation of 1953, when the soaring notes of Parry's 'I Was Glad' seemed to confirm the war's consolidation of the Church of England as an integrating force for the entire nation.

Yet Anglican foundations were insecure. Amidst the hurrying life of great cities, people were seldom without light, never silent, never undistracted, always beset by diverse beliefs and priorities. The stars were seldom noticed, the weather's impact dwindled, the frontiers of medicine and science advanced inexorably, and the concerns and even the language of religion seemed increasingly alien. Urbanization fosters secularization not by abolishing fear, but by concentrating attention on the supposedly removable fears stemming from human action, leaving little room for the believer's immovable fears of what the Almighty might do. Towards religion, big-city life fostered scepticism, relativism, and indifference, so that even reflective irreligion seemed redundant. The prevailing mood of tolerant pluralism that had denied nonconformity its sting and had cleared the way for Catholic advance was not distinct from indifference to organized religion of any kind: the two were linked. By 1950 Rowntree and Lavers were apprehensive: concerned about the impact of religious decline on social reform, they feared that 'we are living nationally on what might be called 'moral capital accumulated in the past'[3].

None the less, Christians were still then well entrenched in intellectual and cultural life, with T.S. Eliot and John Betjeman prominent in literature, and Stanley Spencer painting at Cookham. Symbolic of the continuing affinity

---

[2] See baptismal statistics in A.H.Halsey (ed.), *Twentieth-Century British Social Trends* (Macmillan, Basingstoke and London, 2000), pp.652–3.

[3] B.S.Rowntree and G.R.Lavers, *English Life and Leisure. A Social Study* (Longmans, Green and Co., 1951), p.226; see also p.356.

between art and religion was the performance of Britten's 'War Requiem' at the opening in 1962 of Basil Spence's Coventry Cathedral, adorned as it was with John Piper's stained glass and Graham Sutherland's tapestry. Nor had Christianity yet vacated the intellectual high ground. Overtly Christian scholars – Jacob, Knowles, Powicke, Southern – were distinguished medieval historians, and under Edward Evans-Pritchard (converted to Catholicism in 1944) the social anthropologists were becoming less distant from Christianity. Yet if Christianity had been really powerful with intellectuals, it would have evoked the sort of equal-and-opposite reaction that had emerged in the Victorian period, whereas the twentieth century did not match the Victorians' resourcefulness and serious-mindedness in devising or discovering alternatives to Christian orthodoxy. Few indeed were the twentieth-century equivalents of the Owenites, phrenologists, positivists, theosophists, spiritualists, or secularists – groups with wide and deep influence in this sphere. This contrast reflects a diminishing felt need for such options. Now that religion's artificial defences had been so greatly eroded, the British Humanist Association showed few signs of growth: from the 1960s to the 1990s its (mainly English) membership hovered between two and three thousand[4]. Much more ominous for organized religion than militant irreligion, however, was a quietly growing indifference. The religious challenge to Oxford philosophy's secular mood was on the wane, and the agnostics Ayer and Russell had by the 1960s become the heroes of progressive youth.

Morality had long provided Christians with a special role in public life, but during the 1950s the social scientists were beginning to mount a challenge with their more empirical and pragmatic approach. There was diminishing room for the high-toned confrontation on abstract values that the clergy had earlier favoured: experts now filled the air with their statistics, social engineering replaced moral uplift, and concern with short-term expedients subordinated longer-term

---

[4] I am most grateful to its Executive Director, Hanne Stinson, for a valuable run of statistics provided on 15 Dec. 2005.

(let alone other-worldly) priorities[5]. The shifting tone of the debate on hanging in the 1950s exemplifies the trend. The shrewder abolitionists now emphasized the practical and empirical case against hanging. The strength of their argument had been highlighted by three recent and questionable hangings for murder: of Timothy Evans in 1950, subsequently proved unjust; of the unarmed 19-year-old Derek Bentley in 1953, but not the 16-year-old Chris Craig who had the gun; and of Ruth Ellis in 1955 for shooting a lover whose kicks in the abdomen had caused her to miscarry. In 1956 the House of Commons on a free vote backed the suspension of hanging, but was overruled by the Lords. Far from resisting the trend, the bishops who contributed to the Lords debates were three to one against abolition in 1948, but unanimously backed abolition in 1956[6]. When the government introduced the Homicide Act in the following year, Archbishop Fisher shifted his position: in 1948 he had taken an absolutist position, advocating selective hanging according to the degree of iniquity, but in 1957 he adopted a utilitarian stance whereby hanging would apply only to those types of murder where it was likely to deter. The Act divided murder into capital and non-capital categories, the former being murder as a calculated means to an end; the distinction proved so difficult to operate that the experience of attempting it converted some judge advocates of hanging into abolitionists[7]. This further reinforced the case for complete abolition: suspended for five years in 1965, hanging was abolished in 1969.

In these years the behavioural sciences' wealth of knowledge about human motivation, in alliance with a humanitarian ethic, was sending personal moral responsibility into retreat before a growing belief in environmental determinism[8]. In

---

[5] This discussion owes much to C.Davies, *Permissive Britain. Social Change in the Sixties and Seventies* (Pitman Publishing, 1975), pp.14–24, 36.

[6] H.Potter, *Hanging in Judgment: Religion and the Death Penalty in England from the Bloody Code to Abolition* (SCM Press, 1993), pp.175, 193–4.

[7] For a good discussion see C.Davies, *The Strange Death of Moral Britain* (Transaction Publishers, Brunswick, N.J., 2004), pp.70–5.

[8] As Archbishop Runcie complained in his interview with Bernard Levin, *Times*, 30 Mar. 1987, p.10.

March 1969 the *Times* claimed that no debate about euthanasia could now assume an absolute ban on taking human life in all circumstances: such discussion must accept that 'human happiness, the avoidance of suffering, compassion, and the full realization of human capacities are the chief goods to be sought in inter-personal behaviour'[9]. Even Mary Whitehouse's non-denominational National Viewers' and Listeners' Association in effect transferred blame for individual misconduct to the pressures of a polluted moral (rather than an unjust social) environment. The traditional religious emphasis on girding up the individual to resist inner temptation was giving way to the pursuit of more earthly causes. Yet although Christians might acquire publicity and a comforting sense of relevance by taking the political option – through attacking Apartheid and opposing the Bomb in the 1950s, or through championing the inner city against the Thatcher governments in the 1980s – such a strategy risked diverting effort from the Christian's distinctively individual, moral and other-worldly contribution, besides, the impulse behind such activism could just as well be secular as Christian.

The Archbishop of Canterbury's commission on urban priority areas, *Faith in the City* (1985), provided a focus for religious protest against the Thatcher government. Yet here too the Christian found no hiding-place from the social scientists. They were already in the 1950s publicizing the complex of motive that in practice governs decision-making, whether political and social, or personal and moral: the individual and collective choice between right and wrong no longer seemed straightforward. Furthermore, by the 1980s British economists were turning away from the statist remedies that the Church was espousing. In an increasingly specialized world, the Christian emphasis on sin and individual reclamation seemed unduly simplistic and lacked useful expertise. It was no longer clear that in the public sphere the Christian had anything distinctive to offer. Religion could remain prominent in public affairs only to the extent that public policy's formulation did not seem to require professionalism. The amateur's involvement in public questions within a society that valued expertise risked dividing congregations and neglecting the churches'

---

[9] *Times*, 24 Mar. 1969, p.9 (leader).

own speciality: other-worldly concerns. As Archbishop Carey later confessed, 'archbishops... are not expert in assessing the practical effects of different political or economic options'; he thought that government criticisms of *Faith in the City* had been 'at least partly justified'[10].

Secular values were not merely external to religion: they had begun to pervade church organization. There was a decidedly secular preoccupation in the 1950s and 1960s with rationalization: with how best to deploy the Church of England's resources. By then it was clear that its predominantly rural parish structure must adapt to population change and ongoing urbanization. Already in 1949 the merging of declining rural parishes to conserve resources had begun with the creation of a single pastoral unit around South Ormsby in Lincolnshire. In the 1960s team ministries for enlarged parishes and group ministries for amalgamated parishes seemed the solution. More directly subversive were the theologians who some saw as secularizing their subject's priorities. In 1962 Alec Vidler, Dean of King's College Cambridge, and a self-described 'sceptic in faith's clothing'[11], assembled ten Cambridge theologians in his volume *Soundings* (1962). Unlike the 'liberation theology' then prominent in Latin America, this movement was not socially radical, but its intellectual radicalism seemed subversive enough at the time, especially when publicized by Bishop Robinson. 'My God, John Robinson's written a book which is going to cause mayhem', the future Archbishop Runcie allegedly declared[12], '- he's going to tell the world the sort of things *we* believe!'

Robinson's controversial *Honest to God* (1963) included much autobiography and thinking aloud. In any debate between Christians and humanists, he wrote, 'most of my sympathies are on the humanist's side': the Christian apologist's outmoded language and unhelpful images actually turned people away[13]. God should no longer be portrayed

---

[10] *Times*, 15 Nov. 1996, p.8.
[11] Obituary, *Times*, 29 July 1991, p.16.
[12] To John Montefiore, as cited in H.Carpenter, *Robert Runcie. The Reluctant Archbishop* (first published Hodder and Stoughton, 1996, Sphere paperback ed. 1997), p.159.
[13] J.A.T.Robinson, *Honest to God* (SCM Press, 1963), p.8.

as 'an old man in the sky', if only because space research seemed now to be leaving him 'no vacant spaces': God was not 'out there', but within each of us. Opposing any clear distinction between God and man, between the religious and the secular, Robinson felt that the Church should not be 'a walled garden'; instead, he aimed to extend lay influence within it and project the Christian message beyond the experts and the professionals to the many outsiders who could yet be drawn in[14]. Describing the Christmas story as myth, dismissing black-and-white approaches to sexual morality as too simplistic, sceptical about the continued vitality of the institutional church, he weakened support for any one of his good causes by championing too many others. His loosening of the barriers to faith did not produce the desired religious revival, and by the late 1960s he feared that the clergyman was doomed to remain a mere 'manager of a religious club', stripped of the educational, cultural and welfare roles that were now performed more effectively elsewhere – and reduced to offering only 'one line, which nobody much wants'[15]. In his radical and influential *The Sea of Faith* (1984) the Cambridge theologian Don Cupitt went so far as to abandon God 'as an objectively existing superperson'. In place of the theological concepts which now failed to carry conviction, he recommended a 'religion...wholly of this world, wholly human, wholly our own responsibility'; Christianity, he thought, should now be preoccupied with political activism and moral crusading[16]. Bishop Jenkins of Durham was among the Church leaders who urged the laity to dilute traditional Christian doctrine. Having sufficiently outraged Conservatives with his political views, he compounded his sins by explaining how theology had itself become secularized. By 1988 the virgin birth and the empty tomb had been questioned[17], and in 1993 hellfire went the same way. Few theologians rejected Jenkins's ideas, but some wondered whether he was prudent to publicize them[18].

---

[14] Quotations from *Honest to God*, 13–14, p.140.
[15] 'The Exploding Church', *Observer*, 14 Apr. 1968, p.7.
[16] D.Cupitt, *The Sea of Faith: Christianity in Change* (British Broadcasting Corporation, 1984), pp.270, 273.
[17] *Times*, 4 Apr. 1988, p.5.
[18] *Independent*, 15 Dec. 1993, p.3. *Guardian*, 15 Dec. 1993, p.3.

The church buildings which Robinson viewed as such an encumbrance brought tourists (secularized pilgrims) within the churches' very gates. Visiting the more notable religious buildings primarily for recreational and aesthetic reasons, tourists, with their noise and numbers[19], complemented on the ground the intellectually secularizing impact of 'comparative religion' within university theology departments. The churches began charging for entry, for why should a dwindling number of worshippers maintain the crumbling fabric of the fine buildings whose role was now largely secular? By August 1973 Salisbury Cathedral, eager to preserve its spire, was charging non-pastoral visitors for entry[20]. And if churches remained important centres for music in the 1980s, this was primarily because they could accommodate an organ, an orchestra, a choir, and a large audience in an aesthetically pleasing setting.

Easier travel brought an intellectual hazard still more insidious, for mass immigration from non-Christian countries in the 1950s and 1960s brought closer to home the sort of challenge that nineteenth-century Christians had usually encountered only in the overseas mission field: the relativism prompted by the coexistence of different religious beliefs, all held fervently. Immigrants help to explain why by 2005 Christian church attendance was declining more slowly in London than elsewhere in England[21]. Of those in the census of 2001 who declared their attitude to religion, 79% in England and Wales were Christian, 3% Muslim, 1% Hindu, and 15% said they had no religion[22]. In a multi-faith society some Christians by 2005 even felt obliged to defend Christmas (re-named 'Winterval' in 1998 by well-intentioned Birmingham councillors) as a Christian festival, despite its pagan origins[23], and Archbishop Carey in the following year argued that, given the great changes that had occurred since

---

[19] See the complaints of Edward Knapp-Fisher, Archdeacon of Westminster Abbey, in *Times*, 1 Sep. 1980, p.17.
[20] *Guardian*, 2 Aug. 1973, p.1.
[21] *Economist*, 23 Sep. 2006, p.33.
[22] Calculated from *Times*, 14 Feb. 2003, p.4.
[23] Including the former Archbishop Carey: see Alan Powell's letter in *Times*, 21 Dec. 2005, p.14.

1953, the next monarch would need to be crowned in 'a much more interfaith coronation service'[24].

Religious conflict, central to Victorian education debates, had subsequently faded, but in the 1960s Asian immigrants to the UK unexpectedly revived it. To quote the *Times* in 1969, 'nobody's interest can be served by teachers of doubtful religious faith trying to provide traditional Christian instruction to Sikh and Muslim children', so 'what is required is to move more towards the comparative study of different religions'[25]. University students of religion were reaching a similar destination for less practical reasons. Central to this shift was Ninian Smart, professor of religious studies at Lancaster University from 1967 to 1982. He estimated that in the mid-1950s only sixteen people in British universities had taught religions other than Christianity, whereas by the end of the century his approach (initially controversial) was taken for granted[26]. Given the scale of worldwide migrations, he was working with the tide, and capitalized upon the trend by using his political influence and media skills in the 1970s to get comparative religion into primary- and secondary-school syllabuses. His energy ensured that Lancaster became a powerhouse for promoting worldwide the multi-dimensional study of his subject.

II

Under capitalism, wrote Karl Marx, 'national one-sidedness and narrow-mindedness become more and more impossible, and from the numerous national and local literatures there arises a world literature'[27]. By the nineteenth century the UK had already acquired its role as intellectual entrepôt between Europe and English-speaking peoples worldwide. As an influence on British intellectual life, internationalism made its way somewhat more easily in the nineteenth-century years of free trade, empire, and relatively free admission to the United

---

[24] *Sunday Telegraph*, 4 Jun. 2006, p.6.
[25] *Times*, 19 Nov. 1969, p.11 (leader).
[26] Obituary, *Independent*, 5 Feb. 2001, p.6.
[27] K.Marx, *The Communist Manifesto* (first published 1848, Ed. H.J.Laski, Allen and Unwin, 1948), p.125.

Kingdom than in the more constricted years after 1945. Yet four interacting influences prolonged the nineteenth-century trend: the utilitarian arguments for English as an international language; the ongoing impact of the natural sciences, necessarily global in their outlook, and to a lesser extent of the social sciences; the intellectual and cultural impact of refugees from Hitler; and the growing ease of international travel.

For several reasons the English language was well suited to an international role. Although between the wars English and French had been the two official languages at the League of Nations, the earlier powerful interaction of natural science and industrialization – first in Britain, and then in the USA – helped to make English the language of science. The nineteenth-century breadth of British trade and imperial connections ensured that English speakers were geographically dispersed; indeed, for some multilingual postcolonial developing countries (India, for example), the English language was a major uniting feature. Writers in ex-colonial territories were in a dilemma: the literature of traditionalist nationalism focused on what was distinctive: on the land, the people and the local languages. But this limited the impact of these writers, even within their own country, let alone worldwide. The literature of modernizing nationalism incurred the reverse difficulty: English was often the only language which could both unite the country and reach out towards world influence, but with weaker local resonance[28]. English has other advantages, however: it is relatively easily pronounced, there are many short words, and its syntax has simplified while evolving. True, its spelling often does not reflect its pronunciation, as spelling reformers of the 1940s consistently emphasized when pressing for it to become a world language. Yet this drawback did not prevent UK publishers in 1952 from producing 375 book titles per million of the population – fewer than seven small European countries could boast, but more by a large

---

[28] For good discussions of this see B.King, *The New English Literatures – Cultural Nationalism in a Changing World* (Macmillan, London and Basingstoke, 1980), pp.53, 57, 149. B.King (ed.), *Literatures of the World in English* (Routledge, 1974), p.137. D.Crystal, *English as a Global Language* (Cambridge University Press, Cambridge, 1997), p.115.

margin than the combined figure for the USSR and USA[29]. It was a reflection of the English language's world role that a higher proportion of the books produced in Britain in 1952 (more than a third) was exported, mostly to Commonwealth countries, than in any other of the seven countries surveyed, including the USA[30]. For similar reasons, Britain came very low when rated against other countries for the proportion of translations among the books it produced: the more books a country produced, the fewer it needed from elsewhere[31]. Teaching English became prominent among Britain's late twentieth-century invisible earnings: 6–800 schools in the UK taught it as a foreign language by 1989, most of them in London and the south-east[32]. English-speaking was radiating out in three circles: the first and core circle, where English was the first language, consisted of the USA, the UK, and the British colonies; the second and wider circle embraced the colonies of non-white settlement, where English was often the second language; the third circle, whose population was growing fastest, embraced countries like China, Greece and Poland with no British colonial inheritance, where the inspiration to learn English was purely utilitarian[33].

In 1939 J.D. Bernal had asserted the claims of natural science in his widely-read and trenchant *The Social Function of Science*: scientific research simultaneously benefited mankind, he said, because it solved the problem of scarcity and was 'profoundly satisfying' to the researcher[34]. He wanted research placed at the heart of science teaching, whose career ladder should enable the lab assistant to join the new profession of research scientist. National barriers had no relevance for the natural scientist's subject matter, nor were the

---

[29] R.E.Barker, *Books for All. A Study of the International Book Trade* (UNESCO, Paris, 1956), p.21; the survey covered all countries producing more than 3000 titles.
[30] Barker, *Books for All*, p.24.
[31] R.Escarpit, *The Book Revolution* (Harrap and UNESCO, London and Paris, 1966), p.99.
[32] B.McCallen, *English: A World Commodity. The International Market for Training in English as a Foreign Language* (Economist Intelligence Unit, 1989), p.35.
[33] Crystal, *English as a Global Language*, p.54.
[34] J.D.Bernal, *The Social Function of Science* (first published Routledge, 1939, 2nd. ed. 1940), p.94.

diagrams and statistics central to his researches tied to any one nationality. In so far as language was required, Bernal yearned for a modern equivalent of Latin as a single means of communication between scholars, and held out the hope that this might be 'Basic English', an idea which four years later attracted even Winston Churchill[35]. Help was at hand, for Hitler's expulsion of Jewish scientists and his failed bid for world domination ensured that English became the postwar international medium for natural science without even needing to become 'basic'. Whereas in the 1920s a scientist needed to know German, fifty years later English had become the language of international scientific conferences. The 1940s were the physicists' great moment, and the Hiroshima bomb was alone sufficient to advertise their power. Refugees from Hitler made a major contribution here – for example, in building up Oxford's Clarendon Laboratory as a centre for the study of low-temperature physics[36]. Germany's defeat in two world wars and the USA's industrial might consolidated the role of English as the language of the natural sciences, which were growing fast. Whereas Bernal had seen pre-war nationalism as ominously fracturing the internationalism of natural science, the postwar generation witnessed an Anglo-American free trade in ideas and products. Britain was well placed to combine her defence-related American and Commonwealth scientific links with her slowly recovering scientific contacts in Europe, and English had by then become a world language.

There was a long postwar afterglow whereby wartime radar research, for instance, prompted major and ongoing advances in spectroscopy, and research into nuclear physics helped to build up an important scientific research complex south of Oxford. Although physicists and engineers gained greatly from the emphasis on defence in government-funded research, they also gained from the efforts in the 1950s to switch from coal to nuclear fuels. As with all rapidly growing

---

[35] Bernal, *Social Function of Science*, p.302. For Churchill see *The Diaries of Sir Alexander Cadogan O.M. 1938–1945* (Ed. D.Dilks, Cassell, 1971), p.543 (12 July 1943).
[36] J.Morrell, *Science at Oxford 1914–1939. Transforming an Arts University* (Oxford University Press, Oxford, 1997), pp.369–70, 381, 401–32 provides rich detail.

subjects, physics attracted huge investment in capital equipment and personnel, and dissolved into sub-specialisms. Already by 1938/9 arts and social sciences were a minority, and their proportion continued to fall thereafter, whereas the proportion in pure and applied science among the staff of British universities had been rising for decades[37]. Given the twentieth-century expansion of pure science in British universities and the continued strength of applied science, the typical university teacher was now a technologist[38]. There was a tenfold real increase in government expenditure on civil science between 1945/6 and 1962/3[39], with rapid growth in both university-based science and government-sponsored civil and defence research. The launch of the Soviet Sputnik satellite on 4 October 1957, by advertising Russian scientific prowess, made the democracies all the keener to spur on their own scientists. The advance of radio astronomy prompted the eye-catching Jodrell Bank radio telescope; it came into operation in 1958 and symbolized Britain's continuing intellectual vitality and aspiration. The enhanced interest in applied science, especially engineering, reflected the growing concern in the 1960s about Britain's relative economic decline. In 1960 Lord Hailsham, as Conservative minister responsible for science, thought pure scientists now looked down on engineering, rather as interwar classicists had looked down on natural science, and equally mistakenly[40]. There was all-party recognition of the need for a changed outlook. The Wilson government's national plan in 1965 ascribed much of the weakness in British manufacturing to 'a shortage of engineers and... insufficient attention to the importance of engineering design'; it aimed through the Ministry of Technology to raise their status, improve their training, and deploy them more effectively[41]. Scientists required massive investment in capital equipment and in the

---

[37] A.H.Halsey (ed.), *Trends in British Society since 1900* (Macmillan, London and Basingstoke, 1972), p.216.
[38] A.H.Halsey and M.A.Trow, *The British Academics* (Faber, 1971), pp.156–7.
[39] T.Wilkie, *British Science and Politics since 1945* (Blackwell, Oxford, 1991), p.49.
[40] *House of Lords Debates*, 9 Nov. 1960, c.429.
[41] *The National Plan* (Cmnd.2764, H.M.S.O., 1965), p.49.

people who could operate it, so that scientific and technical workers were proliferating faster than any other white-collar occupations: if the number of lab technicians almost doubled between 1951 and 1966, the number of scientists and engineers more than doubled[42].

In the careers of many natural scientists, national boundaries had always been permeable and were now diminishingly relevant. Sir Richard Woolley's preoccupation was consistent: to discover how the laws of physics determine the working of the universe. His distinguished career was conducted in four countries: his first degrees came from Cape Town and Cambridge, his doctoral research was in California, and he held posts as Director (1939–55) of Mount Stromlo observatory in Australia, 11th Astronomer Royal (1956–71) in Britain, and Director (1971–6) of the new South African Astronomical Observatory. To be preoccupied with notching up national scores and 'firsts' would be childish, and would also be misleading about how natural science advanced after 1945. In so collaborative and capital-intensive an enterprise too much energy should not go into unravelling who was the first to discover what and when. 'DNA was still a mystery, up for grabs,' the American James D.Watson recalled of the early 1950s, 'and no one was sure who would get it.'[43] He and his older English colleague Francis Crick, brilliant in scientific dialogue, sparked off one another, and in April 1953 published in *Nature* the key paper which proposed DNA's double-helix structure, subsequently of the greatest diagnostic and forensic importance. The second major British breakthrough in biotechnology also occurred in Cambridge. In 1975 it too was first announced in *Nature*: the hybridoma technique evolved by the immunologists George Kohler (born in Germany) and the Cesar Milstein (born in Argentina) for producing monoclonal antibodies.

The debt owed to Hitler by the natural and social sciences, and by the arts in Britain was huge. Jewish immigrants of the 1930s eventually endowed Britain with thirteen Nobel prizewinners, 63 Fellows of the Royal Society, and 31

---

[42] Halsey (ed.), *Trends in British Society*, p.114.
[43] J.D.Watson, *The Double Helix. A Personal Account of the Discovery of the Structure of DNA* (Weidenfeld and Nicolson, 1968), p.4.

Fellows of the British Academy[44]. Without the conductor Fritz Busch and the producer Carl Ebert, the Glyndebourne Festival Theatre's rejuvenation of British opera in the 1930s could hardly have occurred; and without its first artistic director Rudolf Bing, the Edinburgh Festival might never have been launched. Refugees infused British cultural life with European perspectives, pushing further forward the attack Albert Prince Consort had launched a century earlier on British intellectual and aesthetic insularity. For however worldwide her seaborne trading and other relationships, Britain's cultural connections had been relatively narrow even before 1914 and in some ways narrowed thereafter. Hitler helped to change this. The Warburg Institute, transported from Germany to London in 1933 and incorporated into London University in 1944, helped to enrich the UK with the wealth of European art and culture. Within this context, such distinguished London-based German-Jewish refugee scholars of art and architecture as Ernst Gombrich, Edgar Wind and Nikolaus Pevsner could flourish in the 1940s. The qualities shared by the entrepreneur and the scholar – commitment, specialization, postponed gratification, perception of opportunity – were notably combined among those German Jewish refugees who so profoundly influenced British postwar scholarship and publishing, especially art publishing. The immigrants Paul Hamlyn, André Deutsch, Peter Owen, Max Reinhardt and George Weidenfeld all launched their own publishing houses. Hamlyn, born in 1926 and the son of a German-Jewish paediatrician, reached Britain with his family in 1933, and at twenty-two was selling from a barrow in Camden market books that were destined eventually to reach a mass market. Deutsch, son of a Hungarian Jewish dentist who reached Britain in 1939, set up as a quality publisher in 1945. The Hungarian Jewish publisher Bela Horovitz, who moved from Vienna to Oxford, operated at a still more elevated level, re-establishing the quality art publisher Phaidon in Britain. In 1949 the Jewish immigrant Eva Itzig, who had fled Germany in 1938, joined her third

---

[44] P.Pulzer, 'Foreigners: The Immigrant in Britain', in W.E.Mosse, *Second Chance. Two Centuries of German-Speaking Jews in the United Kingdom* (J.C.B.Mohr, Tubingen, 1991), p.8, n.4.

husband Walter Neurath in founding Thames and Hudson, thus creating the firm which became the world's leading publisher of art and illustrated books[45].

The growth of a global market in talent ensured that intellectuals whose talents were marketable, especially natural scientists, were not securely tied to their country of birth, and that economic motives reinforced the political for moving between countries. By the late 1950s Britain was slipping in the world's wealth-ranking, and wage differentials within Britain had long been flattening. If really able managers, scientists, technologists and entrepreneurs were required – the rare oil-capping talents of a Red Adair from Texas[46], for example – they would move only if paid at the worldwide going rate. The so-called 'brain drain' from Britain had begun well before 1963 – the year of the *Oxford English Dictionary*'s first citation of the phrase – in the context of young British scientists and technologists lost to the USA. Of British natural scientists with recent doctorates between 1952 and 1961, 16% moved permanently abroad, a growing number to the USA, which absorbed 7% of the total; by 1963 the USA had also permanently recruited twenty Fellows of the Royal Society[47]. Whereas with the Commonwealth there was a balance between intellectual exports and imports, few American scientists thought it worth moving permanently to Britain.

Given the growing ease of travel after the 1960s, however, intellectuals keen to remain in their country of birth could periodically sample what was available elsewhere. International academic exchange was common enough by 1975 to be satirized in David Lodge's novel *Changing Places*. International conferences and 'international reputations' were now in vogue. Furthermore, internationalism was increasingly built into the procedures of the natural and social sciences, both in subject matter and in collaboration between dispersed researchers. Cross-cultural comparisons

---

[45] Obituaries of Hamlyn, *Guardian*, 3 Sep. 2001, p.18; Deutsch, *Daily Telegraph*, 12 Apr. 2000, p.31; Eva Neurath, *Independent*, 3 Jan. 2000, p.5.
[46] Obituary, *Times*, 9 Aug. 2004, p.25.
[47] *Emigration of Scientists from the United Kingdom. Report of a Committee Appointed by the Council of the Royal Society* (Royal Society, 1963), pp.10, 12.

were becoming integral to research in medicine and the social sciences. In the natural sciences such international collaboration was necessary if only because essential equipment was so expensive, especially in astronomy and physics: hence collaborative projects such as JET and CERN. Among many instances of collaboration can be cited the sort of cross-country social and medical research that involved eliminating cultural variables: demographic research into the influences on family size, criminological research into the impact of penal systems, or medical research into the impact of smoking and diet. One distinguished career exemplifies the growing international links between medical research and humanitarian impulse: that of the Liverpool-based bacteriologist Allan Downie, who pressed the World Health Organization into campaigning against smallpox, a disease that in the 1960s was killing ten million people a year, yet which has produced no case since 1978[48].

With late twentieth-century advances in the media – from radio to television to the internet – it was becoming ever easier to absorb influences from elsewhere without moving from one's country of birth, for the media were decidedly internationalist in tendency. Television enhanced the domestic impact of overseas correspondents, instantly reporting those memorable events of the 1960s: student radicalism in California, the Vietnam War, and Russian tanks in Prague[49]. What sociologists call 'fugitive terminology' – novel but ephemeral words and phrases flitting round the world – flourished within the teenage underground of the 1960s. So-called 'media moguls' had begun to appear: the Canadian Roy Thompson bought the *Sunday Times* in 1959, for example, and the *Times* seven years later. In 1969 the Australian Rupert Murdoch bought the *News of the World*, then in 1969 the *Sun,* which he converted into a successful tabloid; then in 1981 he bought the *Times* and the *Sunday Times*. But the really powerful cultural influence at this time was American.

---

[48] C.S.Nicholls (ed.), *Dictionary of National Biography 1986–90* (Oxford University Press, Oxford, 1996), p.109.
[49] See Crossman's comments on this in his *The Diaries of a Cabinet Minister. iii. Secretary of State for Social Services 1968–70* (Hamish Hamilton and Jonathan Cape, 1977), p.172 (4 Aug. 1968).

Direct American influence on the interwar BBC had been small[50], but the BBC lost its monopoly of television in 1955, and there followed a rush of American media influence, first on television and from the 1960s on the radio as well. With the advent in the 1990s of the internet, home-based international intellectual collaboration could attain new heights

III

Secularization, the natural and social sciences, and meritocracy fed into the third overriding intellectual tendency after 1945: professionalism. If the upper classes in Britain survived the 1940s only precariously, the postwar middle classes went from strength to strength. Cohesion might be the hallmark of other social classes, but fragmentation was integral to the middle-class bid for supremacy, and they felt free to subdivide at several levels. Physics and chemistry might be declining after 1970 as distinct areas of study, for instance, but they were unobtrusively growing through combining with adjacent subjects into new specialisms such as biophysics, biomathematics, and biochemistry. Likewise with the professions, that major middle-class redoubt. There the source of status lay in certificated admission qualifications and training courses which simultaneously excluded and evangelized. To police them, 'qualifying associations' had been forming between 1910 and 1950 at the rate of two dozen per decade, so that by mid-century engineering accounted for a quarter of their total, management and administration for a tenth and accountancy for a twelfth[51]. Traditionally trained outside the universities, whose bias lay towards theory rather than practice, the professions in Britain gradually enhanced their status by incorporating university courses into their qualifications, thereby lending a more vocational emphasis to university curricula and research. William Baxter, for example, was the UK's sole full-time professor of accounting when he arrived at the London School of Economics in 1947,

---

[50] A.Briggs, *The History of Broadcasting in the United Kingdom. ii. The Golden Age of Wireless* (Oxford University Press, London, 1965), p.109.
[51] G.Millerson, *The Qualifying Associations. A Study in Professionalization* (Routledge, 1964), p.183.

but by 1971 there were twenty[52]. Repeatedly dividing and recombining in response to a ceaseless quest for enhanced professional status, the professions assumed that their institutional self-interest coincided with that of the community as a whole. They deployed their expertise to discredit amateurism among the classes higher up, and with their meritocratic examinations they extended an escalator to the self-improving and the talented among the masses lower down. Although secularization removed or demoted some religious professionals, the growing prestige of science recruited professional numbers with hordes of engineers, surveyors, draughtsmen, architects, designers, technicians and laboratory workers.

The middle-class meritocratic triumph required a selection process which substituted formally assessed achievement for birth and personal connection, thereby converting schoolteacher and examiner into allocators of life-chances. The middle-class battle-cry from the 1940s onwards was 'modernization': the need to promote national security and prosperity through invoking measured merit. This outlook shaped the enthusiasm from the 1950s for comprehensive schools: they were envisaged as devices for ensuring that merit would at last attain its full potential. The pursuit of merit also transformed the mood and social role of the UK's independent schools and universities after 1945. At mid-century an examination-tested professionalism seemed likely soon to destroy classbound barriers to personal achievement. By such means could be fended off the relative national decline that threatened the UK, which was seemingly ill-endowed with natural resources and needed to live off its wits. This outlook informed both major political parties, moulded in their outlook as they were from the 1950s to the 1970s by the belief that votes were best won through focusing on the corporatist centre-ground. Occupying such territory were both Harold Wilson (prime minister from 1964 to 1970 and from 1974 to 1976) with his utilitarian pursuit of planning, efficiency, institutional reform and social opportunity; and Edward Heath (prime minister from 1970 to 1974) with his respect for European innovation, his undoctrinaire

---

[52] Obituary, *Times*, 7 Aug. 2006, p.44.

outlook, and his pursuit of power through conciliation and pragmatism. In the 1960s scientists' identification with merit and modernity, and their rationalistic affinity with the ideal of planning, made an alliance with the Labour Party seem natural. The novelist C.P. Snow, son of a shoe-factory clerk, was one among many of natural science's twentieth-century socialist enthusiasts from H.G. Wells onwards. 'If there had never been a case for socialism before', said Wilson in his first speech to the Labour Party conference as leader in 1963, 'automation would have created it': technology 'left to the mechanism of private industry and private property, can lead only to high profits for a few, a high rate of employment for a few and to mass redundancy for the many'[53]. Nor did anyone question the need for meritocratic promotion among doctors or among individuals and teams in the footballer's world, which in the 1960s was reconstituting itself into a nationwide meritocratic hierarchy. The meritocratic thrust persisted for the rest of the century, transforming university admission criteria, moulding the careers of the Social Democratic Party's voters and parliamentary candidates in the 1980s[54], pervading the re-shaped parties of Margaret Thatcher in the 1980s and of Tony Blair in the 1990s, and ensuring that by 2000 the honours system had shed most of its feudal associations.

Nowhere more than in universities was the middle-class capacity for growth through fragmentation, for social mobility through measured merit, more in evidence. Academic 'subjects' were continually combining and re-combining as specialization advanced, and a growing fashion for interdisciplinary courses and structures in the 1960s – epitomized in the structures adopted in the new university at Sussex – both reflected and fostered such developments. Research now moved up among the university teacher's priorities, and natural science provided the fashionable model for collaboration in government-funded interdisciplinary and group

---

[53] H.Wilson, *Memoirs. The Making of a Prime Minister 1916–64* (Weidenfeld and Nicolson, 1985), p.197.
[54] I.Crewe and A.King, *SDP. The Birth, Life and Death of the Social Democratic Party* (Oxford University Press, Oxford, 1995), pp.274, 281, 293.

projects. The impact of so huge an influx on the overall culture, priorities, and even style and vocabulary of universities was profound; research, often collaborative and costly, became ever more central to their role. Their rapid expansion during the 1960s denied first-degree courses much of their earlier cachet, and academic status increasingly required a higher degree. In all British universities the postgraduate student was gaining ground: whereas 11% of male and 10% of female full-time UK university students were studying for research degrees in 1950/1, these figures by 1967/8 had risen to 17% and 13%, respectively[55]. Between 1950/1 and 1970/1 the number of full-time postgraduate students at British universities rose fourfold, and the number of higher degrees awarded almost sixfold[56]. The taste for graduate study also reflected the need felt by a growing academic profession for a more standardized way of recruiting itself. British universities by world standards operated on an unusually high staff/student ratio. In 1951/2 there were 9,869 full-time staff in British universities, but three times as many twenty years later. Inevitably the proportion of staff drawn from Oxford and Cambridge declined, and as the academic hierarchy elongated, the proportion of readers and senior lecturers rose[57]. A career-ladder had emerged within and between universities with increasingly standardized recruitment, structures, procedures, and funding arrangements.

The social sciences, which disappointed many high hopes of the 1960s, illustrate the multi-layered fragmentation that was now accelerating within the middle class as a whole, but also within the intellectual worlds which lay at its meritocratic heart. There was first the fragmentation within academic life between areas of scholarly study, each with its esoteric language, its admired exemplars and its special concerns. Internationalism was increasingly built into the

---

[55] Halsey (ed.), *Trends in British Society*, p.222.
[56] R.Simpson, *How the Ph.D. Came to Britain. A Century of Struggle for Postgraduate Education* (Society for Research into Higher Education, Guildford, 1983), pp.165–6.
[57] W.A.C.Stewart, *Higher Education in Postwar Britain* (Macmillan, 1989), p.284. A.H.Halsey (ed.), *British Social Trends since 1900. A Guide to the Changing Social Structure of Britain* (Macmillan, Basingstoke and London, 1988), pp.283, 286.

procedures of the natural and social sciences, both in subject matter and in collaboration between dispersed researchers. Fragmentation was also occurring at a deeper level, between intellectual life as a whole and other sections of the national elite: political, economic, religious, even recreational – for sport's growing professionalism was eroding the universities' once powerful status in team games. Political scientists distanced themselves from practical politics by focusing upon political theory and adopting abstruse approaches to empirical inquiry. Economists forsook the book for the journal article, and practical relevance for arcane abstraction. Theory and sophisticated numeracy, not empiricism and practical utility, were their signposts to status. No longer for them the 'big issues' tackled by economists in the tradition of J.S. Mill, Marshall, Keynes and Meade.

With natural science promoting a 'Germanic' zeal for professionalism in research, the 'learned journal' was throughout the twentieth century gradually ousting the less specialist quarterly and monthly reviews which had been so central to Victorian intellectual life; even the influence of the serious 'generalist' weekly journals was waning by the 1960s. Academic professionalism was accumulating a wealth of expertise – not just in the natural sciences, but in such subjects as musicology, psephology and the history of art and architecture, and a wealth of new reference works was building up long before the internet burst upon the scene in the 1990s. The nationwide system of university and public libraries undermined the role of the secondhand bookshop, and the professionalization of the literary critic in university departments of English further threatened those leisured and moneyed 'men of letters' who had somehow survived rising taxation and inflation. University teachers in English literature, especially when influenced by the Cambridge academic F.R. Leavis, showed a growing part-time interest in producing and reviewing fiction, as became manifest when reviewers in the *Times Literary Supplement* lost their anonymity in 1974[58]. Peter Hall claimed that Leavis, despite disliking the theatre, wielded even there

---

[58] D.May, *Critical Times. The History of the 'Times Literary Supplement'* (Harper Collins, 2001), p.425.

'more influence [...] than any other critic'[59]. Creative writers did not always welcome Leavis's pronouncements. When Leavis declared D.H. Lawrence alone worth consideration among modern novelists, J.B. Priestley expressed alarm at this 'sort of Calvinist theologian of contemporary culture' with his acolytes forcing authors 'to undergo some kind of customs and passport examination[...] with narrowed gaze, tight lips, service revolvers'[60]. Philip Larkin regretted that academic professionalism had since the 1920s called forth the kind of poetry that required elucidating: there were, he thought, all too few Betjemans and Dylan Thomases who could yoke poetry to the general public[61]. In this climate the Harold Nicolsons, the Philip Toynbees and the Cyril Connollys could survive for a time as broadcasters on the Third Programme and as literary critics in weeklies or Sundays like the *New Statesman* and the *Observer*, but the integrated and educated elite that had once spread out from country house to subscription library, from country rectory to London club and London Library, was now fragmenting and fading. Hence the widespread discussion in the 1950s about whether 'popular culture' would fill the gap.

A professionalism of sorts was also spreading through the publishing world, where a quiet revolution occurred in the 1950s and 1960s. The strength of British postwar publishing, amateur or not, emerges from statistics for 1952. Although the USSR surpassed the UK in the total number of volumes produced, the UK produced far more volumes than any country outside the USSR, even including the USA. Volumes published in English accounted for a fifth of the world's total production, and a third of the volumes produced in the UK went overseas, a higher proportion than were exported from any other country[62]. In all categories the total output of titles issued by British publishers between 1951 and 1970 (including reprinted or new editions, which in both years contributed

---

[59] P.Hall, *Peter Hall's Diaries. The Story of a Dramatic Battle* (ed. J.Goodwin, Hamish Hamilton, 1984), p.347 (18 Apr. 1978).
[60] *New Statesman*, 10 Nov. 1956, p.580.
[61] A.Motion, *Philip Larkin. A Writer's Life* (first published Faber, 1993, paperback ed. 1994), pp.344–5.
[62] Barker, *Books for All*, pp.22–3.

more than a quarter of them) almost doubled[63]. The utilitarian share of the book titles published by a country declines as its industrialization advances, and by 1953 44% of the titles produced in the UK fell into the non-utilitarian categories of fine arts, recreation and literature[64]. The history of firms such as Faber and the Hogarth Press illustrates how blurred had been the interwar boundary between recruitment to publishing and writing, and this attractively amateur affinity between publisher and author persisted well into the 1950s. Authors and publishers did not qualify as professionals, because they lacked the professional person's exclusive status, formal entry qualifications and standardized career pattern. Yet neither were they committed entrepreneurs: author and publisher both relied on personal flair, but by no means all sought to maximize profits, and many authors were no more than part-timers because they needed the income that came from a second occupation.

Three developments from the 1950s brought significant change to what later came to seem this gentlemanly world of small British publishing firms. There was first the linked decline of the private circulating library and the rise of the public library. In 1937 Mudie's had been the first private circulating library to go, and in 1957 was followed by Day's Library; W.H. Smith succumbed in 1961, the Times Book Club in 1965 and Boots Book Lovers' Library in 1966. By then most of the small shop-based twopenny libraries had also vanished, and only Harrods' Subscription Library remained[65]. The rise of the public library, much faster in Britain than in France, increasingly complemented its initial self-improving purpose by catering for leisure needs. In the late 1950s some still refused to use them for fear that the books would be soiled or transmit infectious disease, but by the mid-1960s they had become 'one of the great middle-class institutions

---

[63] *Mumby's Publishing and Bookselling in the Twentieth Century* (6th. ed.), p.220.
[64] Barker, *Books for All*, p.20. See also Escarpit, *Book Revolution*, p.37; the book contains ample fascinating statistics.
[65] J.G.Olle, 'The Lost Libraries', *Library Review*, Autumn 1966, p.455. R.Findlater [pseud. For K.B.F.Bain], *What Are Writers Worth? A Survey of Authorship* (n.p., 1963), p.9 claimed that in that year there were still about 4000 shops lending books at a weekly charge.

in this country'[66]. They could well have killed off book-buying but for the second major publishing development: the paperback. Allen Lane, its leading pioneer, had always seen himself as 'converting book-borrowers into book-buyers'[67], and in the 1950s Penguin's educational thrust had not yet drained away. The first Penguin classic, Homer's *Odyssey*, translated into modern English by E.V. Rieu, came out in 1945 and by 1960 had sold a million copies – a total also reached in 1978 by Coghill's rendering of Chaucer's *Canterbury Tales*[68]. Penguin eventually got caught up, however, in the third major publishing development of these years: the Americanized commercialism of the 1960s. By the late 1950s the firm faced stiff competition from paperback publishers further downmarket, and hardback publishers were by then publishing paperbacks from their own backlists. After changes among Penguin's top personnel, Tony Godwin, who in Charing Cross Road's 'Better Books' had established a modern and more stylish bookshop, moved into and up Penguin's hierarchy. The firm transformed itself from a private limited company to a public company in 1961, and Americanized glossier covers swept through the paperback trade. Its total number of titles grew sixfold during the 1960s, and in 1970 paperbacks accounted for two-fifths of the sales revenue in book publishing[69]. By then few people bought a book primarily because it was a Penguin book: the brand had lost its distinctiveness, and in 1970 the firm was absorbed into the huge Longman Pearson Group.

So internationalism and professionalism impinged as much upon publishing as upon intellectual life generally after the 1950s. By the 1970s American influence was especially important. The rapid postwar expansion in the output of British

---

[66] Lord Francis-Williams, *House of Lords Debates*, 30 Jun. 1964, c.544; see also Baroness Wootton, c.539.
[67] Quoted in S.Hare, *Penguin Portrait: Allen Lane and the Penguin Editors 1935–1970* (Penguin Books, 1995), pp.117–8.
[68] *Mumby's Publishing and Bookselling in the Twentieth Century* (6th. ed.), p.163. J.Sutherland, *Reading the Decades. Fifty Years of the Nation's Bestselling Books* (British Broadcasting Corporation, 2002), p.22.
[69] R.Stevenson, *The Oxford English Literary History. xii. 1960–2000: The Last of England?* (Oxford University Press, Oxford, 2004), p.137. S.Laing, 'The Production of Literature', in A.Sinfield (ed.), *Society and Literature 1945–1970* (Methuen, 1983), p.128.

publishers could hardly be maintained thereafter, yet growth continued rapidly enough: 79% for total titles and 42% for reprints and new editions between 1970 and 1987[70]. The small publishing concern, with small print-runs, diverse products, and a relative unconcern with management and marketing, could not survive invasion from the huge American publishing machines, and the 1970s and 1980s saw an almost complete turnover of the leading publishing personalities. The combination of rapid inflation, bad labour relations, falling library demand and rising oil and paper costs compelled extensive mergers and rationalizations. From 1974 British publishers were subjected to a literary equivalent of the 'Top of the Pops', American in origin: the bestseller list. Furthermore, there was a growing practice of manufacturing bestsellers according to a formula, especially when aimed at television. The former academic Henry Babbacombe, in Bradbury's *Cuts*, discovers that 'writing for television was teamwork', and that in the production team 'everyone else was there to change everything else that everyone else did'[71]. With the private lending libraries vanished, the secondhand book trade in decline, university libraries cutting back, and the paperback fully established, everything depended by the 1990s on what barcoded paperbacks the publishers could tempt readers to buy from airport lounges, railway stations and readers' supermarkets such as W.H. Smith, closely monitored as they were by stock control.

Yet the supermarket publisher did not entirely oust small but literate and well-connected delicatessen publishers and booksellers who knew their market, could back hunches, and cater for significant minorities: it had been a regime creative enough (and sufficiently 'professional', in its way) to survive multinational commercialism. So rather than the monoliths completely taking over, publishers in the 1970s and 1980s witnessed continuous shrinkings and expandings, mergers and secessions. From the 1980s publishing costs fell markedly, and that too helped the small publisher, just as the internet placed the secondhand bookseller on an entirely

---

[70] Calculated from statistics in *Mumby's Publishing and Bookselling in the Twentieth Century* (6th. ed.), p.220 supplemented by figures in Publishers Association, *Quarterly Statistical Bulletin*, Mar. 1988, p.19.
[71] M.Bradbury, *Cuts* (Hutchinson, 1987), pp.76, 78.

new and more promising footing. Library purchasing of books continued to grow till the mid-1970s, but went into marked decline thereafter till the universities started expanding from the late 1980s. Authors could no longer be reticent: media-boosted publicity was important for sales, and authors had to be seen at poetry readings, literary 'events', book festivals, chat programmes and book signings. The age of book-prize ballyhoo had arrived, with the Booker Prize (for a British author of a fictional work published in Britain within a named period) first awarded in 1968. From Cheltenham in 1949 to Hay-on-Wye from the late 1980s the literary festival, too, had arrived: amateur at first, but with an increasingly hard-nosed and commercial dimension[72]. One scholar can, however, be cited to stand for the many in the humanities who after 1970 remained undistracted by the pursuit of publicity or fashion, and was professional in the best sense: devoting decades of dedication to an abstruse but important subject. In the late 1930s the Cambridge biochemist Joseph Needham became interested in Chinese culture through his graduate student (much later his wife), Lu Gwei-Djen. In 1950 he planned a seven-volume study of *Science and Civilization in China*. Four of its volumes had been published by 1971, and thereafter it grew into a huge multi-authored collaborative project backed by a growing collection of material; in 1987 this was housed in its own library within a research institute devoted to the subject. It was a 'professional' achievement as substantial, original and significant as any other that the twentieth century had witnessed.

IV

The 'professional' intellectual specialization and fragmentation on the scale so far described, especially when buttressed by secularization and internationalism, were not unequivocally beneficial – not least because they prompted an equal-and-opposite fourth trend: populism. The trend towards intellectual specialization led Sir George Thomson in 1955 to pronounce it so far advanced that 'professional liaison officers between specific fields' would be needed to enable even scientists to

---

[72] D.J.Taylor in *Guardian*, 25 May 2002, Saturday review, p.3.

communicate with one another; as for the general public, popularizers would be essential[73]. Given that researchers are by no means always the best or most eager publicists of their work, the need for gifted intermediaries to improve the public understanding of the natural sciences was becoming urgent. Fred Hoyle met the need in astronomy, with broadcasts and books beginning with *The Nature of the Universe* (1951), an outcrop of his Third Programme broadcasts in 1950. There he coined the phrase 'big bang' to describe the idea that the universe had been created in a massive explosion. Television was particularly helpful to zoology, generating spinoffs in the form of popular books like Michaela Denis's *Leopard in my Lap* (1957) and Joy Adamson's *Born Free* (1961). In the humanities, too, the media set out to interpret the professionals to the public. Television serials of major fictional works ensured an even wider readership for the literary canon than before, while the New Left and the campaign for 'cultural studies' were pushing forward the broader literary agenda pioneered by George Orwell, Raymond Williams and Richard Hoggart into new and fruitful directions. From the 1960s history, too, was opening out towards a wider public with help from A.J.P.Taylor, the History Workshop movement, industrial archaeology (with its array of volunteers), and the vogue for 'oral', family and 'contemporary' history. In the 1970s history won still more enthusiasts through the 'heritage' industry, with abundant custom from tourists and leisured pensioners. Constitutional and diplomatic history were by then in decline, whereas the history of the 'common people' – social, labour and economic history – flourished. Towards the end of the century, television did for history what it had earlier done for archaeology: it helped to satisfy a mass popular thirst for knowledge about a subject whose professional scholars were unable or even unwilling to slake it. Unexpected audiences suddenly emerged for historical programmes of a wide-ranging and well-presented visual kind.

All this was encouraging, and in 1945 it was still widely hoped that democracy and high culture could be reconciled. Radio at first seemed potentially helpful. The Leavises and

---

[73] Sir G.Thomson, *The Foreseeable Future* (Cambridge University Press, Cambridge, 1955), p.147.

the ABCA-nurtured adult educationists still laced their leftish contempt for London's literary potentates with faith in the likely impact on British culture of democratized access to education and leisure. If *Scrutiny* ceased publication in 1953, this was partly because it seemed no longer needed, so wide had been the Leavises' influence. Nonetheless, by the late 1950s commentators like Hoggart felt the need to distinguish between popularization and populism: they were worrying about the impact of commercialism on popular culture, and about the 'knowing, permissive treason of the clerks': the educated people who thought it fashionable to go along with falling standards[74]. As early as 1930 F.R. Leavis had claimed that films 'involve surrender, under conditions of hypnotic receptivity, to the cheapest emotional appeals', and that radio 'tends to make active recreation, especially active use of the mind, more difficult'[75]. Similar comments were made in the 1950s about television, which like so many earlier recreational innovations became a target for the moralists. It was widely alleged that television's audiences would be more passive. Furthermore, politicians in the 1960s found it difficult to project their message less because of deliberate bias, more because the mass media seemed increasingly to demand a rapid and often purely visual impact. Tony Benn, in many ways himself instinctively populist, nonetheless complained in 1968 that news was telescoped, fragmented, oversimplified, spiced up and trivialized. Immediacy and impact were now of the essence. For similar reasons newsreaders by 1979 were adopting emphases unfamiliar to their seasoned exemplar Alvar Lidell in 1979: 'news has a right to be boring and dull on occasion. The thing that must be ruthlessly avoided is *synthetic* excitement'[76]. It was not only the viewers and listeners who were allegedly being corrupted. In 1987 Bradbury's *Cuts* redirected to the media his satirical portrayal of amoral, extravagant life-styles that he had earlier applied to universities; in the insincere and meretricious world of the media,

---

[74] e.g. Richard Hoggart, 'Speaking to Each Other', in N.Mackenzie (ed.), *Conviction* (MacGibbon and Kee, 1958), pp.130–1.
[75] F.R.Leavis, *Mass Civilisation and Minority Culture* (Minority Press, Cambridge, 1930), pp.9–10.
[76] Letter in *Listener*, 3 May 1979, p.620.

the academic-turned-scriptwriter is taken up, taken over, exploited, soiled and ultimately disposed of. By then the roles of the Workers' Educational Association and the national press were becoming increasingly recreational, and it was claimed that if 'quality' papers were losing circulation more slowly than the rest, this was only because they were going downmarket in search of more readers.

A twofold change was occurring in the relationship between education and social class. On the one hand the traditions of working-class self-education were being eroded by a meritocratic educational system which sucked up working-class talent and deposited it in the middle class, and probably also in London. On the other hand, the middle classes were losing their self-confidence in cultural leadership. Alertness to accent and language frequently accompanies shrewdness in assessing where power is thought to lie. The dominant middle-class tendency for at least a century had been to deploy language and accent as a filter when admitting recruits from below and as a bridge towards middle-class mobility further up. The word 'toilet', for example, was for decades a talisman of working-class status among the devotees of 'lavatory' (or, increasingly by the early 1970s, 'loo'[77]). Mike Leigh's television play *Abigail's Party* (1977), with his wife Alison Steadman in the lead role as the obnoxious Beverly, compellingly captured the traditional middle-class approach to social mobility, which involved aping what were thought to be upper-class attitudes and language. Yet the play was already slightly out of date, for significant middle-class groups had by then begun to look lower down for their speech models. Influential sections of the middle class by the 1970s, especially among the young, were prepared to compromise on language and culture. Whereas earlier middle-class generations had hoped to educate their new (working-class) masters towards congenial voting habits and the mass adoption of high culture, later generations opted for a populist rejection of 'elitism' (a term increasingly used pejoratively) in favour of supposedly working-class accents, vocabulary,

---

[77] On which see Viscount Ridley, *House of Lords Debates.* 2 July 1974, c.204.

syntax, recreations and attitudes[78]. Middle-class snobbery was becoming inverted.

A temporary proletarian cult had been seen before: among energetically sincere left-wing Oxford undergraduates in the 1930s[79], for example, or among middle-class national servicemen in the 1950s. By the 1970s, however, influential sportsmen and media personalities lent new force to the cult, which also received useful backing from the philologists; furthermore, under male rather than female influence, this cultural shift was becoming permanent[80]. Middle-class people had long imitated working-class speech – half affectionately, half patronizingly – but such mimicking was not now at all facetious, and aimed to reduce rather than accentuate social distance. So, unusually among linguistic trends, fashions set below were travelling socially upwards: acquired glottal stops and a colourful vocabulary now began to lace so-called 'estuary English'[81], the watered-down version of Cockney that issued from more and more young middle-class mouths throughout England. Slowly the 'received pronunciation' of Oxford University and the BBC ceased to be the passport to career success, and even came to be seen as itself an 'accent'. By the 1990s the English language was experiencing 'convergence in grammar and vocabulary but divergence in phonology'[82]. A 'strange, inward-looking proletarianism' was widespread even at the top of the Labour Party in the 1970s[83], a decade in which much deference was paid to the trade unions. Roy Jenkins and some of his followers became suspect within the labour movement as much for their accents as for their Europeanism, and C.A.R. Crosland felt the need to compensate for his patrician tones by refusing as Foreign

---

[78] See P.Howard, 'Elite Force in the War of Words', *Times*, 25 Aug. 1978, p.10.
[79] C.Mayhew, *Party Games* (Hutchinson, 1969), p.26.
[80] J.C.Wells, *Accents of English. i. An Introduction* (Cambridge University Press, Cambridge, 1982), p.105.
[81] A phrase originating with David Rosewarne, 'Estuary English', *Times Educational Supplement*, 19 Oct. 1984, p.29.
[82] Professor Peter Trudgill to author, 31 July 1997.
[83] David Marquand, 'Inquest on a Movement. Labour's Defeat and its Consequences' in *Encounter*, July 1979, 13*.

Secretary to wear a white tie[84]. This decidedly Oxford-accented politician also affected something of a proletarian style, together with alleged footballing enthusiasms and frequent references to his Grimsby constituents. Inverted snobbery of this type owed something to the Labour Party's disappointments with what had emerged from the Wilson cabinets in the 1960s, where university-trained intellectuals had wielded much influence, and to which all the rationality of socialism-as-planning had been so central. It owed more to the salience (which exaggerated the reality) of trade-union power within British politics in the 1970s. A desire to escape such tendencies was one factor causing the Social Democratic Party to break off from the Labour Party in the early 1980s, and also contributed to the outlook of 'New Labour' in the 1990s.

The persistence of populist attitudes among late twentieth-century British intellectuals also reflects worldwide influences, most notably American youth culture in alliance with the mass media. When Elvis Presley died in August 1977 the BBC broke into its evening programme schedule to announce the fact – an action which a *Times* leader thought 'not inappropriate'[85]. In the 1980s comic strips invaded the *Guardian* and filled a *Sunday Times* supplement, and by the end of the decade the scholarly and somewhat earnest treatment of pop music that the underground counter-cultural press of the 1960s had pioneered re-surfaced in the national broadsheet dailies; they pursued their younger readers with deeply ruminative articles on the skills and even thoughts of footballers and pop singers. It was becoming important for intellectuals to be able to claim that they had a football team to 'follow', and in some intellectual circles it became fashionable even to lace conversation with meaningless (because redundant and misapplied) obscenities. Fuck's journey towards acceptability in the media, for example, had provided milestones along the high road to sixties culture: in the *Observer* in 1960, the theatre critic Kenneth Tynan first thrust it into the Sunday papers in the context of the *Lady Chatterley* trial, and in 1965 provoked a national furore

---

[84] *New Statesman*, 19 Nov. 1976, p.707.
[85] 'A Singer of Social Significance', *Times*, 18 Aug. 1977, p.13.

when he was the first to utter it in a BBC programme on 13 November late at night; the much less flamboyant Alastair Hetherington, editor of the *Guardian*, was the first editor to allow the word into his paper[86]. By the 1990s 'fucks' quite frequently regaled intellectual gatherings, though the BBC presenter Anna Ford in 1997 ran into trouble for describing a fictional character in the serial programme 'The Archers' as 'a shit'[87].

The media were important for infusing populism into spoken intellectual discourse, given the approachable manner required on television. The unstructured dialogue encouraged by the relative impermanence and haste of e-mail and the mobile telephone later fostered written informality. Populism and commercialism were interlinked. The problem was not confined to the commercialism which had led Penguin Books in the 1960s to dilute their distinctive educational role. Almost immediately on the launching of commercial television, considerations of sheer survival had forced it to move rapidly downmarket in 1955–6[88], and by the 1960s ITV had a much stronger following lower down in society than higher up[89]. American television demonstrated how, quite apart from programme content, the periodic intrusion of advertisements shortened the attention span and trivialized the overall mood. In the 1960s commercialism ineluctably permeated radio as well, throwing the BBC by the 1970s on the defensive. Its one-time central place in British life, consolidated by the Second World War, was now doubly undermined: first by the compulsory and accelerating loss of its monopoly but, second, by its voluntary abandonment of a distinctively standard-setting role: its licence-based mass funding now seemed to require rivalry with ITV for audience ratings.

---

[86] K.Tynan, *The Life of Kenneth Tynan* (Weidenfeld and Nicolson, 1987), pp.178, 236. Obituary of Hetherington, *Guardian*, 4 Oct. 1999, p.16.
[87] *Daily Telegraph*, 2 Apr. 1997, p.6. See also the survey of manners cited in *Times*, 17 Sep. 1991, p.2.
[88] B.Sendall, *Independent Television in Britain. i. Origin and Foundation, 1946–62* (Macmillan, London and Basingstoke, 1982), pp.328–9.
[89] Halsey (ed.), *Trends in British Society*, p.557 (figures for 1960–1 and 1968).

A somewhat similar release from restraint was occurring in late twentieth-century religion. At the same time as the electorate was becoming more volatile in its party-political allegiances and the bookshops were filling with self-help manuals, a supermarket of religious faith was developing in which individuals made up their own religion; they sought like all religions to make sense of the inexplicable, but depended much less heavily on guidance from formal or educated hierarchies. The idea of personal choice within a religious supermarket owed something to the growing prevalence within the UK of several non-Christian religions often fervently held. At just the point when nonconformity had entered rapid decline, its logical consequence – the individual's self-determined designer-faith, shaped to suit personal need – became increasingly feasible and acceptable. In the House of Lords debate of 18 January 1979 on unidentified flying objects, for example, both reason (embodied in a determinedly rationalistic Lord Trefgarne) and guided unreason (embodied in an anxious Bishop of Norwich, Maurice Wood) felt on the defensive against this newest of supernatural commitments. Trefgarne was convinced that such sightings could usually be explained 'by logical scientific theory', and that the rest would become so 'if our knowledge were more advanced or if we had more information about the sightings'. As for the Bishop, he insisted that Christ has 'literally a galactic significance' and that 'all the far corners of the creative world, right out further than we can ever see or even know by radio, are within the plan of the Creator'; he feared the 'climate of credulity' and 'ersatz spirituality' developed in UFO groups, which drew their members 'into a sub-Christian, and... sometimes a non-Christian cult', obscuring 'basic Christian truths'[90].

The so-called 'new age' beliefs were by the 1980s advancing in the most affluent parts of the country, most notably southeastern England, whose residents were tempted to migrate to remoter parts (in Wales, the Lake District and Northern Scotland) where they could more effectively commune with

---

[90] *House of Lords Debates*, 18 Jan. 1979, cc.1253 (Trefgarne), 1270–2 (Wood).

natural forces[91]. Eclectic in belief, amorphous in structure and ideas, 'new age' enthusiasts owed much to the irruption in the 1960s of influences from oriental religions; they also fed upon the widening scepticism about natural science and its effects which from the 1950s fuelled green, animal liberation and anti-nuclear movements. 'New age' adherents grew numerous enough for bookshops to set aside special shelves: at a time when religious titles were slowly declining in their share of the books published in Britain, titles on occultism doubled during the 1960s as a proportion of religious titles, and continued slowly to rise thereafter, up to 1990[92]. The Glastonbury festival originated in 1970 as a free and countercultural event, somewhat mystical in tone, with an attendance which by the early 1990s had risen to 75,000[93]. From 1974 the annual Stonehenge free festival was staged during the summer solstice, a focus for the 'New Traveller' culture; ten years later it was attracting 70,000 people. There was much concern in the 1980s about drugs, squatters and public order, however, not to mention the security of Stonehenge, and in 1985 the festival was forcibly dispersed by the police. The Public Order Act (1986) temporarily ended the British free festival movement, though the authorities could not prevent the many illegal rave parties that sprang up in increasingly remote locations during the late 1980s[94].

Concern about populist trends in education, the arts and humanities were summed up during the 1980s in the phrase borrowed from the USA: 'dumbing down'. It marshalled complaints that were by no means new. Already by 1869 Matthew Arnold was complaining about the lack of objective literary and cultural standards[95], and in 1887 he viewed W.T. Stead's 'new journalism' as 'feather-brained', like the

---

[91] S.Bruce, *Religion in Modern Britain* (Oxford University Press, Oxford, 1995), p.114.
[92] Halsey (ed.), *Twentieth-Century British Social Trends*, p.667.
[93] See the website *www.netcomuk.co.uk/~drbob/glasto/whatisglastonbury.html*, consulted on 6 Apr. 2005.
[94] See www.efestivals.co.uk/festivals/stonehenge/2001/historyopinion.shtml, and *http://news.bbc.co.uk/1/hi/entertainment/music/3662921.stm*, both consulted 6 Apr. 2005.
[95] 'Culture and Anarchy' in M.Arnold, *Complete Prose Works* (Ed.R.H.Super, University of Michigan Press, Ann Arbor), v (1965), pp.147–8.

democracy it served[96]. The 'yellow press', as championed by Gissing's enthusiastic Whelpdale, aimed at 'the quarter-educated' new generation being turned out by state schools, 'who can just read, but are incapable of sustained attention... their attention can't sustain itself beyond two inches. Even chat is too solid for them: they want chit-chat'[97]. The crusade to uphold standards launched by the Leavises from interwar Cambridge has already been mentioned, and in 1944 the Cambridge historian G.M. Trevelyan expressed deep disillusionment with the results of mass education: 'whether in the twentieth or twenty-first centuries the lower forms of literature and journalism will completely devour the higher has yet to be seen'. Literature and journalism, he said, 'now cater for millions of half-educated and quarter-educated people, whose forebears, not being able to read at all, were not the patrons of newspapers or of books'[98].

Given the late twentieth-century populist climate, self-defence for intellectuals of any type was not easy – especially as they were now fragmented by a professionalism that encouraged them to talk only to each other. In 1932 the historian G.M. Young was already voicing alarm at how academic professionalism and democracy had fragmented the Victorian clerisy; it must quickly be rebuilt, he claimed, 'if our civilization... is to survive the deluge of picture-thinking and mass-suggestion bearing down on us from East and West and always welling up in our midst'[99]. 'Through the gateway of the Competitive Examination we go out into the Waste Land of Experts', he complained in 1936 when discussing the increasing specialization of the 1880s, 'each knowing so much about so little that he can neither be contradicted nor is worth contradicting'[100]. For Trevelyan, as for the Leavises,

---

[96] 'Up to Easter' (May 1887), in *Complete Prose Works*, xi (1977), p.202.

[97] G.Gissing, *New Grub Street* (first published 1891, paperback ed., Oxford University Press, Oxford, 1993), p.460. I owe this reference to my friend Mark Griffiths.

[98] G.M.Trevelyan, *English Social History* (first published 1944, Reprint Society ed. 1948), p.588.

[99] 'Victorian History', in *Selected Modern English Essays. Second Series* (Oxford University Press, London, 1932), pp.276–7.

[100] G.M.Young, *Victorian England. Portrait of an Age* (Oxford University Press, London, 1936), p.160.

the universities became a defensive redoubt, with an 'endowed priesthood' to uphold the cultural standards which were 'otherwise disappearing with the disappearance of all forms of aristocratic tradition'[101]. Yet a century after the 1880s – with the advance of populist fashions, academic specialization, 'grade creep', and a philistine commercialism and vocationalism – the redoubt's fortifications were weakening.

It was to the natural sciences that the most serious challenge from populism came, reinforced with all the power of conspiracy theories and sentimentalism. The late-Victorian concern about vivisection had not gone away, and Hiroshima reinforced the doubts of those who had long questioned any inextricable link between science and progress. Orwell in 1946 had detected a link between science and totalitarianism[102], and the sheer cost of big science, given the British economy's faltering state in the 1950s, evoked doubts. The Campaign for Nuclear Disarmament both divided the scientists and drew its best-known supporters from the arts – so much so, that in the first Aldermaston march in 1958 the publisher Victor Gollancz claimed to have done more business than in the entire previous year[103]. Even when nuclear physics was deployed for peacetime purposes in nuclear power stations, the authorities were nervous of alienating the public by telling it too much about accidents. University students by 1959 were becoming wary of co-operating with mass radiography[104], and in the same year the Nobel-prizewinning biologist Peter Medawar thought he must deploy his Reith lectures against the growing gloom about the natural sciences' impact on ordinary life. Also in 1959, H.K. Beecher's *Experimentation on Man* made much impact with its claims – inflated in M.H. Pappworth's *Human Guinea Pigs* (1967)

---

[101] Quotations from Trevelyan in 1954 and 1955, respectively, in D.Cannadine, *G.M.Trevelyan. A Life in History* (Harper Collins, 1992), pp.233, 236.
[102] G.Werskey, *The Visible College. A Collective Biography of British Scientists and Socialists of the 1930s* (Allen Lane, 1978), pp.287–9.
[103] Ian Rodger, quoted in 'The Road to Aldermaston' (BBC programme, 30 Mar. 1978).
[104] University of Oxford, *Hebdomadal Council Papers*, pp. ccxxxii (Jan.-Apr. 1959), 299; ccxxxviii (Jan.-Mar. 1961), 283.

– that scientific experiment was not confined to animals[105]. It was not long before medical science was hit by the thalidomide tragedy, which heightened scepticism about the medical profession and medical progress.

By the 1960s more people were willing to challenge the doctor's authority. Authoritarian and conservative attitudes still prevailed within hospitals, especially in the relationship between doctors and nurses, but the nurses had a powerful weapon: among the many exposures of National Health Service abuses during the 1960s it was the marginal people – orderlies, student nurses and part-timers – who were the whistle-blowers. Particularly vulnerable to maltreatment were the long-stay patients in relatively isolated and routinized institutions staffed by self-insulated people in the medical profession's backwaters. Less complex societies had often reserved special roles within the community for the eccentric, the mentally subnormal and the very old, but industrial societies gathered them into institutions – often huge and bleak Victorian buildings whose tall chimneys and water towers lent them an air of mystery when glimpsed through the trees from distant locations. As far as the patients were concerned, it was out of mind out of sight, out of sight out of mind, and they were treated like children. It was in mental health and geriatric medicine that the reaction against institutionalizing patients began[106].

This unsystematic twentieth-century critique of the natural sciences built upon the self-help strain that had earlier been so influential in challenges to intellectual authority elsewhere. Its pedigree in the medical sphere was long and highly rationalistic. Late twentieth-century critics of the medical profession carried forward something of the Victorian radical's hostility to the doctor-as-priest, and such perceptions chimed in with the revived wariness of natural science that spread out from Chernobyl and Three Mile Island. The doctors were hampered by the fact that they could not keep delivering breakthroughs on the scale

---

[105] See L.J.Witts's review of Pappworth in *British Medical Journal*, 10 Jun. 1967, p.689.
[106] J.P.Martin, *Hospitals in Trouble* (Blackwell, Oxford, 1984), pp.82, 87, 245, 247.

of the 1940s: sulphonamides might grapple effectively with infectious disease, but the health hazards of old-age – heart attacks, cancer, and bronchial diseases – were far less tractable. Furthermore, new diseases or strains of disease appeared, and were more readily propagated as the world shrank into a global village. The iconoclastic American author Ivan Illich's *Limits to Medicine. Medical Nemesis* (1976) cast doubt on the profession's alleged achievements, argued that the pretensions of 'the medical establishment' threatened health as well as liberty, and claimed that the doctors were turning life 'into a pilgrimage through check-ups and clinics back to the ward where it started'[107]. His alternative was to preach the gospel of medical self-help.

Ian Kennedy acknowledged Illich among those 'to whom my debt is great' in the preface to his widely discussed Reith lectures of 1980[108]. Trenchant, irreverent and quotable, the lectures emphasized the doctor's professional self-interest and questioned his scientific and other pretensions. Through categorizing rather than curing, doctors were allegedly empire-building; through following 'the technological imperative' they had converted the National Health Service into 'an illness service', preoccupied with glamorous cures, big hospitals and mechanistic rather than environmental and holistic approaches to the body[109]; and in matters of birth and death they were straying well beyond their sphere of competence. In recommending preventive medicine, in urging doctors' need to justify their expenditure to the taxpayer, and in emphasizing medicine's subjective elements, Kennedy's analysis was salutary: 'being ill is not a state, it is a status', he declared, 'to be granted or withheld by those who have the power to do so'[110]. His analysis was also timely for Conservatives newly returned to power in 1979 and keen to cut welfare costs. Yet as a lawyer Kennedy was not above empire-building himself, recommending the patient-as-consumer to resort more frequently to

---

[107] I.Illich, *Limits to Medicine. Medical Nemesis: The Expropriation of Health* (first published 1976, Penguin paperback ed. 1977), p.87.
[108] I.Kennedy, *The Unmasking of Medicine* (Allen and Unwin, 1981), p.xi.
[109] Kennedy, *Unmasking of Medicine*, 143. *Listener*, 20 Nov. 1980, p.677; cf. Dr.Peter Draper, Director of the Unit for the Study of Health Policy, Guy's Hospital, *Times*, 3 Sep. 1980, p.1.
[110] Kennedy, *Unmasking of Medicine*, p.8.

the courts, and some of his remedies were vague and impracticable. Equally irreverent towards professionalism was the assault on Freudian theory and medico-biology conducted by the British psychiatrist Garth Wood: in his *Myth of Neurosis* (1983) he denied that 'neurosis' was a useful diagnostic term. He saw the therapist with his alleged expertise and allegedly remedial drugs as self-aggrandizing: the psychiatrist was bamboozling the patient into addictive dependence and dangerous introversion. Self-help through 'moral therapy' would, by contrast, encourage problems to be confronted rather than evaded, and (with friends providing common sense, empathy and experience) would endow the alleged neurotic with the self-respect that health and happiness require.

Re-issued by Penguin as a paperback in 1977, Illich's book adopted a slash-and-burn approach which probably carried little weight in Britain, and Wood's book probably made less impact there than in America, where psychotherapists wielded more influence. Nonetheless, both books reflected widely held fears of the doctor's dominance. Such doubts prompted the late twentieth-century trend for doctors to act upon Joseph Fletcher's insight: to keep patients better informed and to listen to them more often[111]. Furthermore, the AIDS epidemic highlighted the value of informal and lay self-help groups, and the value of paramedical services in reinforcing the doctor from below was increasingly evident. Given the need for rapid action in emergency cases, it was sensible to bring hospital facilities to the patient rather than the patient to the facilities. In heart-attack cases, for instance, Frank Pantridge had realized in 1965 how sensible it would be to equip the ambulance with the defibrillator, carried by all front-line ambulances by 1990[112]. The term 'paramedic', to denote people trained to provide specialist emergency care, originated overseas in the 1960s, but by the 1990s had become a familiar term within the UK. Nurses' status and

---

[111] J.Fletcher, *Morals and Medicine* (Gollancz, 1955), pp.60–1; cf. I.Loudon, J.Horder and C.Webster (eds.), *General Practice under the National Health Service 1948–1997. The First Fifty Years* (Clarendon Press, Oxford, 1998), p.225.
[112] Obituary, *Guardian*, 6 Jan. 2005, 25.

duties were advancing too, both within hospitals and in the general practitioners' new health centres of the 1960s.

By the end of the twentieth century even the doctor's professional ethic was on trial. In a society where reticence was in retreat and the pursuit of celebrity in vogue, the confidentiality that was integral to the professional ethic was vulnerable. Lord Moran provided an early instance of professional betrayal from within when in 1966 he exposed in published diaries his medical relationship with his patient Winston Churchill. But while reticence was built into professional conduct, its abuse for the purpose of cover-up was apparent from a series of hospital scandals and court cases in the 1990s: the climate of fear within a hospital could protect an authoritarian consultant from deserved criticism. These scandals included the controversy about the secret storage of dead children's body parts at Alder Hey Hospital, Liverpool, on a huge scale for years without parental consent[113]; the controversy surrounding the allegedly botched operations performed by the gynaecologist Rodney Ledward; and the 'club culture' among paediatric heart surgeons at Bristol Royal Infirmary which concealed its high death-rate[114]. Most astonishing of all, however, was the exposure of the general practitioner Harold Shipman as having murdered at least 215 patients between 1975 and his arrest in 1998[115]. Hospital league-tables, closer monitoring of prescriptions, and external regulation with more lay participation were among the specific remedies proposed for such scandals, but diminished reverence for the professions was perhaps the most powerful remedy of all.

Alleged 'alternative' or 'complementary' options to professional medicine were by then clamouring for attention. For the UK's indigenous population, the doctor had never fully ousted the patent medicine and the self-help cure; in 1972 about two-thirds of adults surveyed had taken a self-prescribed medicine during the previous two weeks[116]. The

---

[113] *Daily Telegraph*, 31 Jan. 2001, p.2.
[114] For Ledward see *Economist*, 17 Jun. 2000, p.36. For Bristol, *Independent*, 19 July 2001, p.3.
[115] *Independent*, 10 Dec. 2004, p.18.
[116] V.Berridge and G.Edwards, *Opium and the People. Opiate Use in Nineteenth-Century England* (Allen Lane, 1981), p.238.

health store Holland and Barrett was becoming a high-street name, and millions of cod-liver oil, vitamin, garlic, echinacea, evening-primrose oil and other pills were disappearing down the throats of a late twentieth-century nation that hoped thereby to ward off arthritis, the common cold, and heart attacks. Minimally interventionist, holistic in approach, and demanding the patient's active participation, 'alternative' medicine – which included herbalists and the rapidly growing pseudo-profession of aromatherapy – was indeed complementary. Here was another of Prince Charles's campaigns against the professions: his speech to the British Medical Association in 1982 prompted sponsored systematic investigation in the area[117]. Despite continuing professional scepticism, the House of Lords, in debating the subject on 11 November 1987, almost unanimously favoured variants of medicine which seemed ineluctably to be advancing from 'fringe' to 'alternative' to 'complementary'. The general practitioners' hostility was waning: by 1981 8% of them had joined complementary medicine's professional bodies[118], for alternative medicine too was now taking the familiar professional route towards formal association, training, and selection by examination. If the acupuncturists, chiropractors, homoeopathists, hypnotherapists and osteopaths practising in the UK in 1981 were aggregated, they were already one-sixth as numerous as general practitioners. Immigrants fuelled the revival. Hindu immigrants guided by their Vaids, Muslims by their Hakims, were taking directions alien to Western medicine; eighty were practising in the UK by 1981[119]. By the early 1980s complementary medical practitioners were increasing five or six times faster than doctors[120].

---

[117] J.Dimbleby, *The Prince of Wales. A Biography* (Little, Brown and Co., 1984), 306, 309. See also his opening of the Cancer Help Centre at Bristol, *Daily Telegraph*, 16 July 1983, p.1; and his comments in *Times*, 17 July 1984, p.1.
[118] S.Fulder, 'Alternative Therapists in Britain', in M.Saks (ed.), *Alternative Medicine in Britain* (Clarendon Press, Oxford, 1992), p.169.
[119] *Guardian*, 5 Mar. 1979, p.2. S.Fulder, 'Alternative Therapists', p.168.
[120] S.J.Fulder and R.E.Munro, 'Complementary Medicine in the United Kingdom: Patients, Practitioners, and Consultations', *Lancet*, 7 Sep. 1985, p.545. For comparative statistics on its incidence in several Western countries 1985–92 see C.Webster, 'Caring for Health in the UK 1974 to

Much more alarming to the professions, and also to university researchers, was the mounting humanitarian and environmentalist critique of the natural sciences. In 1990 animal-rights extremists planted three bombs, one at Bristol University under the car of a researcher into pain relief. Andrew Blake (a patient shocked by this event) mounted a counter-move. He had been struck at age fourteen by Friedrich's ataxia, and was surprised to find that no organization existed to mobilize patients in support of vivisection for medical research. The pressure group SIMR (Seriously Ill for Medical Research) which he founded in the following year had 800 members or supporters by 2002, the year of his death[121], and his outlook had bucked the anti-doctor trend. Environmentalist pressure threatened nuclear physics. Tony Benn, visiting the huge nuclear reprocessing complex at Windscale as Energy Minister in 1978, was 'struck, on the one hand, by the skill and scientific knowledge of the people who run it and, on the other, by the exceptional vulnerability of such a complicated system'[122]. Its vulnerability was soon revealed: the proposal to make Windscale a centre for nuclear re-processing exposed much hostility in the public debate during 1977–8; nor was it long before man-made disasters vividly advertised the hazards.

Despite their major achievements and their ample funding, many natural scientists felt vulnerable in British public life. Fragmented between their specialisms, preoccupied with their research, they were less adept at self-defence in the 1950s and 1960s even than their increasingly unionized technicians. Snow's lecture on *The Two Cultures and the Scientific Revolution* (1959) made a wide impact with its complaint that in Britain only arts people tended to be described as 'intellectuals'[123]. Similar problems were faced by scientists worldwide, yet there were signs of hope. The natural sciences

---

2001' in C.Webster (ed.), *Caring for Health* (3rd. ed, Open University Press, Buckingham, 2001), p.229.

[121] Obituaries in *Independent*, 29 May 2002, p.18; *Daily Telegraph*, 22 Jun. 2002, p.25.

[122] T.Benn, *Conflicts of Interest. Diaries 1977–80* (ed. R.Winstone, Hutchinson, 1990), p.310 (9 Jun. 1978).

[123] C.P.Snow, *The Two Cultures and the Scientific Revolution* (Rede lecture, Cambridge University Press, Cambridge, 1959), p.3.

had now so diversified that the complaints against 'big science' – far from entailing no science at all – simply entailed a shift from old to new areas of scientific growth: problems arising in one area of natural science would be answered in another. Scientific expertise was now required even to conserve humanitarian and environmental values. By the 1960s the ecological sciences, for example, had already begun to fertilize the public's growing preoccupation with the environment, just as epidemiology and nutrition were by then providing the necessary background for revitalizing preventive medicine. If in addition to marshalling newly found relevant expertise the scientists could bring greater energy and skill to explaining what they were doing, and to mobilizing in self-defence, there was no reason why a fervent but misguided populism should prevail against them. There was consolation, too, in the fact that the natural scientist's problems were not new. The conflict between science and religion had been central to nineteenth-century intellectual life, and in the late-Victorian conflict over vivisection it had reached its most acute form, yet this had not prevented the scientists from prevailing and even (in the twentieth century) flourishing as never before. By cautiously – and when necessary, courageously – deploying the facts in alliance with clear reasoning and a healthy scepticism about passing fashion, they retained hopes of prevailing again.

On the expert system of popular journalism

Martin Eide

Popularization and power – notes on the postwar Norwegian context

The power of journalism and its authority should be regarded as particularly important in modern societies;[1] consequently, an adequate theory of society and a relevant one of power should be able to account for the role of journalism. It is about time to place journalism on the agenda for historical sociological discussions of power and democracy. In my view, this mission cannot be properly accomplished unless we take popular journalism seriously.

Within modern social theory, society is frequently conceived of as constituting different sections or fields and diverse systems or networks with reciprocal relations and floating boundaries. Communication and dissemination between these different fields or systems should then be decisive – and the role of journalism should call for considerable awareness.

Furthermore, in modern social theory, power is frequently conceptualized as a relational phenomenon. Power is not a capacity possessed by an agent once and for all; neither is it permanently anchored in certain social structures. Power appears in multiple and floating ways and typically displays itself through discourses and prevailing logic. Accordingly,

---

[1] The introductory argument of this article draws on the introduction to M. Eide (ed.), *Til dagsorden! Journalistikk, makt og demokrati* [A Point of Order! Journalism, Power and Democracy], Gyldendal, Oslo 2001.

journalism and the impact of journalistic logic on social actors' courses of action should be of central interest in an updated social theory of power.

Questions about journalism and power address important dimensions of the general debate about power in the social sciences.[2] First, journalism is of paramount importance to agenda-setting power. Second, journalism is of relevance to the power implied in non-decisions and issues that never reach a public agenda. Thirdly, journalism is decisive in questions of ideology, hegemony and symbolic power. In short, none of these three dimensions of power can be properly understood if the role of journalism is neglected.

The first national project to study power relations in a Norwegian context in the early 1980s concluded that power had moved away from the parliamentary arena and towards the corporative system; power had thus moved from the electoral channel towards the organizational one.[3] A second national project of the same kind recently concluded that power has now to a greater extent moved towards the market and the legal or judicial system.[4] Journalism has accompanied these movements of power: firstly, through more comprehensive coverage of public administration; secondly, through greater coverage of economic issues; thirdly, through a kind of journalism that emphasizes people's rights in different capacities – especially as consumers but also as citizens; and fourthly, journalism's relation to the market has become more manifest through a general process of popularization.

Of equal importance is a fifth feature of the relationship between power and journalism, namely the fact that journalism has become an intimate and imperative part of the exercise of power. A journalistic logic has come to be an indispensable requirement for any social actor who wants to achieve something in this world. To succeed, one must think journalistically, and this skill is no longer exclusive to

---

[2] S. Lukes, *Power: A Radical View* (Macmillan, London 1974). O. Petersson, *Makt i det öppna samhället* [Power in the open society] (Carlssons, Stockholm 1989).
[3] NOU 1982:3 *Maktutredningen. Sluttrapport* [Norwegian Official Reports. On Power. Final Report].
[4] NOU 2003:19 *Makt og demokrati* [Norwegian Official Reports. Power and Democracy].

journalists. In a way, nowadays every social institution is a media institution.

Hardly any modern institutions or social actors are untouched by the prevailing media logic, existing media conventions or journalistic modes of operation. Accomplishing a goal is more and more a matter of adapting to and taking advantage of media logic. The logic of journalism is expanding, and journalistic power is mobilized by any agent with the slightest ambition in the political field as well as other social arenas. The ability to think journalistically and act in compliance with prevailing media logic is as common outside the mass media as within it. This omnipresence of media logic originates from an implicit, special kind of power, which is more indirect and concealed than the more salient agenda-setting capacity of modern journalism. Journalistic power is a matter of managing the logic of journalism.

Today this logic takes precedence over the political position of the individual journalist: journalism has a professional bias, more so than a political bias in any traditional sense. Although Journalists usually vote for leftist political parties more often than does the average voter, this accounts for less of the journalistic power than the fact that all journalists subscribe to a journalistic logic and a certain professional ideology. Journalism, indeed, has become an ideology in itself, and journalistic influence on power relations has been conceptualized through a model of 'chaotic flow'. Journalists have become 'agents of instability rather than of control', the British media sociologist Brian McNair states.[5]

Journalistic ideology is based on a very simple cosmology, on a rather simplistic image of society. Its construction starts from the premise that on one side of society there are the powerful, while on the other we find the common people. Between them, there are journalists, whose job is to serve the people and challenge the powerful.[6]

---

[5] B. McNair, *The Sociology of Journalism* (Arnold, London 1998), p. 165.

[6] O. Petersson & I. Carlberg, *Makten over tanken* [Power over the Mind] (Carlssons, Stockholm 1990). O. Petersson, 'Journalistene som klass, journalismen som ideologi' [The Journalists as a Class, Journalism as Ideology], in T. S. Edvardsen (ed.), *Media og samfunnsstyring* [The Media and Administration of Society], Fagbokforlaget, Bergen 1994.

Society thus consists of three groups of actors: power brokers, ordinary people and journalists – in other words: sources, audiences and newsrooms. Consequently, all sources not of the people are considered power brokers. And the worst-case scenario, in the journalistic view, is if the powerful are allowed to address the innocent people directly, without any journalistic intervention. Journalists are crucial intermediators and interpreters between the mighty and the people, according to the professional ideology of journalism. Journalists would consider their being regarded not as independent critics of power, but as a part of that power, as unfair.

Journalism as ideology frequently emerges in the form of a special blend of populism and elitism:[7] on the one hand, the audience is flattered and popular commitment is celebrated; On the other, it is emphasized that a turning point always emerges when the journalist takes charge. It is the media's actions that really matter.

A central element in the recent expression of this ideology is the conception of the journalist as an advocate for his or her audience. In the representative plot here, the journalist appears as the fearless knight, who seems to be able to bring about a solution and happy ending on behalf of the audience member. While the journalist is either the hero or the Good Samaritan, the role of the antagonist might be played by the representative of the health-care system, the civil servant, the bureaucrat – or the intellectual...

In a Norwegian context the popular press has led the fashion of pursuing this modern journalistic ideology. To understand the role of dominant journalism, we need to relate changes in journalism to wider changes in society and culture: we need to understand the processes of popularization. Referring to the postwar public sphere, my case in point will be Norway's best-selling newspaper, *Verdens Gang* (VG). [8]

---

[7] O. Petersson & I. Carlberg, *Makten over tanken.*
[8] Cfr. M. Eide, *Blod, sverte og gledestårer. VG 1945–1995* [Blood, Print and Tears of Joy, VG 1945–1995] (Schibsted, Oslo 1995). M. Eide, 'A new kind of newspaper? Understanding a popularization process,' in *Media, Culture & Society*, vol. 19 (2), Sage, London 1997, pp. 173–182.

It entered the public arena with declarations of independence and impartiality in 1945. A new mentality of cooperation and solidarity, fostered by people's experiences of the war, was manifest in this new paper's programme; its declared ambition was to become an arena for political debate, indeed, *the* main arena for informed political discourse in postwar society. The paper proclaimed its great political interests, but had no party-political inclination.

VG's prehistory, as well as its manifest ideology, has striking parallels to those of the French elite paper, *Le Monde*, and other liberal European newspapers rooted in the resistance movement. However, the following history of *VG* demonstrates important discrepancies between it and *Le Monde*.

Throughout the 1950s, the paper's bourgeois leanings became more and more obvious, although it was not linked to any political party. Equally importantly, the newspaper simultaneously underwent a process of popularization, characterized not least by a conversational journalistic style and an emphasis on 'human-interest' material. In 1952 *VG*, now an evening paper, entered the non-subscription market and took up competition with the other major popular newspaper in Norway, *Dagbladet*. In 1963 *VG* went tabloid and a popularization of the paper's journalism ensued. Its success in market terms did not, however, emerge until the paper was taken over by new owners, who from 1967 invested heavily in the paper. A tremendous market success evolved: in 1981 *VG* became Norway's best-selling newspaper, a position which was strengthened in the years to come.

This process of popularization implied an additional disembedding from other sources of authority. For instance, *VG* had, by the time of its founding, invested symbolic capital in the emerging expert system of the new social sciences and declared that it would link to and use their results. This attachment turned into a detachment parallel to the popularization of the newspaper. Instead of relying on other expert systems, the newspaper formed its own expert system, becoming a master of its own domain.

The Kings Bay incident in 1963 illustrates this[9]; it refers to a mining accident in the Kings Bay pit on the arctic archipelago of Svalbard, where 21 lives were lost. Due to this, a major political crisis was created leading to the resignation of the Labour Party, and bringing a bourgeois government into power for a few weeks in the autumn of 1963. After the election of 1965 it was time for a more lasting bourgeois government, in power for more than a full election period. The Labour Party State was history.

The Kings Bay incident heralded the more self-conscious attitude – the new footing – of Norwegian political journalists in general. First, the political crisis was provoked by the media breaching a press ban on an investigative report. Second, the political critique of the Government by the press grew considerably sharper throughout this incident, and *VG* was a driving force. Thirdly, the change of government led to the Labour Party's monopoly on Cabinet information being lifted. With a coalition government consisting of four parties, the latitude for strict information strategies was limited.

A systematic examination of *VG's* coverage of Kings Bay from May to December 1963 offers a striking picture of a more self-confident kind of journalism. Expert systems are conspicuously absent from the newspaper's columns. Considering the emphasis at the time on the political regime changing and the Labour Party State possibly declining, it is remarkable that the newspaper does not to any visible degree rely upon external analytical capabilities or commentators. However, the newspaper does not hesitate to characterize the misdeeds of political actors. In an editorial on the very last day of 1963, *VG* referred to 'disclosures of political incompetence and administrative incapability, of lacking knowledge and crying naivety, of lack of control, outrageous nonchalance and outstanding complacency.' Generally, the newspaper's coverage of the Kings Bay affair eagerly insisted on the correctness of its own interpretations and points of view.

---

[9] A more comprehensive analysis can be found in M. Eide, 'Power on the Threshold of the Interview Society. Journalism, Politics, Popularization', in M. Ekström, Å. Kron & M. Nylund (eds), *News from the Interview Society*, Nordicom, Gothenburg 2006, pp. 79–92.

On a more general level and in a longer perspective, it may be argued that the natural sciences have possessed academic hegemony in relation to this newspaper's journalism. During the postwar period of reconstruction in particular, an engineer-oriented approach was dominant. From the social sciences, the expert system of law was later mobilized, especially in important debates about economic regulations and military stand-by arrangements in the fifties. However, the new social sciences never came to play the central role supposedly attributed to them in the newspaper's programme; its neglect of them can probably be explained by indicating that major parts of the Norwegian social sciences either became too closely linked to power or too closely linked to Labour. Alternative traditions, on the other hand, were either too subversive and critical to please *VG's* political taste. The relevant expert systems were then the legal profession and engineers.

VG's coverage of the Kings Bay incident also instructively demonstrates that 'journalistic independence' may take different forms. There is a vast divide between the idealistically motivated independence of the early postwar years, and the aggressive independence of 1960s political journalism. A process of popularization had altered the concept of journalistic independence. A new professional footing – new forms of journalistic involvement and participation – appear.

This is true, even though the shift in journalistic styles is less obvious in the paper's political journalism than in its other journalistic domains, where informal modes of address and a journalistic conversationalism are cultivated more intensely. These processes also started much earlier and gained more pace in genres other than the political one.

An examination of *VG's* coverage of the Kings Bay incident demonstrates two other significant aspects of popular political journalism. First, a keen focus on the human aspects of the politicians' behaviour seems obvious. Second, it is striking how the newspaper itself becomes a political agent and ascribes to itself a high profile in this regard. Shifts in journalistic authority are at issue here.

The 1960s represented a time of fermentation in politics and journalism, as well as in the relationship between the two. In a Norwegian context these processes of change manifested themselves in the cessation of what has been labelled 'The Labour Party State' and in the breakthrough of a particular kind of popular journalism, one which to a considerable extent established itself in relation to the new medium of television. These processes constituted a new balance of power between politicians and journalists.

Against this background it is of importance to study the subsequent changes in the nature of political journalism. First, political news is no longer privileged. Although political coverage by the popular press is still extensive and rather serious, compared to what may be found elsewhere in what is called tabloid journalism, Parliament remains an important news beat and the official agenda is still reflected, the living room and private sphere are of equal importance in generating top stories.

Second, a kind of service journalism has encroached into the domain of political journalism. The journalistic assessment is clear and simple: in the domain of politics, the reader also needs guidance, clarity and political consumer information to be able to pursue his or her interests. The conception cultivated of the role of journalism is that the journalist is on your side; he or she pushes politicians to come up with clear arguments and effective solutions.

Third, political journalism is characterized by the generally prevailing melodramatic framework of the popular press with its emphasis on drama, conflict, personalities and emotions. It is also imbued with a quest for the human touch; politicians become human beings in a way, while the voters become customers.

Political journalism is subject to what Richard Sennett has called 'the tyranny of intimacy'.[10] When these symbolic forms succeed to the extent they do, it must be due to factors other than mere speculation in the poor taste of readers. There must be a certain *social* sounding-board for this kind of dissemination of politics. When commercially successful modes of address are directed towards consumers, clients and individuals, rather than towards citizens – this might be due to an erosion of the citizen-role. It does then

---

[10] R. Sennett, The Fall of Public Man. On the Social Psychology of Capitalism, Random House, New York 1976.

not matter that much whether readers are politically active or not; those who experience a lack of power can be offered politics as human drama. Moreover, political parties tend to converge ideologically: hence, the personal capacities of individual politicians become more important in the political process. Furthermore, melodramatic political journalism can be conceived of as a popular protest against an abstract and theoretical understanding of society.[11]

Although such factors may *account* for the breakthrough of this kind of popular journalism, they cannot *justify* it. A melodramatic understanding of politics is bound to be a misunderstanding.[12] A journalism that consistently offers 'the experiences of the individual as the direct and unmediated key to the understanding of the social totality' fails to offer a proper understanding of politics and society.[13]

An orientation towards everyday life and a disembedding from traditional news beats and news conventions contribute to a new kind of journalistic self-confidence. Journalism is its own expert system, a knowledge regime in its own right. Journalistic power has gained new and different ground – a new foundation – throughout the process of popularization.

For many decades, the most popular slogan in the journalistic community has been that of 'independence'. Indeed, independence from political parties was the first matter of concern in the professional arsenal of modern journalism. Later, this liberation was followed by a slogan claiming independence from sources and a struggle against what has been labelled 'the tyranny of sources'. It is problematic that the relationship between journalists and sources is defined first and foremost as a power struggle; if such proclaimed independence from sources is prioritized over the knowledge

---

[11] J. Gripsrud, 'The Aesthetics and Politics of Melodrama,' in P. Dahlgren & C. Sparks, *Journalism and Popular Culture*, Sage, London 1992, pp. 84–95.
[12] Gripsrud, 'The Aesthetics of', p. 91.
[13] C. Sparks, 'Popular Journalism: Theories and Practice', in P. Dahlgren & Sparks (eds.), *Journalism and Popular'*, p. 41.

required to investigate a case; if professional independence is reduced to superficial posturing.[14]

It is also problematic when journalistic creativity is mobilized first and foremost in the dramaturgical arrangement of news at the expense of investigative creativity and serious efforts to learn about how the world is put together. It is important – for the journalist as well as the public – to question the prevailing media logic. Since power is so closely related to media logic and media dramaturgy, it is crucial to understand and criticize journalists' dramaturgical work – the staging of issues and events – the endeavour that definitely turns the journalist into a key actor in the modern public sphere.[15]

From rhetoric as well as dramatic art, we know that tension is created by contradictions and conflicts. On the one hand we have the protagonist, and against him the antagonist, earlier actions or external circumstances outside his control. The protagonist's own mistakes can cause defeat. Or the opposite: a strike of luck can turn the situation, or an act of rescue can bring salvation and a happy ending.

It is not the events themselves, but the presentations – the ways the story and the actors are directed and arranged – that are crucial. This arrangement is most efficient when it is conducive to excitement, surprise, controversy and reconciliation, when the earlier events and actions constitute preconditions for what is happening at the moment.

In a play, this is accomplished through the dramatic construction – the succession of scenes and acts. In the mass media the same effect can emerge through serial-like presentations of a case's developments. The audience is kept in suspense with effective cliffhangers. This technique is by no means reserved for fictive television serials.

The test of a good piece of drama is how well the processing of events and the portrayals of actors are interwoven – how the personalities of the principal characters constitute

---

[14] M. Eide, 'Det journalistiske mistaket' [The Journalistic Fallacy], in *Sociologisk forskning* [Sociological Inquiry], no. 3/98, Örebro University, Örebro 1998, pp. 123–142.
[15] Cfr. M. Eide & G. Hernes: *Død og pine! Om massemedia og helsepolitikk* [Damn! On Mass Media and Health Policy], Fafo, Oslo 1987.

choices that create new situations that in turn give birth to new choices or change their qualifications. And the actions must stem from their interests and feelings, their ideals and their fear.

The reservoir of dramatic archetypes is probably relatively restricted in modern journalism. Furthermore it seems reasonable to claim that certain mass media specialize in certain archetypes or classes of principal characters...

At any rate, journalists usually have the upper hand in the dramaturgical arrangement of public issues. They possess a privilege in confronting other social actors and setting up confrontations between public figures. They exercise their dramaturgical and narrative power through an ability to provoke reactions in social actors and institutions.

In addition to this substantial dramaturgical power, the journalist can also act as a *reviewer*, as a *critic* of the play performed by the sources or actors in the media drama. For the participants in a media event, the rule of the game is not only to act in order to get the most favourable publicity through the event itself; it is as important to get a good review, to be proclaimed the winner of a public confrontation or at least to gain sympathy and support through the journalistic interpretation of the appearances on the media stage.

Occasionally there is more at stake. A media appearance can be a disclosure, even a scandal. The journalistic dramaturgy is then of particularly great importance. Armed with a heavy burden of moral pathos, journalists then act as custodians of conscience, to use a phrase coined by James Ettema and Ted Glasser.[16] Or to put it another way, the journalists act as a modern priesthood, even though they have no salvation to offer unfortunate participants in a media scandal or a media drama of destiny. The significance of scandals is considerable in 'a world where visibility has been transformed by the media and where power and reputation go hand in hand'.[17] Scandals matter. And journalists are the masters of the moment. They are in charge.

---

[16] J. Ettema & T.L. Glasser, *Custodians of Conscience. Investigative Journalism and Public Virtue*, Columbia University Press, New York 1998.
[17] J. B. Thompson, Political Scandal. Power and Visibility in the Media Age, Polity, Cambridge, 2000, p. xi.

But their superiority will always be challenged by other media strategists and sources knowledgeable in the rules of the game. As indicated, journalists are not the only masters of media logic; skills in media logic abound in a modern media society.

Journalism can be regarded as a framing and interpretative machinery. Intellectuals' talk is among the raw material in this enterprise. The relation between intellectuals and the media is a matter of changing power relations which calls for a historical understanding. To do this, it is important to account for the role of popular journalism and be sensitive to different kinds of popular journalism. To me it is obvious that there are *vast differences* on the one hand between a tabloid paper of the kind that is not a *news*paper at all, but an entertainment medium, and on the other hand, a tabloid newspaper that still provides news in a traditional sense, and conveys political information – also in a traditional sense. A historical perspective is certainly required to understand schizophrenic newspapers on this score.

To conclude, a process of popularization may be instrumental in the making of an influential expert system. Intellectuals and other social agents' roles in the public sphere are profoundly challenged by the expanding expert system of popular journalism.

The intellectuals' ideal: British views of Scandinavia in the 1950s and 1960s

Glen O'Hara

In 1965 the Danish writer Henrik Stangerup argued that 'we are experiencing today in Scandinavia one of the most important experiments in world history'. 'That may sound pretentious', he continued, 'yet it isn't. The Scandinavia of today is the world's *avant-garde* society. What is taking place among us will happen in other countries tomorrow, as soon as they have reached a comparable level of freedom and welfare'.[1] This concept was spread by experts and policy entrepreneurs of all types, from labour economists to educationalists, and from lawyers to social scientists. One writer praised Sweden with these words in 1970: 'any book on Sweden's social and economic structure tends to read like a paean of statistical superlatives. This would be wearisome. But Sweden deserves her reputation. In so many ways she is ahead of the rest of us'.[2] This chapter will attempt to ask exactly when, why and how these ideas were influential within the British policymaking community, using evidence from government, private and pressure group papers to reveal the contours of these ideas.

---

[1] A. Ruth, 'The Second New Nation: The Mythology of Modern Sweden', in S.R. Graubard (ed.), *Norden: The Passion for Equality* (Oslo: Norwegian University Press, 1986), pp. 250–1.
[2] P. Austin, *The Swedes: How They Live and Work* (Newton Abbot: David and Charles, 1970), p. 9.

The importance of international experts

The role of expertise and policy advice is a newly fashionable one among historians. Their influence, their means of persuasion, and the 'networks' of contacts they draw upon, have all become novel topics of historical research in recent years. Patricia Clavin has recently labelled this structure a 'honeycomb', a multitude of spaces filled and refilled by groups, ideas and movements, and written of this 'transnationalism' as 'first and foremost about people: the social space that they inhabit, the networks they form and the ideas they exchange'. Rather than focussing on nation states, a rather narrow frame of reference, she and her collaborators have begun to delineate some of the most important political, financial and economic communities of the twentieth century.[3] International relations theorists, no less than historians, have been forced to rethink their ideas in an era notable for the rise of nongovernmental organisations. Authors such as John Boli and George M. Thomas have pointed out the need for a new history of 'world culture' based, not on traditional states and politicians, but on the 'organizational dimensions of the world polity, that is, structures that embody, express, transmit and transform world culture'.[4]

'Honeycombed' networks of intellectuals carried great political weight in the post-war period of managed economies and welfare states. A.W. Coats has shown how economists' sophistication, numbers, connections and persuasiveness assisted in the adoption of their views; the same might be said of social scientists.[5] It may be possible in what follows to identify a relatively small number of thinkers who formed, in Peter Haas' influential treatment, an 'epistemic community'. These expert networks, relying on their advanced understanding and privileged knowledge, share normative and causal beliefs, as well as notions of validity and

---

[3] P. Clavin, 'Defining Transnationalism', *Contemporary European History* 14 (2005), pp. 422, 438.
[4] J. Boli and G.M. Thomas, 'Introduction', in J. Boli and G.M. Thomas (eds), *Constructing World Culture: International Nongovernmental Organizations since 1875* (Stanford: Stanford University Press, 1999), p. 4.
[5] A.W. Coats, 'Economic Ideas and Economists in Government', in D.C. Colander and A.W. Coats, (eds) *The Spread of Economic Ideas* (Cambridge: Cambridge University Press, 1989), pp. 110–15.

views of which policy instruments might work.[6] Boli and Thomas' 'culture', the very wide paradigms of how the world either does or should work, was built partly by just these types of people.

One thing that international networks of intellectuals gave to policy was clarity in the guise of numbers: in this period, national statistics ranging from Gross National Product to the number of graduates being produced by each state's education system. J. Adam Tooze has written of statistics as a 'cultural artefact', an 'integral part of the economic and social world, which they seek to describe'; in an alternative formulation, they are 'the vocabulary of social analysis and grids of categories into which bureaucracies attempt to fix the continuous mobility, tensions and dynamics of society'.[7] Statesmen had realised the role of statistics in modern statecraft since at least the sixteenth century: one early example might be William Petty's famous 'Down Survey' of 29 Irish counties, which followed in the wake of Cromwell's conquest of that country, and which was as much about assessing rent dues and imposing English claims as anything else.[8] In another national context, the Napoleonic surveys of French geography, along with the foundation of a Statistical Bureau of the Republic in 1800, were both indications of the perceived power of information in binding a young and threatened nation together.[9] The power of statistics was always available to their academic or expert producers and guardians, a reality that shaped the twentieth-century welfare state even more acutely than state policy in the seventeenth to nineteenth centuries. In every field where policy intellectuals used Scandinavian influences to shape British policy during the 1960s, numbers were among their weapons of choice.

---

[6] P.M. Haas, 'Epistemic Communities and International Policy Coordination', *International Organization* 46 (1992), pp. 2–3.
[7] J.A. Tooze, *Statistics and the German State 1900–1945: The Making of Modern Economic Knowledge* (Cambridge: Cambridge University Press, 2001), p. 3; S. Woolf, 'Statistics and the Modern State', *Comparative Studies in Society and History* 31 (1989), p. 604.
[8] M. Poovey, *A History of the Modern Fact: Problems of Knowledge in the Sciences of Wealth and Society* (Chicago: University of Chicago Press, 1998), pp. 120–2.
[9] A. Derosieres, *The Politics of Large Numbers: A History of Statistical Reasoning* (Cambridge, Mass.: Harvard University Press, 1998), pp. 31–4.

What, then, decided whose ideas were influential, when, and why? The political scientists Randall Hansen and Desmond King have suggested a threefold explanation of why some ideas are taken up by governments and some are not, and their model may be thought helpful here. According to Hansen and King, the first requirement of an idea's adoption is that there is 'a synergy between ideas and interests'. The second is that 'carriers' of the new ideas possess crucial institutional positions. The third condition for policy adoption is that those ideas come at a propitious time for their survival and adoption.[10] What follows is an attempt to use the threefold Randall and King typology to analyse the adoption – or non-adoption – of Scandinavian political and economic policies in the era after the Second World War.

British enthusiasm for Scandinavia

There can be no doubt that the Scandinavian example was constantly mused over and analysed by the British elite, for this archetype was always in the back of decision makers' minds. In almost every field of economic and social policy, whenever alternatives to British practice were mooted, Scandinavia was put forward as a model of progress. When members of Labour's National Executive Committee visited three of Scandinavia's Social Democratic Prime Ministers during 1963, they reported back that 'their governments have a wealth of experience (particularly Sweden) which the Labour Party would do well to study'. The Swedes seemed to have answers in fields as diverse as 'trade union organisation, incomes policies, social security, town planning, defence, including the Western Nuclear deterrent, and civil defence'.[11]

Health care can be given as one more specific example. As far back as 1933 Somerville Hastings, the sometimes Labour MP and medical Socialist who helped to found the Socialist Medical Association, had called attention to the

---

[10] R. Hansen and D. King, 'Eugenic Ideas, Political Interests and Policy Variance: Immigration and Sterilization Policy in Britain and the US', *World Politics* 53 (2001), p. 262.

[11] *Harvester Archives of the British Labour Party* (hereafter *HABLP*) series one, part two, fiche 225, Rd: 494, Visit to Denmark, Sweden and Norway by Walker, Shore and Ennals, June 1963.

Swedish model. 'What we want', he wrote, 'is a State Medical Service providing at the cost of the rates and taxes, the best that medical services can give... There is nothing unusual... in such a service. They have it in Russia and they have it in Sweden'.[12] Sweden's relatively early choice to socialise medicine and spread the burden between employers and workers, rather than just provide more state funding for the sick, helped for many years to make the country a popular example. When Conservatives tried to think radically about the future of the National Health Service (NHS) in 1961, even their relatively free-market Research Department was impressed. Officials primed members of the relevant policy committee with the thought that the 'burden of contributions towards health insurance fell... principally on the employee in Denmark, Norway, Sweden and Switzerland; and principally on the employer in France and Italy. Only in the UK did the main burden fall on the State'. The implication, that British workers could and should pay more, was clear.[13] Such ideas had already been extensively discussed in a special Cabinet Committee on the future of NHS finance.[14] Right wing, as well as left wing, observers were impressed. It was also not only the form of socialisation that was admired. George Godber, the Government's Chief Medical Officer during the 1960s, singled out Swedish diagnostic and technological progress when he pressed the Treasury for more capital spending in 1966.[15]

More generally, the way in which Scandinavian governments and economies had stood up to the Depression lent their methods political and empirical support. Instead of being helplessly in power like their British colleagues during the crisis of 1929–31, the Swedish left was not only in

---

[12] J. Stewart, *'The Battle for Health': A Political History of the Socialist Medical Association, 1930–1951* (Aldershot: Ashgate, 1999), p. 59.
[13] Conservative Party Archive, Bodleian Library, Oxford, CRD 2/29/9, CRD memorandum to Policy Committee on the Future of the Social Services, 'Comparative survey of European social services', November 1961.
[14] See e.g. National Archives of the United Kingdom, Kew, London (hereafter NAUK) CAB 134/2051, MPNI memorandum to Official Committee on Health Service Finance, 'Health services in other countries', 27 April 1960.
[15] NAUK T 227/2970, Godber paper, 'The cost of recent advances in medical sciences', January 1966.

opposition, but also in possession of new ideas. In parallel with Keynes, leftist politicians such as Ernst Wigforss had worked out their own version of 'Socialist freedom' – supported by government underwriting of demand and employment, rather than nationalisation – and were thus in a strong political position when orthodox financial approaches failed to address the crisis. The Social Democrats were able to govern Sweden in alliance with the Agrarians, with very few breaks, for decades to come.[16] Sweden, and to a lesser extent Norway, became exemplars of what Esping-Andersen has termed the 'universalist' welfare state, bolstered by 'strong universalist trade unions... [and] a labour party capable of dominating the political coalition of farmers and workers that... permitted social democratic ascendance'.[17]

The American journalist Marquis Childs became an influential proponent of Sweden's interventionist methods. 'Sweden's recovery has been one of the most remarkable phenomena of the depression', he wrote in 1936. The country's index of industrial production rose by four per cent between 1929 and 1934, and even unemployment fell back from its mid-1920s levels. Childs singled out the role of public works programmes, a skilled workforce, and investment in industry as sheltering Swedish businesses even while the rest of the world economy was collapsing.[18] The Fabian Society sent a high-level team to study this example in the summer of 1937, a group that included Hugh Gaitskell, G.D.H. Cole, D.V. Glass, the London School of Economics' (LSE) demographer, and Richard 'Otto' Clarke, later Second Secretary at the Treasury and Permanent Secretary of the Ministry of Technology. They, too, concluded that Swedish public works projects had helped that country to weather the Depression.[19]

---

[16] L. Lewin, 'The Debate on Economic Planning', in S. Koblik (ed.), *Sweden's Political Development from Poverty to Affluence, 1750–1970* (Minnneapolis: University of Minnesota Press, 1975), pp. 285–7.
[17] G. Esping-Andersen, *The Three Worlds of Welfare Capitalism* (Cambridge: Polity, 1990), p. 167.
[18] M. Childs, *Sweden: The Middle Way* (New Haven: Yale University Press, 1936), p. 194.
[19] G. Wilson, 'Public Works Policy', in M. Cole and C. Smith (eds.), *Democratic Sweden* (London: Routledge, 1938), p. 91.

These plans to tackle unemployment became elements of a secular faith, that of Scandinavia – Sweden in particular – as an egalitarian exemplar and success story. For their part, postwar Swedish Social Democrats were actually often rather sceptical about high universal flat-rate benefits, paying as they did for expensive middle-class pensions rather than providing for working-class voters. High universal benefits did, however, prove very popular with the public. Sweden's vast size and regional economic disparities also precluded any calculation of a 'poverty line' that could be targeted with means-tested income support. Given these facts, Swedish Social Democrats decided to throw their lot in with the universalist scheme. Britain's relatively low levels of benefits, targeted at the poor and stigmatised as support for failure, rather than claimed 'as of right', began to pale in comparison.[20]

This example was in Richard Crossman's mind when he launched his bid, in 1969–70, to invest state pension funds in industry, and to build up a British state superannuation fund with graduated benefits for higher earners. Sweden's supplementary pensions had been introduced in 1959, and were intended to top up pensions so that they amounted to two thirds of wage earners' income while in work.[21] Crossman was cheered by Tage Erlander's assurances, at a dinner held by the Swedish Embassy in London, that this was both an uncomplicated and a popular scheme. 'I began to realize', wrote Crossman in his diary, 'how lucky the Swedes were to get on to national superannuation early. They didn't have to tell the electors any details of their scheme or its costing'. He spent five days in Sweden during December 1968, studying their system.[22]

By the late 1950s, Britain's elites were beginning to lose confidence in themselves, and to question their relative

---

[20] P. Baldwin, *The Politics of Social Solidarity: Class Bases of the European Welfare State 1875–1975* (Cambridge: Cambridge University Press, 1990), pp. 135–41.
[21] Austin, *The Swedes*, pp. 84–5.
[22] R. Crossman, *The Diaries of a Cabinet Minister, Vol. III: Secretary of State for Social Services 1968–1970* (London: Hamish Hamilton, 1977), p. 206, diary entry for 30 September 1968.

performance.²³ This generally fulfilled the third of Randall and King's explanations for policy change – that new ideas emerge at propitious times. Such was British 'declinism', the belief that the United Kingdom was heading inexorably downwards on almost any measure, that almost any other model seemed attractive. In contrast to British amateurism and incompetence, the Scandinavians were supposed to be expert, efficient and organised. Per Kleppe, Norwegian Minister of Finance from 1973 to 1979, commented on this in 1976 when he argued that there were 'watertight bulkheads' preventing British governments from drawing on proper economic advice, while in Norway, a new economic policy had been developed free of 'conventional thinking'. In 1969–70, there were more economists employed within Norway's much smaller government service than there were in the whole of Whitehall.²⁴ Peter Bierve, director of that country's statistical bureau, reinforced this case in his 1959 book on *Planning in Norway*. Though outcomes had not always matched statisticians' projections, he demonstrated that there was no consistent planning bias towards overoptimism or undue pessimism. And, he argued, Norway's statisticians were improving their accuracy all the time.²⁵ Scandinavia, it appeared, had solved the riddle of low inflation, high and consistent economic growth, supporting a welfare state that was generous but did not stifle effort and innovation, and which was managed by a numerate class of expert technocrats. Britain, it seemed, would inevitably have to copy this example.

British ambivalence

Despite these unfavourable comparisons, some fundamental ambivalence was evident both within and between British

---

[23] See J. Tomlinson, 'Inventing "Decline": The Falling Behind of the British Economy in the Post-War Years', *Economic History Review* 49 (1996), pp. 731–57.
[24] T. Bergh, 'Norway: The Powerful Servants', in A.W. Coats (ed.), *Economists in Government: An International Comparative Study* (Durham, NC: Duke University Press, 1981), p. 133 and table 1, p. 146.
[25] P.J. Bierve, *Planning in Norway 1947–1956* (Amsterdam: North Holland Publishing Company, 1959), p. 333.

policymaking communities: Clavin has drawn our attention to such countercurrents by writing about 'repulsion, rather than attraction' in other examples.[26] Admirable though some Scandinavian domestic policies might be, it remained the case that only the Norwegians were seen as truly reliable military allies. The Swedes, their martial reputation marred by staying out of the Second World War, were a neutral country that Britain's leaders had no wish to emulate. The idea of becoming a 'greater Sweden' simply did not appeal, either morally or – more immediately – in terms of the influence Britain could bring to bear on nuclear weapons negotiations. 'If we did not go into [the] EEC', Quintin Hailsham confided to Selwyn Lloyd in 1962, 'he feared we would become neutral. There would be a Sweden, Switzerland, UK neutral group. We would have to give up nuclear weapons'. One of the main elements of Britain's 'place in the world' would be at risk.[27]

As Hailsham's private views made clear, the very reason why British politicians wished to join the EEC was so that they would *not* become like the Swedes or, an alternative that seemed even worse, the Swiss. As Britain's Foreign Office negotiator wrote back to Rab Butler in 1964: 'it has for long been commonplace to envisage the role of a "greater Sweden" as one of the alternatives before us. I feel it is in fact, in the long run, the only option open to us unless we can establish a satisfactory relationship with the European Community'.[28] Civil servants deprecated the idea of retreating behind the walls of a 'fortress Britain' and an economically protectionist policy when the Wilson Government considered its European options in 1966. 'The adoption of such a course', they argued, 'by a country which, unlike Sweden or Switzerland, has not opted for a role of international neutrality would clearly relegate the United Kingdom to a position of secondary influence in world affairs'.[29]

---

[26] Clavin, 'Transnationalism', p. 424.
[27] Churchill College Archive Centre, Cambridge, SELO 4/22, Selwyn Lloyd diary, 26 October 1962.
[28] NAUK T 312/1011, O'Neill to Butler, 'Britain's Future Relationship with the EEC', 24 July 1964.
[29] NAUK CAB 134/2705, Secretaries' memorandum to Ministerial Committee on Europe, 'Future relations with Europe', 4 May 1966.

Deeper fears were also intertwined in Britons' views of Scandinavia. As so often, the novelist Graham Greene touched on his countrymen's most profound concerns when he visited Stockholm in the summer of 1933. He was there to ruminate on the future shape of his novel *England Made Me*, which was to be set in Sweden. As he later wrote in *The Spectator*, despite that city's beauty, there was a certain undertow of pride, violent self-assertion, and not least, of hypocrisy. 'Our little country, our little country, the Swedish lawyer and the Swedish publisher kept repeating', he wrote, 'with sentimental humility and a deep hidden arrogance... in his formal houses, the Swedish pacifist supported war between races. He grew excited at the thought of Russia, spoke of the glory of a war of extermination'. 'So clean, so clean': Greene remembered the Swedish middle classes' self-interested praise of the working people they kept giving 'just enough to live on'.[30]

Greene's portrait of the decadent English in *England Made Me*, including the corruption of the supposed Old Harrovian Anthony Farrant, is hardly flattering about Britons themselves. But the Swedes come out of his fictional treatment remarkably badly, especially in the figure of the monstrous businessman Krogh, afraid lest anyone find out about 'the American monopoly which even his directors believed to be still in the stage of negotiation'. Krogh was in fact based on the person of Ivar Kreuger, who before his death in 1933 controlled three quarters of the world's trade in matchsticks, and who thought little of manipulating his near-monopoly, or of negotiating with unpleasant *regimes*.[31] It is important to bear Greene's reservations in mind, for identifying enthusiasm for Scandinavian policies should not be thought to mean that influential Britons wanted uncritically to copy Nordic society as a whole.

---

[30] N. Sherry, *The Life of Graham Greene, Vol. I: 1904–1939* (Harmondsworth: Penguin, 2001 edn.), pp. 489–90.
[31] G. Greene, *England Made Me* (London: Heinemann, 1935), p. 51.

Wages policy

Despite such ambivalence at general political and cultural levels, one area in which Scandinavian countries were thought to be world leaders was in wage bargaining. Nationally applicable annual deals were struck there between centralised trade union federations and employers' organisations, a scheme that was supposed to allow national macroeconomic needs to be taken into account along with individual sectors' demands. The Social Democrat economists Gosta Rehn and Rudolf Meidner gave their name to the 'Rehn Meidner model', in which consensual, universal pay scales for similar jobs would replace annual free-for-alls, and social advances would lessen unions' demands for higher wages.[32] Adopting this system was generally thought to encourage wage restraint, the more efficient use of resources, higher productivity, and better industrial relations more generally. Michael Shanks, author of Penguin's *The Stagnant Society* and an influential commentator on Britain's perceived economic decline, was very clear that 'we need to move towards the sort of centralised annual bargaining between unions, government and employers which exists in the Scandinavian countries'.[33] Some well-placed civil servants, for instance the Ministry of Labour's Permanent Secretary James Dunnett, shared these hopes. Dunnett told his staff in 1964 that annual wage rounds co-ordinated across each industry, rather than at company or plant level, could strengthen the hand of the TUC and employers' groups over separate unions and firms. 'If this could be done', he wrote, 'we would be moving towards the kind of annual or biennial confrontation that takes place between the unions and the employers in Sweden'.[34]

This presented the Conservatives, in government in the early 1960s and desperately searching for some *modus operandi* with the unions, with a problem. For Scandinavian-style incomes policies relied on an atmosphere of co-operation, as well as the mechanics of centralisation. John Hare, Harold

---

[32] P. Swenson, *Fair Shares: Unions, Pay and Politics in Sweden and West Germany* (Ithaca: Cornell University Press, 1989), pp. 130–3.
[33] M. Shanks, 'Labour Philosophy and the Current Position', *Political Quarterly* 31 (1960), p. 253.
[34] NAUK T 230/689, Dunnett to Helsby, 'Incomes policy', 6 October 1964.

Macmillan's Minister of Labour when the Prime Minister began his fruitless pursuit of a 'new course' in 1961, told Parliament that he recognised that 'these systems have relied on the mutual agreement of employers and workers. Without that agreement neither system would work. Our traditions are somewhat different... But I do not think it impossible that we here at home can work out in agreement methods suited to our own circumstances and national outlook'.[35]

The Government therefore arranged for trade unionists to visit Sweden in October 1962, so that they could study the Swedes' methods.[36] Most of the TUC's Economic Committee met Swedish trade unionists, civil servants, ministers and industrialists, but the British Ambassador was gloomy as to the impact of this visit:

> I do not think they or any of the other members have yet any clear idea how to make use of Sweden's experience in the TUC's deliberations about economic and wages policy and the structure of the trade union movement. I have the impression that most of the delegates were thinking of using what they saw here rather to improve and develop the organisation and work of their individual unions, and by enhancing inter-union co-operation to move toward a more effective organisation at the centre, rather than as material for any direct reorganisation of the TUC.[37]

The TUC, whose delegation included George Woodcock, the TUC's Secretary General, as well as Frank Cousins and Len Murray among other TUC luminaries, was in fact entirely unpersuaded of the need to change its own plant-level practices. They focused on the 'atmosphere' of co-operation, to the exclusion of some of the structural policies that had helped to foster that mood. 'Active manpower policy', for instance, was warmly welcomed, but not really brought into the TUC's analysis of how incomes policy worked. The pamphlet that

---

[35] *House of Commons Debates*, vol. 651, col. 1072, 18 December 1961.
[36] H. Pemberton, 'Relative Decline and British Economic Policy in the 1960s', *Historical Journal* 47 (2004), p. 996.
[37] NAUK CAB 134/1902, Secretaries' memorandum to Economic Steering (Incomes) Committee, 'Trades Union Congress visit to Sweden', 3 December 1962.

eventually emerged from this visit was written by Jack Cooper, General Secretary of the National Union of General and Municipal Workers. It was extremely sceptical about the centralised bargaining system. 'It would certainly be a mistake', Cooper wrote, '...to conclude that if we remodel [any] aspect of our system on the Swedish pattern we shall achieve the same measure of success'. He settled for blaming employers' lack of co-operation.[38] Randall and King's first explanation for policy changes, a 'synergy between ideas and interests', was not met. The British system of industrial relations granted enormous independent power to the individual unions whose representatives went on the trip to Stockholm; they were not about to give up their privileges to anyone, least of all in alliance with a Conservative Government.

On entering government in 1964, Labour was less encumbered by ambivalence over government intervention than the Conservatives. While in Opposition they had even considered a Swedish-style 'wealth tax', in order slowly to nationalise parts of the economy that the party thought were being badly managed by old-style management. The wealth tax fused contemporary ideas about incomes policy and social ownership. The Rehn-Meidner approach, whereby high corporate tax levels would choke off the ability of fast-growing firms to concede high wage demands, and thus reduce wage drift and income 'leapfrogging', also lent itself to such an approach. Wealth taxes might further contribute to 'mopping up' excess demand, as well as encouraging an egalitarian approach in a country in which high wages by themselves could not truly transform individuals' lifestyles. They might also give governments more resources with which to offer social policy concessions to the unions.

The 'Swedish' plan was outlined to the relevant National Executive sub-committee by Nicholas Kaldor, one of Labour's most important economic advisers. The Swedish wealth tax, he pointed out, began at an annual 0.5 per cent of each individual's net worth, and steadily increased to 1.8 per cent. A slice of inherited wealth, and company profits,

---

[38] J. Cooper, 'Industrial Relations: Sweden Shows the Way', *Fabian Research Series* 235 (1963), pp. 30–1.

was therefore nationalised.³⁹ The money raised might even have been used to buy up shares in industry, a much more radical idea proposed by the Socialist thinker Arthur Lewis in *Socialist Commentary* in 1955.⁴⁰ But Labour chose not to take up this idea, preferring to bring in a Capital Gains Tax that would not fall on individuals' stock of wealth, but rather on their new earnings from profits. The alternative of a 'Swedish' wealth tax had proved simply too radical for Labour to contemplate. Labour's adherence to traditional nationalisation and controls, along with the fear that investment might be lowered by shifting resources from savers to those more likely to spend and consume, ensured that James Callaghan as Chancellor did not adopt the idea.⁴¹

All the same, Andrew Shonfield's influential 1965 book *Modern Capitalism* demonstrated what Labour hoped to achieve by pursuing some 'Swedish' methods. This would not necessarily include wage restraint, since well-placed Scandinavian workers were busy making double-digit wage claims. But emphasising Swedish successes did provide a basis for promoting an 'active manpower policy', combining the familiar Scandinavian elements of increased government help and organisation in the fields of industrial training, retraining and relocation. 'An atmosphere is created in the course of... long and detailed negotiation', Shonfield wrote of centralised wage bargaining, 'covering a wide area of industrial and economic policy, which leads easily to a discussion of methods of achieving a more productive use of labour in various fields'.⁴² Sir Eric Roll, Permanent Secretary of Labour's new Department of Economic Affairs (DEA), received the same advice from his officials after a DEA visit to Sweden in April 1965. After long meetings with the Swedish Labour

---

³⁹ *HABLP*, Labour Party Research Department Memoranda, Series one, part two: RD 508, 'The tax on wealth in Sweden', July 1963. See B. Jackson, 'Revisionism Reconsidered: "Property Owning Democracy" and Egalitarian Strategy in Post-War Britain', *Twentieth Century British History* 16 (2005), pp. 427–8.

⁴⁰ W. Arthur Lewis, 'The Distribution of Property', *Socialist Commentary* (December 1955), pp. 365–7.

⁴¹ M. Daunton, *Just Taxes: The Politics of Taxation in Britain 1914–1979* (Cambridge: Cambridge University Press, 2002), pp. 286–301.

⁴² A. Shonfield, *Modern Capitalism* (Oxford: Oxford University Press, 1965), p. 209.

Market Board and Ministry of Finance, officials 'found the Swedish incomes policy something of a disappointment. Despite elaborate machinery, they still continue to get wage drift and rising prices'. But the DEA advisers agreed with Shonfield as to the wider gains of centralised negotiation and organisation. 'By far the most important lesson for the UK', they wrote, 'is to be found in their [the Swedes'] labour market policy'. Swedish unions were thought to be much less resistant to change when they could see the gains they were receiving for their co-operation – not that this helped British policymakers to bring labour market policies together with prices and incomes intervention.[43]

In the final analysis, the Scandinavian influence on incomes policy was limited by what Jim Tomlinson has termed the 'iron quadrilateral' constraining all policy innovation in Britain: free collective bargaining, tripartite decision-making, parliamentary sovereignty and traditional nationalisation.[44] The Scandinavian example threatened all of these. At the most sensitive point, wages policy, where each partner was threatened by 'Nordic' innovations, the interested groups rejected reform. There was no 'synergy', in Randall and King's terms, and the TUC's attitude in 1962–63 is only one case in point. The failure went deeper, too, reflecting the inherent problems of applying an archetype to actual policies outside the country in which ideals first became real. The particular circumstances that had helped the system gain purchase in Scandinavia – the Depression, centralised employer and trade union organisations, a strong commitment to the high taxes, benefits and supply-side action that helped make the system work – were simply not present in the Britain of the 1960s.[45]

---

[43] NAUK EW 16/24, Jukes to Roll, 8 April 1965.
[44] J. Tomlinson, 'The Iron Quadrailateral: Political Obstacles to Economic Reform Under the Attlee Government', *Journal of British Studies* 34 (1995), pp. 90–111.
[45] On 'the particular combination of institutional arrangements' see T.L. Johnston, *Collective Bargaining in Sweden: A Study of the Labour Market and its Institutions* (London: Allen and Unwin, 1962), p. 336. See also Swenson, *Fair Shares*, pp. 137–8.

Education policy

The next policy arena in which Scandinavians were influential was education. In education, too, Sweden itself had been what Gunnar and Alva Myrdal, the husband-and-wife team of economist and social scientist, called a 'laboratorium' of progress. 'The young are the future', Gunnar declared: '[it is] youth's difficult privilege to think freely and presumptuously about that which belongs to the future'. Gunnar published *An American Dilemma*, on race and prejudice in the USA, and drew on the American Progressives' work: he had spent the worst of the Depression in the US as a Fellow of the Rockefeller Institute.[46] In *An American Dilemma*, he showed how much Scandinavian social democracy owed to American social science, as well as to the planning and administration of Roosevelt's experimental 'New Deal'. Gunnar, indeed, ended his study of discrimination and black exclusion with an extraordinarily confident assertion of the future of the social sciences. 'The social sciences in America', he wrote, 'are equipped to meet the demands of the post-war world.... The social engineering of the coming epoch will [prove]... that "human nature" is changeable and that human deficiencies and unhappiness are, in large degree, preventable'.[47]

Alva Myrdal's research ran along similar and complementary lines. She sat on the Social Democrats' School Commission, which reported in 1948. The Commission's recommendations were very clear, and they formed the blueprint for decades of reform. Though they took many years to bring to fruition, depending on further reports in the 1950s and 1960s, the general outlines were as follows. There should be one curriculum; one school for all children; one nine-year programme, with a strong input both of citizenship and economic skills for all. There should be no false distinction between academic and vocational life, and there should be a strong role for the individual teacher and his or

---

[46] T. Tilton, *The Political Theory of Swedish Social Democracy* (Oxford: Clarendon Press, 1991), p. 145.
[47] G. Myrdal, *An American Dilemma: The Negro Problem and Modern Democracy* (New York: Harper, 1944), p. 1023.

her skills, rather than centralising *diktats*.[48] The Myrdals' general influence, transmitted by the presence of countless Scandinavian educationalists throughout the international educational bureaucracy, as well as numerous universities and think tanks, stands as an important example of Randall and King's second explanation for policy change – the institutional position of the 'carriers' of new ideas.

Many of the British left's most important themes of the coming decades can be found in the Social Democrats' 1948 prescription. These include the role of schools in fostering grassroots research, social citizenship, 'child centred learning' and teachers' role as social scientists, 'learning co-ordinators' and 'action-based' moral leaders. 'Research-action', by which anthropological studies of different techniques at grass-roots level would form the basis for future national policy, was a particularly important innovation associated with the School Commission and the Myrdals. This, too, was to become influential in Britain.[49] Sweden did not move immediately to a comprehensive system, and its government in fact managed a long period of transition between 1948 and, finally, 1970. In the interim, years of fruitful local research would provide the basis for moving forward. This gained in scale and importance as time went on. 144 local authorities originally declared that they were ready to join these experiments, from which 14 were initially chosen. However, as the years passed, more and more councils joined. When the projects started in the academic year 1949–50, 2,483 pupils were included. By 1955–56 there were 84,941, and by 1961–62 436,595.[50]

Sweden had always pioneered educational research, embodied for instance in Carl Cederblad's work on the 'folk high schools' of adult education in the 1930s and 1940s. Torsten Husén had shown in the early 1950s that selective education for exams could *change* and *lift* measures of intelligence such as IQ among those chosen for academic schools, moulding and reinforcing social divisions

---

[48] E.S. Lyon, Modernity, *Social Science and Educational Engineering: Alva and Gunnar Myrdal and the 'Swedish Model' of School Reform* (London: South Bank University, 1999), pp. 39–43.
[49] *ibid.*, pp. 13, 21–38.
[50] P. Söderberg and S. Marklund, *The Swedish Comprehensive School* (London: Longman, 1967), p. 20.

rather than reflecting inherent ability. This insistence on both theory and data now became a constant, and a pervasive, theme in writing about the 'Scandinavian model'. Particularly influential were findings of Husén, at the Stockholm School of Education, and his collaborators. Husén himself went on to become head of the UNESCO Institute in Hamburg, which later moved to Stockholm, and to chair expert conferences under the aegis of groups such as the International Association for the Evaluation of Educational Achievement.[51] His influence was as important in detail as it was in the rarefied world of international advice. Nils-Eric Svensson, in work suggested by Husén, his academic supervisor, grouped Stockholm's schools into three categories: those in which students would work in mixed ability groupings for four, six or eight years. But 'in no instance could we note any distinct superiority for homogeneous or heterogeneous groups', he concluded. Any superiority the pupils in the early streaming schools may have brought over from their previous, more privileged education 'had been reduced to practical nullity by the time all pupils reached grade 8 and 9'.[52] The comprehensive experiment, it seemed, could proceed without worrying about the effects of teaching very different pupils in the same class.

Other scholars buttressed the analysis. The Gothenberg 'youth project', which ran from 1948 with a sample size of more than 10,000 young people followed up every few years, backed up the idea that there was a 'reserve of ability' – itself originally a Swedish phrase – that could be uncovered in a more egalitarian system. This would be revealed once the surface layers of outward confidence and social standing had been stripped away, a function which selective education had not yet been able to perform. 'The results imply', wrote Allan Svensson in 1971, 'that pupils with a positive attitude towards higher education, and who claim to feel at home and confident in the school situation, succeed better in both Swedish and mathematics than their results on intelligence

---

[51] T. Husén, *An Incurable Academic: Memoirs of a Professor* (Oxford: Pergamon, 1983), pp. 83–4.
[52] N-E. Svensson, *Ability Grouping and Scholastic Achievement* (Stockholm: Almqvist and Wiksell, 1967), pp. 169, 176.

tests give reason to expect'.⁵³ Those going into academic education were not necessarily the best and the brightest; it was advisable, therefore, to keep teachers' options open throughout school careers. What was to be taught in those schools was also covered. The Swedish Government's committee of inquiry made recommendations for the curriculum from 1957 to 1961, which were later included in the subsequent 1962 Education Act. In parallel with this, the Swedish Industrial Council for Social and Economic Studies, sponsored by industry and commerce in association with the trade unions, brought out reports on maths and Swedish (1960), physics and chemistry (1962), and civics (1965).⁵⁴

Robin Pedley, at that time Director of Exeter University's Institute of Education, recommended exactly this approach for Britain. He provided the preface for one book by the head of Sweden's National Board for Education with a particularly strong statement of this approach. 'Sweden went ahead with a national plan', he wrote, 'while experiment in England was undirected and piecemeal... Sweden's methodical approach enabled the familiar arguments to proceed alongside planned development'. 'Research in Sweden', he continued, 'has... been most useful in helping to get the details of reorganisation right, and [establishing the] lines of development *inside* the comprehensive school'.⁵⁵ Maurice Kogan later put this succinctly in an interview with Edward Boyle, the Conservative Education Minister in the early 1960s who allowed experimentation with the comprehensive model. Boyle was only two years in office, rather different according to Kogan from

> Swedish social democratic educational planning, in which there were five years of research by Husén and the rest, then a five-year period in which they matched schools in Stockholm to see how comprehensivization worked, and then a change of law and then a ten-year plan concerted

---

⁵³ A. Svensson, *Relative Achievement: School Performance in Relation to Intelligence, Sex and Home Environment* (Stockholm: Almqvist and Wiksell, 1971), p. 138.
⁵⁴ T. Husén and G. Boalt, *Educational Research and Educational Change: The Case of Sweden* (New York: Wiley, 1968), pp. 45–6.
⁵⁵ Söderberg and Marklund, *Swedish Comprehensive*, ix, xi.

between the Royal Swedish Board of Education and the Ministry of Finance to get the thing off the ground. This was, in fact, a cycle of twenty years over which a major piece of social engineering was achieved.[56]

Pedley praised Swedish comprehensives themselves in his Pelican Original, *The Comprehensive School*, in 1963. He acknowledged that many of the old Swedish *gymnasia* now educated young people from 15 to 19, making the reorganisation of the lower schools less of a problem than in England and Wales. Rather than some grammar schools being threatened with actual closure, as in Britain, the Swedes had simply shifted their role to cater for older children and young people. Still, it was an important part of his case that he could cite Husén and Svensson's work showing that 'children from poorer homes have responded most strongly to the superior advantages of the comprehensive school over the Swedish equivalent of the "modern" school; [so] there is nothing to be said for grouping together children of average and below-average capacity'.[57] John Vaizey took up the same theme, from the same evidence, in his 1962 Penguin Special *Education for Tomorrow*, though the details he gave were not precisely accurate:

> In a carefully-controlled experiment in which the city of Stockholm was divided into two, one half going over to the common school, while the other half remained divided into grammar schools and schools for children of lesser ability, the common schools have proved to be academically more successful with all groups of ability except, in the initial years, with boys of high ability from the working class. Even this group has now caught up, and it seems probable that their original retardation was due to the reorganisation of the schools and the consequent disturbance of their academic careers.[58]

---

[56] M. Kogan (ed.), *The Politics of Education: Edward Boyle and Anthony Crosland in Conversation* (Harmondsworth: Penguin, 1971), p. 77.
[57] R. Pedly, *The Comprehensive School* (Harmondsworth: Penguin, 1966 edn), p. 164.
[58] J. Vaizey, *Britain in the 'Sixties: Education for Tomorrow* (Harmondsworth: Penguin, 1962), p. 59.

The Swedes' influence was not limited to simply talking to their fellow academics. Anthony Crosland, the Labour Education Secretary responsible for issuing the administrative circular on which the comprehensive system was based, later remembered that 'we weren't starting completely *tabula rasa*. The Swedes had been going at it for some time, and I got Professor Husén to come to Curzon Street and talk to us all. He was wholly in favour of our pushing on as we were doing'.[59]

It was not only comprehensives, and Sweden, that caught the imagination of British experts. Willis Dixon, Secretary of the University of London Institute of Education, also highlighted Norway's achievements. In particular, under their 1959 Education Act, the Norwegians had succeeded in greatly reducing the number of elementary pupils in single schools with only one or two different classes containing children of different ages. By 1963 the Norwegians had ensured that less than one per cent of pupils were in undivided schools, and only 11 per cent were taught in schools with four or fewer divisions. Norway was nearly as committed as Sweden to the single nine-year school, though the country came to that conclusion later in the 1950s; and Oslo encouraged local experimentation in much the same way Stockholm approached the problem. Works such as Dixon's *Society, Schools and Progress in Scandinavia*, published in 1965, brought these achievements to a British audience.[60]

The idea of strong central direction gained hold in Britain during the early 1960s, especially among educationalists frustrated at the apparently slow rate of progress. The university sector felt this development most acutely. 'At the moment the universities receive their grants from the University Grants Committee, which is run by a handful of permanent staff', Vaizey argued in 1962. 'We need a strong central council for planning', he argued: 'Sweden, France, Holland and the USSR have such bodies'. Vaizey also thought that comprehensive schools would help to boost the numbers applying to university.[61] The Organisation for Economic Co-Operation

---

[59] Kogan (ed.), *Politics*, p. 190.
[60] W. Dixon, *Society, Schools and Progress in Scandinavia* (Oxford: Pergamon, 1965), pp. 121–3.
[61] Vaizey, *Britain in the 'Sixties*, p. 68.

and Development (OECD), though relatively sceptical about Scandinavian economic policies, was also impressed with the quality and manner of Swedish educational planning. In its 1967 report on Swedish education, the OECD pointed out that in 1965 Swedish government departments had been encouraged to plan for the longer term. 'One of the results of this re-organisation', they pointed out, 'was the creation in every ministry of a new unit, the planning and budgetary secretariat'. Not only did the Ministry of Education have its own planning unit, but it also sat on the Educational Planning Council with the much-vaunted Labour Market Board, the Treasury, the universities, the unions and the employers. This allowed all concerned to work on statistics for future policy, follow up expert commissions' recommendations, oversee the research for which Sweden was becoming famous, and to support 'horizontal' work that cut across apparently different policy areas. The OECD praised Sweden's 'rolling' reform process, since it was pragmatic, based on evidence, and capable of adjustment when circumstances or research demanded.[62] Norway, too, as Dixon pointed out, had its own Council for Experiments in Schools.[63]

This zeal for experimentation, and new methods, extended to school architecture as well as the curriculum and teaching methods. Britain's Ministry of Education issued one of its *Design Notes* on Swedish school-building in 1968. A mixed team of civil servants, architects, Her Majesty's Inspectors and local authority officials visited that country in November 1967, and spent a week studying Swedish methods. A day with the Swedish Ministry's chief planners and architects was followed by visits to a wide range of new schools and community buildings. Though their enthusiasm was restrained, the planners were clearly impressed with the provisions for both younger and older pupils. Primary-school pupils were often taught via the new 'open plan' methods, with 'informal arrangements of tables, plenty of space, and generous opportunities for display'. Older pupils' buildings were being assessed by a characteristic set of pilot projects,

---

[62] OECD, *Educational Policy and Planning in Sweden* (Paris: OECD, 1967), p. 347–8, 357, 367.
[63] Dixon, *Society, Schools and Progress*, p. 126.

about which the Ministry was as enthusiastic as the OECD. 87 unitary 'comprehensive' schools were being assessed to see how different modes of mixed-ability teaching could be supported by architectural means. The visiting team were shown one video which showed 'a school project based on glass' in which 'the pupils were seen working in small groups, each one assigned to a particular aspect of the study'. The light and movement allowed by the glass and steel buildings facilitated this type of work.[64]

Scandinavians were certainly not alone in their 'planned' approach to education, but they were a useful example to cite when bidding for money. When the Home Universities Conference called on the Government to expand Higher Education in 1958, they made their case on the basis of the demographic 'bulge' that, due to the postwar baby boom, threatened to overwhelm the system.[65] But by 1963, educationalists at the Economics of Education Conference funded by the International Economic Association Conference were citing international statistics that seemed ever more relevant to Britain as a country thought to be in economic decline. In Britain 4.5 per cent of the age group were at university, but the figure was ten per cent in Sweden, let alone the 20 per cent registered in the USA.[66] Lord Robbins' Committee on Higher Education visited Sweden in October 1962, spending three days there, and its conclusions chimed in with those of the economists. Sweden's participation rate, even allowing for higher numbers of part time and teacher training students in Britain, was marginally higher than Britain's; she was building very quickly for student accommodation; she would be stretching her lead slightly into the 1970s.[67] 'When we compare published plans for future development', Robbins argued, 'many other countries are far ahead of us.

---

[64] NAUK ED 173/4, *Design Note* 4, 'A visit to some Swedish schools, 1967', 1968, pp. 25, 27.
[65] On which see G. O'Hara, '"We Are Faced Everywhere With a Growing Population": Demographic Change and the British State, 1955–64', *Twentieth Century British History* 15 (2004), pp. 243–66.
[66] M. Sanderson, *The Universities and British Industry 1850–1970* (London: Routledge, 1972), p. 393.
[67] Cmnd. 2154, *Higher Education* (London: HMSO, October 1963), pp. 40, 43, table 20, p. 46.

If, as we believe, a highly educated population is essential to meet competitive pressures in the modern world, a much greater effort is necessary if we are to hold our own'.[68]

These ideas were spread by *ad hoc* contacts, such as Husén's visit to London and the Department's trip to see Sweden's school-building projects. But they were also more consistently disseminated by academic conferences based around themes very familiar from Scandinavia's educational experiments: the 'pool of ability'; the economic gains to be expected from education spending; and education as training for citizenship. One such conference was that on 'economic growth and investment in education', organised by the Brookings Institute in Washington DC during October 1961. Vaizey was there, as well as the civil servants W.A.B. Hopkin from the Treasury and Antony Part from the Ministry of Education. Rehn was also present, as well as Kleppe, at that time Under-Secretary of State at Norway's Ministry of Finance. Ingvar Svenilson, Stockholm University's Professor of Economics, gave a paper to this conference in which he stressed all the familiar themes. 'One thing that can be said with some confidence', he argued, 'to those who fear the effect of quantitative expansion on quality is that there is certainly a much larger "reservoir of ability" than has yet been tapped'.[69] The same conference was addressed by Sven Moberg, the civil servant head of Department at the Swedish Ministry of Education. He, too, stressed some of the elements of Sweden's education system that the OECD found so appealing. In this case, it was the planned and rational approach:

> Educational policy is regarded as an important tool for the achievement of basic social aims such as equality, security and general welfare. Educational planning, therefore, is likely to become an increasingly important and integral part of national economic planning.[70]

---

[68] *ibid.*, p. 268.
[69] OECD, *Policy Conference on Economic Growth and Investment in Education* (Paris: OECD, 1962), Vol. II, p. 34.
[70] *ibid.*, Vol. IV, p. 34.

Altogether, Sweden's influential adult education and training system, her comprehensive schools, universities and decision-making system made a formidable case for more research, centralisation and planning. Other Scandinavian countries played a much less important role in the British educational debate, except when any elements similar to the Swedish model were noted as implicit support for her experimental and egalitarian approach. Some educationalists even used that integrated system as a shorthand for the perceived triumph of the northern nations as a whole. 'The small size of population of each country may contribute to [a] feeling of intimacy, of "togetherness"', wrote Willis Dixon. Schools provided an introduction to 'a way of life which everyone, according to his means, his tastes and inclinations, can share with his neighbours'.[71]

Though Scandinavian models were not always copied, and Britain for instance introduced comprehensives at very short notice compared to Sweden, the appeal and the model were nonetheless vital as signposts and exemplars of what could be achieved: as indicating, in short, the line of march. As Lewis Spolton, Lecturer in Education at University College, Swansea, put it in 1967:

> In 20 years the framework of a new pattern has been carefully erected. From any point of view it is a formidable undertaking. But the Swedish policy-makers believe the pace of change is such that waiting for something to evolve is no longer possible; what is required is a national system geared to buttress economic growth.[72]

That judgement flowed from Scandinavians' position at the heart of international advisory bodies, as well as their direct contacts with British politicians and civil service planners. Both allowed the 'carriers' of new ideas, Husén and the Myrdals among them, to spread their influence.

---

[71] Dixon, *Society, Schools and Progress*, p. 28.
[72] L. Spolton, *The Upper Secondary School: A Comparative Survey* (Oxford: Pergamon, 1967), p. 172.

The ombudsman

Next on the list of policy experts' influence must come the creation of Britain's Parliamentary Commissioner for Administration or 'ombudsman'. This was a tradition borrowed from the Scandinavians, and one deeply rooted in the Scandinavian idea that the state and individual are bound together in a shared, common project. For Scandinavian Social Democrats, the creation of the good citizen, aware of his or her own responsibilities to the state as well as the state's own duties, required an awareness of 'civics'. This was apparently required for family, as well as civic, life. In her wartime book on Sweden's falling population and perceived population crisis, Alva Myrdal argued that the country needed 'an expansion of civic studies to include more of the factual fundamentals of the art of living in families'.[73] Such courses were also thought to be needed within schools. The Swedish Social Democrats' School Commission, upon which Myrdal sat, indeed recommended the creation of the new subject of 'civics' in their proposed comprehensive experiments, and the subject was eventually included in the national curriculum.[74] By the 1960s the ombudsman had become an example of such 'civics' in action: he or she was an avenue of complaint against sloppy or poorly thought through administrative action, as complaining to the ombudsman did not necessitate expensive and lengthy recourse to the courts.

British interest in an office of civil complaints was encouraged by the so-called 'Crichel Down affair' of 1949–54. This was a case in which the Air Ministry had transferred land to the Ministry of Agriculture, which it had then sold on in 1949 without reference to the Air Ministry's previous promise to two local landowners that they would have first call on the sale. No laws had been broken; there had been no corruption; but the officials involved had acted peremptorily and ignored administrative procedures. The subsequent Franks Report recommended a much stronger system of administrative tribunals, and a central Council to supervise

---

[73] A. Myrdal, *Nation and Family: The Swedish Experiment in Democratic Family and Population Policy* (London: Kegan Paul, 1945 edn), p. 183.
[74] Söderberg and Marklund, *Swedish Comprehensive*, p. 18.

their operation.[75] This was at least a partial admission that, given its administrative complexity, the welfare state could not operate checked only by the courts and MPs. The idea of an ombudsman who would take complaints therefore gained ground, a process that was only helped by the fact that New Zealand adopted the idea in 1960. New Zealand's decision was critical; as an English-speaking Commonwealth country, and one that had the same common-law traditions as England, this development showed that it was not just Scandinavian countries that could gain from the innovation. When Donald Johnson, the Conservative MP who was one of the first parliamentary advocates of the idea, pointed out in one debate that 'there is an Ombudsman for Norway', he did not fail to add that 'New Zealand has just appointed one. We even hear about rumours of interest behind the Iron Curtain – in Poland'.[76]

The proposal was, once more, not without its crosscurrents and opponents. Justice, a pressure group of international lawyers, published a report calling for the creation of an ombudsman in 1961, making the issue one of immediate political relevance. Justice's report contained seventeen pages which dissected the Scandinavian example in great detail.[77] But Henry Brooke, the Conservative Home Secretary, told the Home Affairs Committee of the Cabinet that British ministers, and the British courts, could be trusted in a way that foreigners could not. Ministers ran their departments in Britain, and were directly responsible for their actions, his argument went. In Sweden, where ministers supervised the work of administrative commissions and had a much more hands-off role, some bureaucratic redress might be needed. In Britain, the remedy for government incompetence or inaction could be more political. 'Restraints were imposed by administrative action in Sweden', he wrote: this 'would never be tolerated here without a court order'.[78]

---

[75] G. Sawer, *Ombudsmen* (Melbourne: Melbourne University Press, 2nd edn, 1968), pp. 20–22.
[76] *House of Commons Debates*, Fifth Series, vol. 640, col. 1694, 19 May 1961.
[77] Justice (Whyatt Report), *The Citizen and the Administration: The Redress of Grievances* (London: Justice, 1961), pp. 45–62.
[78] NAUK CAB 134/1992, Brooke memorandum to Home Affairs Committee, '"Justice" report on "The Citizen and Administration"', 10 August 1962.

These differences were used by ministers to reject the idea: Cabinet responsibility, and parliamentary sovereignty, were not to be challenged. The supposed greater powers of civil servants in Scandinavia, as opposed to those in Britain, were to the fore in the Conservatives' public response. Sir Jocelyn Simon, the Attorney General, told the Commons after considering the proposal: 'I understand that in Sweden, the Cabinet takes decisions on matters of policy but the administrative work of implementing that policy is done by public boards, rather like the boards of our nationalised industries. The officials of those boards are answerable, not to the ministers, but to the courts. That is a very different system from ours'.[79] In short, as the Lord Chancellor's Department put it in private, 'the basic idea behind the Scandinavian model... is foreign to our constitutional practice of direct ministerial responsibility to Parliament'.[80]

Such ideas would have to wait until Labour gained power. The creation of a British ombudsman was at the heart of Labour's 1964 election promise to 'set up the new office of Parliamentary Commissioner with the right to investigate the grievances of the citizen'.[81] The party retained its traditional scepticism of anything that seemed like it might become an alternative to ministerial power. Frank Soskice, Wilson's first Home Secretary in 1964, damned the idea with faint praise in the 1961 Commons debates, and argued that departments themselves could usually be trusted to be 'effective'. And the Parliamentary Commissioner covered far fewer areas of government than his northern counterparts.[82] Nevertheless, the Scandinavian example was one reason why the Wilson governments did introduce this reform. Douglas Houghton opposed the idea within Labour's NEC

---

[79] *House of Commons Debates*, Fifth Series, vol. 640, col. 1754, 19 May 1961.
[80] R. Gregory and P. Giddings, *The Ombudsman, The Citizen and Parliament: A History of the Parliamentary and Health Service Ombudsmen* (London: Politico's, 2002), p. 39.
[81] Labour Party General Election Manifesto 1964, *Let's Go With Labour for the New Britain*; cited in I. Dale, *Labour Party General Election Manifestos 1900–1997* (London: Politico's, 2000), p. 124.
[82] M. Winstanley, 'Britain's "Ombudsman" – His Role in the Process of Parliamentary Scrutiny', in A. Morris (ed.), *The Growth of Parliamentary Scrutiny by Committee* (Oxford: Pergamon, 1970), p. 78.

sub-committee on the matter; he argued that he was 'simply not convinced' of the need. Since Houghton was destined to become social security 'overlord' when Wilson finally gained power, his opposition might have been fatal to the scheme. But Labour's permanent research staff, led by Peter Shore, were much more favourably disposed to the idea, and returned fire with a long memorandum laying out the benefits of 'a Commissioner of Rights on the lines of the Scandinavian Ombudsman'.[83] The word 'ombudsman' itself was omitted from the Bill, as well as from the legislation that came after. But the White Paper on which the legislation was based freely admitted that the examples of Sweden, Finland, Denmark, Norway and New Zealand had been studied. Although the schemes would differ in detail, the Government announced, 'the broad objective in each country has been the same'.[84]

Closer inspection reveals again the influence of Scandinavian officials and their international connections. The Danish Ombudsman, Stephan Hurwitz, had been extremely active in promoting the adoption of this system in the late 1950s and early 1960s, giving public lectures on British tours, and talking on the radio's Third Programme.[85] One informed British observer recognised that 'it has been primarily through his talks and broadcasts that such general knowledge as there is on the subject exists'.[86] It was Hurwitz who played the key role in persuading New Zealand's National Party to replicate his office.[87] Dr John Robson, New Zealand's Secretary for Justice, was present when Hurwitz gave a paper on the idea of an 'ombudsman' to an academic conference held at Kandy, Sri Lanka, in 1959. Upon the National Party's accession to office in 1961, Robson was called in by the new Minister for Justice, and interrogated about the Kandy conference. Ralph Hanan, Robson's replacement after his party

---

[83] Labour Party Archive, Manchester, NEC sub-committee files, Home Policy Committee memorandum RD 570, 'The Parliamentary Commissioner or Ombudsman', November 1963.
[84] Cmnd. 2767, *The Parliamentary Commissioner for Administration* (London: HMSO, October 1965), p. 3.
[85] S. Hurwitz, 'The Ombudsman and His Office', *The Listener* 1624 (1960), pp. 835–8;
[86] B. Chapman, 'The Ombudsman', *Public Administration* 38 (1960), p. 303.
[87] Sawyer, *Ombudsmen*, p. 25.

won the 1961 election, later cited Hurwitz's Kandy paper as the reason for his conversion to the idea.[88]

Conclusions: influence and reality

Scandinavians had a number of advantages over other experts. Like Americans, they usually spoke English, which helped Husén, for instance, to influence debates about education. They were extremely prominent in those international advisory bodies that proliferated at this time, as befitted their small-nation status and 'outward looking' approach: Svenilson, Hurwitz and the Myrdals are good examples of this tendency. The Scadinavian welfare state was relatively generous, which appealed to the left, but was relatively contributory, which appealed to the right. Sweden's intermediate status during the Cold War, during which she was clearly identified with the West while retaining her neutrality, boosted the general appeal of the Swedish domestic model across the political spectrum, while causing most British policymakers to reject her international stance. Norway's wartime resistance, and shared military ties with Britain given her membership of NATO, meant that she was not forgotten. Altogether, the Nordic countries made for an impressive exemplar, all the more influential thanks to the physical closeness of the nations just across the North Sea.

But this proximity and attractiveness could not guarantee that Scandinavian ideas were implemented. Comprehensive schooling was largely accepted and implemented by Labour, though the Scandinavian example probably only had a peripheral influence on that process. The ombudsman was clearly inspired by Scandinavian experience. But in areas in which Scandinavian experiences were perhaps even more central, for instance in wages policy, there was less success. This was mainly because of the absence of those elements political scientists such as Randall and King have identified, and indeed this paper has proved a useful test of their typology. For deep changes to be possible, ideas and interests

---

[88] J. Robertson, 'The Danish Ombudsman: New Zealand's Precedent', in H. Gammeltoft-Hansen and F. Axmark (eds), *The Danish Ombudsman* (Copenhagen: Ministry of Foreign Affairs, 1995), p. 35.

have to come into line; their sponsors need to be in positions of power and influence; and the timing has to be right in the 'receptor' country for truly radical change. The time was not ripe, even in the 1960s, for a major realignment of British politics along Scandinavian lines. Neither trade unions nor employers wanted the Government to help them decide on prices and incomes, or central national bargaining that they believed would hold back the strongest workers and most efficient firms. The public, and even some more traditional Labour thinkers, were not ready for a wealth tax; pensions reform proved simply too complex, and too politically divisive, to emulate Swedish superannuation.

More generally, this interpretation should alert us all the more urgently to the role of policy networks, and of gradual policy learning, both within and outside bureaucracies. The role of UNESCO in spreading educational ideas, of the OEEC and OECD across the range of economic and social policy, and of international pressure groups such as Justice: these are further lines of inquiry that will repay further study. For despite the failure of the Scandinavian ideal fundamentally to transform British politics, that example remained extremely influential. Comprehensive schooling, and the parliamentary ombudsman, are only two examples of the deep and abiding influence of the Scandinavian countries on British public life.

Norwegian academics as public intellectuals after World War II

Ragnvald Kalleberg

The term 'intellectual' may have several different meanings; here it will be used to refer to a sub-role in the role-set of academics. 'Academics' in my terminology are simply people with an academic education. As public intellectuals they communicate specialized knowledge to lay publics outside of their own specialty. This task has been part of the role-set of Western academics since the Enlightenment. The term 'laity' here includes specialists from other disciplines; a political scientist, for instance, is a lay person when the disseminator is a chemist, and vice versa. Popularization between specialists in different fields, especially when integrated with larger cultural and political publics, is essential in liberal democracies due to the intellectual complexity of our challenges, for instance related to crime or ecology, and the necessity of enlightened public discourses to handle them in better ways.

Contrary to what many academics assume, the high level of general education in OECD-countries today has not made this intellectual role less important than before. In my view, the most adequate understanding of this academic task under contemporary conditions may be acquired if one starts by discussing it in relation only to those with an academic education. If academics do not understand that popularization is essential also today – and even in an imagined society only consisting of academics – and that each one of them (us) in most discussions are lay people, they (we) do not understand the task. This point of view does not in any way imply that communication between specialists and people with no academic education is unimportant.

The paper is focused on Norwegian academics, especially sociologists. Norway's first department of sociology was founded in 1950, and fifty sociologists were educated over the next twenty years. Thirty years after that the number had grown to 1800 (Kalleberg 2000b: 400). Today, around 2700 sociologists have been educated in Norway. Relative to its less than 5 million inhabitants, the number of sociologists in Norway over the last 20 years has probably been larger than in any other nation. Perhaps the influence of sociology in society is also stronger than anywhere else, as suggested by an international evaluation of Norwegians sociology (Allardt et al. 1995:35). (The evaluation group was chaired by a Danish Harvard sociologist, and included leading sociologists from the other Scandinavian countries.) This influence follows to a large degree from the importance of the role of intellectual among Norwegian sociologists.

Academics as intellectuals

In Danish, Swedish and Norwegian, three Scandinavian languages, the term *intellektuell* is used with a number of different meanings, as is the case with the equivalent words in English, German and French. It can be used narrowly to refer to a small group of public figures that over a long period of time has influenced public opinion. They have different backgrounds, such as academic, literary, journalistic or political ones. Examples of internationally known sociologists in this category over the last half century include Robert Merton, Jürgen Habermas, Pierre Bourdieu, Anthony Giddens, Gunnar Myrdal and Johan Galtung. However, the term can be widened to include all people working with cultural production and dissemination; we can then identify teachers, artists, journalists, scientists and the like as typical intellectuals. It may also be meaningful to define the term so that it refers to all citizens in a society. Deliberative democrats might for instance insist that in a given context each and every one of us can use his or her voice to influence an issue on a public agenda.

The basic task for academics as intellectuals is to make knowledge and insights from their discipline understandable and relevant for people outside of the specialty. In Norway it is unusual to call that kind of task an intellectual one. Most Norwegian academics probably think it sounds pompous to define themselves as 'intellectuals' comparable to archetypical 'intellectuals' such as Jan Paul Sartre, Bertrand Russell or John Kenneth Galbraith. Over the course of the last century, Norwegians have most often used the terms *folkeopplysning* (enlightenment of people), *popularisering* (popularization) and *forskningsformidling* (dissemination of research) to identify the kind of activity we are focusing on here. The last term mentioned has been the official one used for this kind of academic work during the last twenty years. Here I shall use these three words and (academic) intellectual as (approximately) synonyms.

Today there is widespread confusion in Norwegian academic and public life over the meaning of the 'dissemination' of research; there is one term, but several meanings. A close look at public white papers and internal discussions at specific institutions reveals that the term *forskningsformidling* is used in an unusually bewildering way. This may lead to an unclear understanding of the task at hand, of the character of institutional and individual activities, of the intended output. To my knowledge, such confusion is also typical of today's discussions in other countries in the OECD-area.

Forskningsformidling is used to refer to at least seven different tasks, activities and end results: 1) scholarly work resulting in publications; 2) teaching and supervision resulting in graduates at different levels ('teaching is the most important type of dissemination offered by this institution'); 3) popularization of scientific knowledge and participation in public discourse resulting in improved cultural and political literacy; 4) expert or professional activity resulting in improvements for a client, such as advising an enterprise or treating patients; 5) PR activity which is supposed to result in improved visibility, status and perhaps even more money; 6) commercialization of scientific knowledge resulting in new processes, products and services; and 7) academics participating in political roles, for instance as members of social movements and participants in local community development. (See Kalleberg 2004, 2005, 2006)

One word often has several distinct meanings in the social and cultural sciences and in general public discourse, and in most situations this is no problem. Because it is so common as a linguistic experience, the basic semantic insight should be widespread, and can easily be formalized in the semantic triangle: A single *term* (word) can express several different *thoughts* (meanings, concepts) and refer to several *things* (practices, states of affairs). Problems regularly emerge when we forget the arbitrary relationship between terms on the one hand, and thoughts and things on the other.

The academic task of being a public intellectual is a central one. To be able to describe, analyze and stimulate such activity it is therefore important to recognize this widespread terminological and conceptual confusion to gain a clearer understanding of the task, individual and institutional practices and intended end results. There are several factors contributing to this confusion, some of them linked to the complexity of academic role-sets, the underinstitutionalization of the task and the strength of a market-management ideology for the last quarter of a century. When trying to organize the main academic tasks into only three groups – such as the Norwegian model of 'research, teaching and dissemination' or the American one of 'research, teaching and service' – it is easy to marginalize or forget certain tasks. In order to achieve more clarity and realism we should instead speak of five basic institutional and individual tasks.

The fivefold academic role-set

The structural position of the university academic, such as a professor at a Scandinavian or American research university, is the basis for a fivefold role-set, reflecting academic disciplines as bundled institutions (Kalleberg 2000a: 229–237). The academic is a researcher, teacher, 'intellectual', expert and academic citizen responsible for institutional governance. All the roles contain several sub-roles, such as the teacher-role including the sub-roles of lecturer, supervisor, participant at seminars or examiner. The end products of the activities of the five main roles are quite different, despite the fact that the same kind of knowledge is largely a necessary prerequisite for performing all of them. Broadly, they may result in scientific publications, graduates, public enlightenment and rationality in public discourse, useful services for clients and well functioning, academic institutions. The importance of the different tasks to institutions, disciplines and individual academics do vary. Some tasks may be lacking or shift over the academic´s life-course. This role complexity leads to confusions in discussions about dissemination.

Obviously, this conception of a role-set is an ideal-type (in Max Weber´s sense); in practice, activities are intertwined and can often only be analytically separated. Especially in the social sciences and the humanities, it is often only possible to distinguish analytically between a scientific and an intellectual contribution. A good example would be Gunnar Myrdal´s *An American Dilemma* (1944), recognized as a splendid scholarly contribution and – despite its more than 1000 pages – widely read. Good examples of such contributors from Norway and the UK are historians and sociologists such as Francis Sejersted, Vilhelm Aubert, Eric Hobsbawm and Anthony Giddens. Obviously dissemination also regularly takes place indirectly, for example by virtue of the knowledge and insights students on all levels take with them to later working life. Such close connections make it understandable that so many simply identify dissemination with both research and teaching.

Even in university systems in which individual academics disseminate a great deal, such as in Norway, the activity as such is under-institutionalized. Compared to teaching activities, there is little or no administrative support, few financial resources and little recording of the actual activity and its influence in the wider society. This low degree of institutionalization contributes to the relative invisibility of dissemination and confusions in discussions about it.

A market-management ideology and corresponding practices became increasingly influential from the mid 1980s in Norway and other OECD countries. Ideas and practices from the business sector were regarded as appropriate even outside of market contexts. In the public sector the new strategies are often labeled *New Public Management*.

Science and higher education should not only be modernized according to these requirements, but were also regarded as essential for competitiveness and economic growth in the new knowledge economy. As it has been (over)stated, earlier the slogan was 'publish or perish', now it is 'patent or perish'. In accordance with this tendency it has become usual to equate dissemination with commercialization, as exemplified in a recent report on dissemination from The Norwegian Association of Higher Education Institutions. Here the main examples of contributions to this third task primarily concerned innovations, patents and the successful commercialization of new scientific knowledge (see Kalleberg 2006). The strong tendency to equate dissemination with institutional communication and PR strategies, including lobbying for academic institutions, also blurs the understanding of the intellectual task.

Using scientific knowledge in commercial and PR activities is important and legitimate. They are anchored in two of the basic roles in the academic role-set: expert activity for the benefit of clients and institutional governance. The expert role is especially easy to see in professional disciplines like medicine, law and engineering, but the role can be important in all disciplines, for instance in the form of advising to clients. Academic PR is an important task for academic leaders, not least for top leaders and their information people. But dissemination is a different kind of task.

It is a form of conceptual misbehavior not to keep the activities analytically separate. We have to say 'analytically' because different disciplinary activities are regularly bundled together in practice. Excellent research can be a value in its own right, but also improve studies and expert activity (for instance, the quality of medical doctors), be the basis for fascinating popularization and contribute to an institution's visibility in society; winning a Nobel prize has a great PR cachet.

Disseminators and debaters. Cultural and political citizens

It is useful to divide the task of academic intellectual into two subtasks, two forms of communication between specialists and non-specialists: the academic as disseminator and debater. In dissemination specialized knowledge and insight is made relevant and understandable for interested people outside of the research specialty. Here the outsider is active in the role of a cultural citizen, for instance as reader of popular science books or listener to radio presentations of research. The role of the specialist here has much in common with the role of a teacher within academies, but the recipient is not a student; as a rule he or she is a person with much less time to spend on understanding the expert's specialized knowledge and insight. Disseminators' ability to present their message interestingly and understandably, but also in a condensed form not requiring too much time, is therefore essential.

The academic may also take part in public discourse and contribute his or her specialized knowledge to a public discussion or be able to place new topics on the public agenda. Here, the academic as debater is communicating with other people in their role as political citizens. The subrole of debater more easily gives us associations of an 'intellectual' than the subrole of disseminator. But the two roles are closely connected and different from situations in which the academic leaves the academic role-set and moves into an ordinary political role. It can be difficult to draw a distinction between disciplinary and political roles, but this distinction is essential both in theory and practice. One would have to be a kind of political Manichean – be it of a pre- or postmodern kind – if arguments in public discourse were just seen as functions of open or hidden interests, only rhetorical instruments for economic, political or religious interests. (In addition such positions lead to self-refuting contradictions, cf. Kalleberg 2007: 145–46, 151–52). To develop feasible reforms in an area, it is as a rule a requirement for political adversaries – as far as possible – to develop a shared understanding of the existing situation based on valid knowledge, for instance regarding climate change.

Norwegian academics as public intellectuals

Norwegian academics have a long history as public intellectuals, dating back to the Danish-Norwegian Enlightenment during the first half of the 1700s (Kalleberg 2008). The towering figure in that period was Ludvig Holberg (1684–1754), a professor at the University of Copenhagen. Holberg was born in the second largest city of the dual monarchy, in the Norwegian merchant town of Bergen. He was unusually productive as a scholar, his collected works amount to 20,000 pages of published text. As a broadly oriented scholar, he contributed to fields we today would situate within the humanities, social sciences, law and theology. He worked within the tradition of natural law as developed by Hugo Grotius, Thomas Hobbes, Samuel Pufendorf and Christian Thomasius. If he were to be described in terms of contemporary categories, it would be apt to characterize him as a historical-comparative, moral sociologist. Holberg was the most widely read author in Norway during the eighteenth century, and has influenced artists and scholars up to the present day. His public influence was partly due to his comedies, still regularly performed, and essays. In his artistic work he (also) conveyed basic natural-law insights. Holberg defined and developed the role of the academic as public intellectual in Denmark-Norway. As an individual he is the most influential academic public intellectual and role model in Norwegian history.

In 1814 Norway became independent from Denmark, acquired its own constitution and was forced into a new union, lasting until 1905, with Sweden. In 1811 Norway's first university was founded. The University of Oslo became a key institution for the political-economic, social and cultural modernization of Norway. Professors at the university and academics trained there were regularly active as public intellectuals and academic professionals, thus contributing to the modernization processes. Some of the results were impressive, also in an international perspective. In 1875 Norway had become the third largest shipping nation in the world, exceeded only by the UK and the USA. Norway was generally ahead of Sweden in the development of democratic institutions and practices, as for instance illustrated by the abolition of the nobility in 1821, strengthened local influence in the municipalities during the 1830s, the early introduction of parliamentarianism (1884) and universal suffrage for men in 1898. Around 1850 everyone in Norway under 50 years of age could read and write, a cultural achievement perhaps at the pinnacle of the European experience. Early sociologists also contributed to these transformations, such as Eilert Sundt (belonging to the same generation as Spencer and Marx), and Sigurd Ibsen (the son of Henrik Ibsen), belonging to the same generation as Durkheim, Weber and Mead.

Norwegian sociologists during the interwar period were also strongly oriented to the task of disseminating sociological insights to wider audiences and to taking part in public discourses. The most influential group worked at The Institute for Comparative Cultural Research, a group of people strongly influenced by Durkheimian sociology. The leading people came from law, history and linguistics. They were intensively oriented towards contributing to peace and international understanding, wanting to heal the wounds after WWI (Holmås 2008).

In 1946 parliament decided that Norway should have a second university, to be established in Bergen. In the Act for this university it was for the first time (1948) stated that popular science and public enlightenment was a third task, in addition to scientific research and academic studies (Forland and Haaland 1996: 255–257). However, this was not the introduction of a new kind of practice, but a formalization of a long national tradition, and a strong local tradition at Bergen Museum, which had been established in 1825. Similar requirements were later integrated into the Acts regulating the other universities. From the late 1980s it is stated in the law pertaining to all Norwegian higher educational institutions that dissemination is a basic task. In the most recent law from 2005 these requirements have become more visible and demanding, also expecting student participation in public discourses (see §§ 1.1, 1.3).

Norway has three national committees for research ethics. The one for the social and cultural sciences is explicit and detailed with regard to recommendations for dissemination (NESH 2006). Six of its guidelines concern this topic, starting with number 42: 'Specialized research groups shall ensure that scientific knowledge is communicated to a broader audience outside of the research community'. These guidelines have been revised three times, based on discussions between representatives from the humanities, social sciences, law and theology, including extensive national hearings. These guidelines have been explicated and developed over many years, based on discussions within the disciplines themselves.

Laws and guidelines are not, however, the same as actual practices. Are Norwegian academics generally active as public intellectuals, disseminators and debaters? As far as the member states of the OECD are concerned, I know of only one set of representative, national surveys documenting this field of academic activity, which would allow one to provide a reasonably grounded answer to such a question. Three comprehensive surveys based on questionnaires that covered all academics in the four traditional universities of Norway (Oslo, Bergen, Trondheim and Tromsø) have been conducted. Academics were asked about their activity in the field of dissemination during three 3-year periods, the first one for 1980–82 (see Kyvik 2004, 2005). From 1998 to 2000, half of these university academics had published at least one popular article and a third had participated in public discourse. Academics in the humanities were the most active as disseminators and debaters. Two-thirds had written at least one popular-science article and almost half had participated in public discourse. University academics in technological fields were the least active.

60 % of the social scientists had popularized and published at least one article, on average 2.4 articles of this kind (Kyvik 2004: 89–101). Half of the social scientists had participated in public discourse, on average with 2.2 articles. The studies document that this level of disseminating and debating activity was relatively stable between 1980 and 2000. However, such a study does not cover all kinds of activities as public intellectuals: Norwegian academics give all kinds of lectures and talks; people are interviewed by the mass media, give talks at schools, for instance for teachers in mathematics in sixth form colleges, sit on panels for public discussions and the like. Some of these activities were also reported in these studies. Half of the Norwegian academics reported that they had at least once been interviewed or been written about in the media (Kyvik 2004: 98). 62% of the social scientists reported that they had been interviewed, 59% said that their research had been mentioned in different kinds of mass media.

It is sometimes speculated that it is the less productive scientists that are active in popularization. However, this is disproved by the studies above. Kyvik has (2004: 99) documented that 'those who publish for a lay public are the most productive in terms of scientific and scholarly publishing.' The different surveys also show that very few academics only published for a lay audience.

In the 3-year period 1998 –2000, social scientists at the four Norwegian universities on average published 7.9 articles as scientists and 4.6 articles as intellectual popularizers and debaters (Kyvik 2005: 96). It has thus been documented that the sub-role of being a public intellectual in the Norwegian university system is quite widely practiced and has been stable for the period focused on. It would be very useful to have similar studies conducted in other countries, thus making it possible to compare nations, institutions and disciplines.

On sociologists as academic intellectuals

The social sciences have generally a much longer intellectual than institutional history. As modern intellectual enterprises they emerged as part of the scientific revolution in Europe during the seventeenth century. As organizational units with permanent positions and an explicit reference to the name of a disciplinary field, such as sociology or psychology, they started to emerge at the end of the nineteenth century and the beginning of the twentieth. The real growth came after WWII. The development of Norwegian sociology fits into this pattern, with a history dating back to the early Enlightenment, although its first department, positions and formalized academic study were founded only in 1950.

The tradition of early sociologists, or precursors to sociology, was to be active as public intellectuals, as disseminators and debaters. The young people that built up Norwegian sociology after the German occupation of Norway ended in May 1945, were shaped by this tradition. This was a generation deeply influenced by their experiences of war and resistance to the Nazi-occupation, with strong pro-democratic convictions and a desire to contribute critically and constructively to the development of a peaceful world and social equality in a democratic welfare society.

The role of being a public intellectual has been a visible and vital part of Norwegian sociology in the decades since 1945. The relative importance and legitimacy of this role in the role-set of Norwegian sociologists seems to be stronger than in some other traditions, such as the American one. This is my subjective impression based on visits to different sociology departments in the USA. Some of the tensions in the discussions of so-called 'public sociology' in the USA seem to back up this comparative remark (see Burawoy 2005 and the following issue of BJS).

This does not mean that all Norwegian sociologists have been regularly active in this role. An interesting exception is the political sociologist and political scientist, Stein Rokkan (1921–1979) (see Hagtvet ed. 1992, Mjøset 2000). He came to social science from the humanities, originally graduating in philosophy with a dissertation on David Hume's social and political philosophy. Rokkan did not do much work in the role of public intellectual; he wrote mostly in English for an international scientific community, and published very little in general journals and papers meant for a general public. In this respect he fits into the American pattern. His influence on the broader Norwegian culture and politics has been indirect, through his scientific publications and generations of students reading him.

Five well-known sociologists, Vilhelm Aubert (1922–1988), Johan Galtung (born 1930), Dag Østerberg (born 1938), Gudmund Hernes (born 1941) and Rune Slagstad (born 1945), may illustrate to some extent the role of sociologists as intellectuals in the Norwegian society. (Also others could have been presented, such as Ottar Brox, Nils Christie, Harriet Holter, Sverre Lysgaard and Thomas Mathiesen, but I limit myself to the five mentioned.) They have all been active in the most visible mass media and each of them has influenced public opinion for at least four decades. They illustrate different themes and styles; and the combination of being productive and recognized (esoteric) scholars and influential (exoteric) intellectuals.

Within a national perspective it is often easier to focus on differences than similarities. Passionate debates have taken place between the sociologists introduced above, for example about positivism in social science. Dag Østerberg and Johan Galtung strongly disagreed with one another during the 1960s, for instance about the possibility of predicting new developments in social life or about the inevitability and desirability of the mathematization of sociology. Other examples can be found in the heated debates about the design of Norwegian universities at the end of the 1980s and in the 1990s, when Hernes and Slagstad occupied conflicting positions.

But by taking a more bird's-eye view and more comparative perspective, for instance by contrasting Norwegian with American sociologists, similarities become visible. All five have been active and influential public intellectuals; they have also researched into or reflected systematically on the role of public discourse and the quality of the mass media. They have all intervened to design and develop institutions – such as new journals, new strategies for publishing houses, the creation of new public discussion forums, active participation in the establishment of newspapers to broaden the spectrum of opinions presented in public discourse – so essential for a vibrant, civil society.

Vilhelm Aubert: The doyen of Norwegian sociology as public intellectual

Vilhelm Aubert has been the most influential Norwegian sociologist after WWII, his position being described with words like 'godfather' and *doyen* (on his work see Kalleberg 2000b; for an autobiographical sketch see Aubert 1989: 9–27). He was trained both in law and sociology. His primary field was sociology of law, but he also researched into several other subfields within the discipline (see Lindblad 1990 for a bibliography). As a young student he was entrusted with an important and dangerous task by the military intelligence organization XU, fighting the German occupation of Norway. XU collected information about German activities in Norway and transmitted them to thr Allied Central Command in London. It has been characterized as 'the most organized and productive intelligence organization operating during World War II' (Kramish 1986:107).

Aubert insisted that social scientists should disseminate their knowledge to wider publics and take part in the general debates in society. He had a clear understanding of the role and its importance. In a preface to a collection of articles, addressed both to the scientific community and wider audiences, he underlined the importance of this task with this strong claim: 'The most important function of sociology is to strengthen and defend rationality in public debate' (Aubert 1982:13). Correspondingly, he generally required that social scientists not only choose research questions that were interesting in a scholarly way, they should also be socially relevant (Kalleberg 2000b: 402- 406). (It is interesting to note that Robert Merton, with whom he had so much in common, did not explicate this in his discussions of problem formulation in sociology, and did not underline the role of public intellectual in the role-set of academics.) Through his own academic practice, Aubert solidified and clarified the intellectual role as a legitimate and necessary one in the role-set of sociologists. The most important way of disseminating sociological knowledge and insight, according to Aubert, was to write so that scientific books and articles could be read also by an interested audience outside of the discipline, scientists in other disciplines included. He was well aware that this was to continue a long tradition in Norwegian academic life, a paradigmatic case being historians.

Through newspaper articles, radio talks and public lectures for associations in civil society, Aubert remained actively engaged in public discourse throughout his life as a sociologist. He was an exemplary public intellectual, addressing a broad range of topics and using many literary genres. The topics indicated his broad interests as a scientist, including price and rationing bills, pacifism and conscientious objection to military service, equality and justice within the legal system, various forms of discrimination on the basis of class, gender and race (the Sámi minority in the North), political surveillance, security policy, university and research policy and the relationship between the developed and the developing countries. As a disseminator, he published articles in scientific journals that could (and also were) read by people outside of the discipline, and also open essays addressed to a larger audience. As a debater, he also employed aphorisms, the small format (such as in his series *Det lille vi* (the small we) in a weekly newspaper), and poems, for instance to express his sorrow and anger about the American warfare in Vietnam. In these formats, his work as a sociologist was fused with his activities as an ordinary citizen in a political role. During the 1950s he contributed regularly to a left-wing social-democratic newspaper, *Orientering*, and had been part of the group that established it and even became the editor himself for one year; he was convinced that the spectrum of opinions presented in the Norwegian debates was too narrow and needed to be expanded.

A central event in the cultural and political life of Norway in the 1960s was the emergence of the cheap paperback book. A small, left-wing publishing house – Pax – was to play a central role in Norwegian civil society during the 1960s and 1970s, stimulating Norwegians as members of reading and debating publics. The very first Norwegian book Pax published was Albert's *Likhet og rett* (Equality and Justice) (1964), a critical study of class prejudices in the Norwegian legal system (cf. also Aubert 1952). This book is an example of excellent dissemination, but being a scientific contribution at the same time. His structural-sociological perspective on the legal system and the class -structure, his focus on social elites in the legal system and a discussion of inconsistencies in legal sanctions (for instance comparing small thefts and large-scale tax evasions) generated heated debates.

One of the reasons for bundling academic activities together in institutional design and complex role-sets, is the possibility for stimulating learning experiences between different kinds of activities (Kalleberg 2000a: 234–237). An example is the way in which research can influence teaching and vice versa. In public debates Aubert also expected to acquire new sociological knowledge and insight, with learning processes regularly moving in both directions. And he did gain new insights during these debates. In the early 1950s he criticized right-wing social democrats for seeing communists and hidden conspiracies everywhere, and for not being able to differentiate between such phenomena and a well functioning liberal public sphere. Later he generalized such political criticism in sociological insights about 'Trojan horses' (Aubert 1982: Ch. 13).

Four influential disseminators and debaters: Galtung, Østerberg, Hernes and Slagstad

Johan Galtung graduated in mathematics in 1956 and a year afterwards in sociology, with a *magister artium* thesis – roughly equivalent to a US PhD degree – on the 'Prison Society'. His thesis was partly based on enforced participant observation for half a year; Norwegian authorities had thrown him into prison because he had demanded to do peace-relevant work instead of military National Service. His main scholarly field of interest has comprised studies of peace, conflicts and conflict resolution. He has also contributed to several other fields, including quantitative methods and theory of science (see Gleditsch 1980 on his production until 1980). With the philosopher Arne Næss, he published his first book in 1955, on Gandhi and his non-violent political ethics. According to the homepage of *Transcend*, a 'peace and development network for conflict transformation by peaceful means', Galtung is now author of more than 1000 articles and 100 books, translated into several languages. He regards his contributions to main elements in a new discipline of peace research – to substantive focus, methodological and theoretical approaches – as his most important scholarly achievement.

Galtung has been active in all five roles in the academic role-set. He has taught throughout his career and is regarded by students all around the world as an enthralling lecturer. He has been active as an expert in stimulating non-violent conflict resolution in different contexts and has developed a general strategy for peaceful conflict transformation (Galtung 2004, 2007). With regard to the academic role earlier identified as institutional governance, he has been an entrepreneur creating and building new institutions. He is one of the main founders of peace research as an academic specialty; he has founded one of the first institutes for peace research (in Oslo) in 1959, and was its director for its first 10 years. Galtung was instrumental in establishing *The Journal of Peace Research* in 1964. During the 1970s he was a professor in peace and conflict studies at the University of Oslo.

The role of the public intellectual has been important for Galtung throughout his career. Up to the late 1970s, he was one of the most visible and influential intellectuals in Norwegian public discourses. He published articles in the mass media and has lectured to all kinds of associations in civil society. In the last three decades he has been a kind of cosmopolitan, influencing public debates in several nations and settings. Even though he visits Norway only a few times a year, he was among the 100 Norwegian professors most mentioned in the Norwegian mass media during 2006 and 2007 (Ballo 2008).

Galtung has not only been active in the media and for institutions in civil society; he has also researched the mass media. In an article with Ruge he documented and analyzed the presentation of four Norwegian newspapers of the Congolese, Cuban and Cypriot crises (Galtung and Ruge 1965). This study is regarded as a modern classic in its field. 'Their study of gatekeeping and selectivity remains even today one of the most influential pieces on news making...' (Zelitzer 2004: 54). The study and general conceptions of peace and conflict studies have stimulated the development in the 1990s of 'peace journalism', and the 'term and the concept were coined by Johan Galtung..' (Lynch and McGoldrick 2007: 250). The ambition of 'peace journalists' is to exert a broad sociological imagination on conflicts – especially by widening the structural and historical perspective on concrete conflicts and the reportage and evaluations in and by the media. Galtung has also tried out other literary genres as the author of *A flying orange tells its tale – a fable for children and everyonee else* (Galtung and Galtung 2007) in which he presents basic insights about conflicts and their resolution.

Dag Østerberg graduated in 1961 with a *magister* thesis on the nature and task of sociology as a science (on his work see Kalleberg 1997; for a bibliography see Sundbø 2003). He was awarded a *Doctor Philosphae* degree – equivalent to the German *Habilitation* – in 1974, based on two historical-systematic studies of Marx and Durkheim. He has been working in fields where sociology and social science overlap with humanistic disciplines, especially philosophy, the history of ideas and studies of classical European music. There is perhaps no other Scandinavian sociologist that has been so much read by Scandinavian students as part of their academic studies, due to his own contributions, his translations and introductions to central sociologists and his condensed presentations of basic sociological concepts. Østerberg has been able to link esoteric scientific fields with general cultural and political public spheres in Norwegian society. His scholarly prose is widely admired for its combination of simplicity and sophistication; it can be read, and has been read, by a much larger public than just the sociological community.

Since the mid 1960s he has been an influential public intellectual; he was widely perceived to be Norway's leading social theorist from the mid 1960s to the mid 1980s. A historian of Norwegian factual prose (*sakprosa*), where scientific texts are essential, has compared him to one of the great heroes of Norwegian history, the explorer, scientist and diplomat Frithjof Nansen: 'If Nansen's book from 1890 is an icon on Norwegian nation building, Østerberg's book *Forståelsesformer* from 1966 is an equivalent icon for a generation of students and intellectuals' (Grepstad 1997: 531; see also Neumann 2007: 273).

As a young student Østerberg was a *kulturradikaler*, skeptical of traditions and believing in positivistic science (Østerberg 1997: 15–16). He quickly realized that this was not a tenable position for a self-reflective sociologist who was not willing to live with self-refuting, performative contradictions. His *magister* thesis from 1961 and an article in the leading Norwegian journal for social science from the same year, were convincing refutations of the positivistic claim that causal explanations and predictions such as the ones found in the natural sciences were possible also in the social sciences. He consequently also argued that the new social sciences could not be the basis for social technologies and social technocratic policies.

The critique of a positivistic understanding of the tasks and practices of the social and cultural sciences and the contributions to a new paradigm were essential. With the philosopher Hans Skjervheim (see Habermas 1984: 111ff; Særbø 2002), he was the main critic in Scandinavia of this understanding of man, society and science, and their interrelationships. This discussion has been one of the most important in Norwegian culture after WWII. This was not only an esoteric discussion of models of man and society and the tasks of the new social sciences, it was also of high exoteric relevance to the use of social science in culture and politics. It became a central element in the transformation of opinions and values associated with what is often referred to as the 1968-generation in Norway (Kalleberg 1998: 60–64, Slagstad 2004: 78–80).

It has often been noted that Østerberg is a left-wing critic of capitalist society; it is less often noted that he is also a conservative radical. He argues that sociology does not only have a critical task, but also a conservative one in not forgetting essential insights from the past. Creativity is required to keep the dialogue with earlier generations alive. He has discussed historical contributors such as Durkheim and Marx as if they were contemporaries, i.e. with a systematic intent. He has also taken the initiative to translate essential works into Norwegian, e.g. works by Marx, Durkheim, Weber, Simmel, Bergson, Cassirer, Merton, Parsons, Sartre and Bourdieu, and written introductions for the specialized and general reader. His argument is that scholarly prose and contributions should be central in our common culture, not locked up in closed worlds of specialists. As a public intellectual he has probably had a stronger influence on Norwegian culture and public opinion as a cultural conservative than as a Marxist critic of Norwegian society.

Gudmund Hernes studied history in Trondheim, economics and sociology in Oslo and was awarded a PhD in sociology by the Johns Hopkins University in Baltimore, where he was productively influenced by Arthur Stinchcombe and (especially) James Coleman. His PhD thesis from 1970 was on the influence of committees at the Norwegian Parliament (*Storting*). He published an article in the world's most prestigious sociological journal, the *American Journal of Sociology,* the same year. Only 30 years old he became a professor of sociology at the University of Bergen. He was involved in the first national study of standards of living and became one of the research directors, together with the political sociologist and political scientist Johan P. Olsen, of a large-scale power study (1972–1982) with a mandate to document and analyze power relationships in Norwegian society (see NOU 1982: 3). One of his special interests was the study of educational institutions and their role in the reproduction of social inequality. (On his production up to 1991, see Larsen ed. 1991: 170–188.)

Hernes has been a part time professor at different institutions, a visiting professor in sociology and research leader at an institution (*Fafo*) with strong links to the most powerful interest organization in Norwegian society, the social-democratic trade-union organization (LO). He is internationally recognized as an excellent sociologist. An indication of this was Robert Merton's desire for Hernes to become a professor at Columbia University after Paul Lazarsfeld's death in 1976. For most of his life Hernes has been an active member of the Labour Party and has had leading political positions, first as state secretary at the Planning Secretariat (1980–81).

He was a cabinet minister at two ministries while Gro Harlem Brundtland was prime minister, first at education (1990–1995), then at health (1995–1997). At the Ministry of Education, he was responsible for all levels, from the primary schools to higher education. In a book about historical trends in Norwegian secondary education, the author claims that no other politician during the twentieth century has so enduringly (re)formed the Norwegian system (Bjørndal 2005: 313; see also Moe 2004 on Hernes as an educational politician). From 1999 he was in Paris for six years, as the director of UNESCO's International Institute for Educational Planning. He was also responsible for coordinating UNESCO's work to prevent HIV and AIDS.

Hernes has been interested in power, the democratization of all sectors of society, social inequality and schools as basic cultural and social institutions for reducing social inequalities. His books and articles have been widely read, by scholars in other disciplines and by society at large. One example is *Forhandlingsøkonomi og blandingsadministrasjon* (Negotiated Economy and Mixed Administration, 1978), focusing on the character of three basic governing systems (the market, state bureaucracy and political democracy), their interrelationships and the possibilities of their both improving and perverting each other. In 1983 he was awarded a prize from one of the research councils (NAVF) for his popularization of social research.

Hernes has contributed to public discourses with articles and talks since the mid 1960s and is one of the most influential Norwegian intellectuals; he now has a regular column in an influential (at least among academics) weekly paper,

Morgenbladet. His style is condensed and elegant and he often uses concrete examples to clarify and develop his main point(s). He employs shrewd rhetorical devices and strategies, and adores alliterations and allusions. Hernes has been active in the design and development of social infrastructure stimulating public discourse. He was a part of the group that established an influential general journal for people on the left of politics – *Kontrast* – in the mid 1960s. In 1980 he was the founding father of *Politisk Forum* (Political Forum), an association in Oslo at which people met regularly to discuss public issues and get new ones on the public agenda.

Hernes is also the author of several entertaining books, taking as their starting point a well-known aphorism that is sometimes called Murphy's Law (whatever can go wrong, will go wrong). It is easy to see links to his scholarly work, his interest in complex situations where different coordination mechanisms may pervert each other, and his interest in the ironies of the unintended consequences of purposive social action. Although no contemporary sociologist has ever achieved being as entertaining to readers as Holberg, Hernes has had a good try.

Rune Slagstad studied theology and philosophy and graduated with a *magister thesis* in sociology (1975) on the Norwegian debate about positivism. 11 years afterwards he earned a *Dr. Philos.* degree with a thesis about *Rett og politikk* (Law and Politics). Slagstad is an interdisciplinary academic having had full or part time professorships in sociology, political science, law and theology (for a bibliography see Sundbø 2005). Slagstad's *De nasjonale strateger* (The National Strategists), his *magnum opus*, was published in 1998. He underlines the importance of ideas and scientific disciplines for the understanding of the Norwegian modernity project. Central in his analysis is the concept of 'knowledge regime', mediated by leading strategists anchoring their primary definition of situations in different academic disciplines, such as law or social science (see Slagstad 2004). In the first period, the 'civil servants' state' (1814–1884), professor politicians and their legal knowledge regime were crucial. In the third modernization period, the 'Labour Party State' from 1945 and until around 1980, the knowledge regime of the modern social sciences was essential both for the constructive design of economic and educational policies and for the critical evaluation and public debate of the sociological criticism of central institutions in society, such as prisons, law courts, universities, the new social sciences, welfare agencies, business enterprises and schools.

Slagstad has been an active public intellectual for the last 40 years. He articulates his points with impressive sociological imagination – combining individual-existential, historical and structural perspectives in descriptions and evaluations – and is a passionate polemicist (see Slagstad 2005). He has received prizes for his eloquence and for his many contributions to public discourse. He was for a period vice-chairman of the SV, the Socialist Left Party. In this position he initiated a large-scale debate about the challenges for a socialist strategy appropriate for contemporary Norwegian conditions. Slagstad is a left-socialist conservative, a socialist with regard to the just distribution of wealth and opportunity, a liberal democrat in politics and a conservative in his insistence on intellectual traditions and quality in culture.

He has been influential in designing and developing institutions important for stimulating rationality in public discourse. He has been an editor at two publishing houses, at *Pax* in the 1970s and at *Universitetsforlaget* (Oslo University Press) in the 1980s. One of the most impressive examples of scholarly dissemination in Norway during the last half century was the publication of *Pax Leksikon* (Pax Encyclopedia), written from an open-minded leftist perspective. Slagstad took the initiative for this encyclopedia, co-edited it (among others with the historian Hans F. Dahl and the social theorist Jon Elster) and contributed with 50 articles he had written himself. As an editor at *Universitetsforlaget* he took the initiative for and edited a series of books called *Det Blå Bibliotek* (The Blue Library). The ambition has been to publish high-quality scientific contributions 'solidly anchored in one or more disciplines', especially from the humanities, social sciences, law and theology, 'that at the same time are oriented to a larger audience' (as it is stated by the publisher). The first book to appear was one by Jon Elster, *Vitenskap og politikk* (Science and Politics, 1989).

Together with Hans Skjervheim Slagstad took the initiative for a scholarly and general public journal, *Nytt Norsk*

Tidsskrift (New Norwegian Journal), founded in 1984. He is the chief editor to this day and has been a prolific contributor. In its first issue the journal defined itself as an 'intellectual meeting place', meant to stimulate argumentative analyses in a field where politics and science, general culture and scientific culture overlaps. The journal has established itself as an important intellectual forum in the public arena.

Creation of public opinion and transformation of communicative power into administrative power

It is useful to distinguish between the informal areas in civil society and formal democratic and legal institutions making binding decisions. Associations and forums where a rational public opinion is formed characterize a well functioning deliberative democracy. The normative term 'rational' has to be understood as a gradual one, it refers to processes of the formation of opinions in forums where relevant arguments are defended, criticized, rejected and modified with reasons. Arguments refer both to descriptive and normative claims. In well functioning deliberative forums given opinions and preferences are not just registered and counted. They are transformed on the basis of convincing reasons. Deliberative processes are not power-free, but are based on the legitimate 'power' of the better argument (Kalleberg 2007: 146). Also in the most fateful power struggles the power of the better arguments can be at work, as when Churchill's and not Lord Halifax's definition of the situation was accepted in the deliberations of the British War Cabinet at the end of May 1940 (see Kershaw 2007: 47–53).

Habermas has developed a sophisticated conceptual framework for the description, analysis and evaluation of opinion- and will-formation in liberal democracies (1996: 341–387, 1998: 273–288). *Public opinion* formed in undistorted forums in civil society can be transformed into *communicative power* by legislating bodies enacting laws or cabinets forming political programs. This kind of power can further be transformed into legitimate *administrative power* by ministries actually implementing laws and political programs. The constitutive normative idea of democratic theory points to a 'self-legislating community, where all members enjoy equal private and public autonomy, so that the addressees of valid laws can at the same time regard themselves as the authors of these laws' (Habermas 1998:281). Habermas is of course aware of the fact that the normative model is not identical to actual practices in existing democracies. But the ambition is at least partly realized, or to express it with a formulation from one of his early studies: *wenn nicht wirklich, so doch wirksam* (Habermas 1962: 47). Another leading theorist of democracy also seeing the idea of democracy as something still to be realized, has suggested to distinguish between 'polyarchy' (existing, partly realized democracies) and 'democracy' (fully realized) (Dahl 1989: 322–341).

The interrelationships between informal processes of discussion in the public sphere and formal decisions and implementation processes in the political-administrative system are crucial. Norwegian sociologists as scientists have been active in identifying problems in society and making them into public issues as disseminators and debaters. Sociologists have often occupied roles as members of governmental commissions close to organized interests, parliamentary processes and ministries. Processes of opinion- and will-formation in such bodies regularly also include bargaining, including designing fair compromises. Two cases in point, linking formal and informal processes, respectively concern a national reform of opening hours in the private and public sector, and a reorganization of the public system of education.

During the first half of the 1980s, a sociologist (Anne Kalleberg) chaired a commission appointed by the government to document and evaluate the existing opening hours schemes; and suggest reforms. She was working at an independent research institute and her object of study was the Norwegian labour market. She also had close contact with different groups in the women's movement. A social-democratic cabinet minister (the economist Per Kleppe), directing the Planning Secretariat, arranged seminars so as to be able to early detect social problems. Social scientists were also invited to present their ongoing research. In 1979 Anne Kalleberg presented a paper at such a seminar, entitled 'The Struggle over Time', documenting that the traditional opening hours of Norwegian working life had become dysfunctional. One explanatory factor was that married women had entered the labour market in the 1970s; this created new time-management problems in combining paid work, housework, shopping and access to public services. Clearly, suggesting changing the regulations for opening hours could create conflicts, not at least in relation to a powerful male-dominated trade-union movement used to a 'normal workday', based on the traditional combination of a male breadwinner with the wife at home.

The commission consisted of 15 people: social scientists, civil servants, trade unionists, and people from employer-interest and consumer groups and agencies. Their mandate comprised a broad set of tasks, including the documentation of existing formal arrangements and actual practices, the evaluation of the costs and benefits of these arrangements, appraisals of arrangements in other nations, recommendations for a new law and suggestions for pilot projects. A public investigation such as this is an interesting forum for argumentation and bargaining; it may for instance be difficult or impossible for employee and employer representatives from a certain branch, say the banking sector, to insist just on their definitions and evaluation of situations. National surveys can quickly produce a different result with regard to what consumers prefer and find problematic about the opening hours of banks. A substantial part of the costs of this investigation were spent on conducting an extensive national survey and several minor research projects conducted by external researchers. The ministry was furnished with a green paper, a *Norwegian Official Report* (NOU 1984: 13), which was sent to the usual national hearing for public debate. Throughout the committee's work, there had also been many public debates about the issues. In the end, Parliament passed a new Act, adjusting opening hours to the fact that Norwegian women had entered the labour market. The 1985 Act made Norwegian opening hours among the most flexible and liberal in Europe.

During the second half of the 1980s Gudmund Hernes chaired another public investigation discussing the design of Norwegian higher education institutions (NOU 1988: 28). One of the suggestions was a new division of labour between the national network of institutions; a plan that resembled the Californian master plan for higher education. The process started with a *kronikk* in one of the national newspapers

(*Dagbladet*), written when Hernes was a visiting professor at Harvard University. A *kronikk* is a kind of public forum, much used by Norwegian academics as public intellectuals; the author is allowed about 1200 words to present a condensed argument. Hernes claimed that the University of Oslo was not fulfilling its potential in research and education, sparking an intense national debate about the quality of Norwegian institutions. When, Hernes, moving from an academic to a political position, became a member of the social-democratic cabinet in 1990, he redesigned important parts of the Norwegian educational system, from primary schools (Norwegian children were to start one year earlier and have one more year of compulsory schooling) to PhDs.

As minister also responsible for the curriculum of 10-year compulsory schooling, Hernes identified the institution of education as a pivotal one, especially in terms of the reproduction of basic cultural and civic literacy, a necessary condition for the legitimate creation and transformation of public opinion in liberal democracies. A general part of a central document, in which it is easy to recognize the Hernes' hand, states that the shared background knowledge conveyed in schools is essential: 'The more specialized and technical our culture becomes, the more difficult it will become to communicate across professional boundaries. Shared background knowledge is thus at the core of a national network of communication between members of a democratic community. [...]Education plays a leading role in passing on this[...] Education must therefore provide the fertile soil for the cultivation of coherent knowledge, skills and outlooks' (KUF 1996). The document expresses an understanding of the importance of designing and maintaining a balance between the different 'orders' of society – in economy, politics and civil society – and the pivotal role of educational institutions in the socio-political and cultural reproduction of Norway as a liberal democracy.

A concluding remark on institutional challenges for Norwegians as cultural and political citizens

The institutional context of an academic intellectual is a public forum, such as a journal (also) read by a general public, a newspaper with arenas for serious public discussions, a radio channel, a broader forum at a university open to contributors from different disciplines and institutions, an association in civil society, an open forum at a school, a museum or a discussion site on the internet. Academics as intellectuals communicate in forums where arguments are essential. The academic is here in dialogue with other people in their roles as cultural and political citizens. The aim is to influence the definition of cultural and political issues with knowledge and arguments, and also seek to get new issues on the public agenda(s). We could also say that the aim is to stimulate enlightened public understanding and contribute to deliberative-democratic discourses (Dahl 1989, Elster ed. 1997).

The primary task for disseminators and debaters is not to sell anything, lobby, make something visible, or manage anything. Their partners in interaction are not customers, clients or other users. As Habermas succinctly observes in an analysis of the deterioration of quality newspapers, where the institutional balance between cathedral and market is tipping in favor of the market: 'Radio and television audiences are not just consumers, that is market participants, but also citizens with a right to participate in culture, observe political events and form their own opinion' (Habermas 2007). One of the unintended consequences of mainstream market-management ideologies and practices is to marginalize and distort cultural and democratic processes. Clients and consumers have become visible roles in the contemporary OECD-world, whereas other basic roles such as being cultural and political citizens have become blurred.

Contemporary threats to processes of enlightened public understanding are depressingly familiar: public space is increasingly filled with commercialization, entertainment, infotainment, news about media celebrities, and the instrumental communication strategies of organized interests through professional lobbying and PR organizations. A recent change to the Norwegian Constitution may become an important initiative to counteract such tendencies; on the basis of a green paper, extensive hearings and public debate, the Norwegian Parliament in 2004 accepted a new, revised article on the freedom of expression (see NOU 1999/2005). There are several interesting elements in the 6 paragraphs of this article, but here the most pertinent one concerns the maintenance and development of an adequate institutional infrastructure for cultural and democratic sustainability: 'The State authorities shall create conditions that facilitate open and enlightened public discourse'. The commission insists that this clearly states the responsibility of the state to ensure that individuals and groups are actually given opportunities to express their opinions. State subsidizing of the mass media, the public funding of schools and universities, public support of the arts, non-governmental organizations, and support for Norwegian and minority languages, are mentioned as examples.

Media power in liberal democracies is so important for essential cultural and democratic processes that it is desirable to have constitutional provisions to stimulate adequately functioning institutions, including an infrastructure within which we can bind ourselves to the mast like Odysseus, taking on the obligations of cultural and democratic citizens, and ensuring an adequate balance between institutions and the great social orders of modern society (market, state, civil society). The institutional task of the dissemination of research and the tasks of individual academics as public intellectuals are located in this broader picture.

References to literature

Allardt, E., T. Gulbrandsen, R. Liljeström, N. Rogoff
 Ramsøy. Aa. B. Sørensen. 1995. *Nasjonal evaluering av høyere utdanning. Fagområdet sosiologi.* /National evaluation of higher education. Sociology/ Oslo: Kirke-, utdannings- og forskningsdepartementet (KUF).
Aubert, V. 1952. 'White-Collar Crime, and Social
 Structure', pp. 263–271, *American Journal of Sociology*, vol. 58, no 3.
Aubert, V. 1982. *Ufred. /Conflict, strife/* Oslo: Pax Forlag.
Aubert, V. 1989. *Continuity and Development. In Law and Society.* Oslo: Norwegian University Press.
Ballo, J. G. 2008. 'Her er professorene mediene liker' /Here
 are the professors preferred by the media/, pp. 8–9, *Morgenbladet*, February 15th to 21st.
Bjørndal, I. 2005. *Videregående opplæring i 800 år – med hovedvekt på tiden etter 1950.* /Secondary education

during 800 years – with a focus on the period after 1950/ Halden: Forum Bok.
Burawoy, M 2005. 2004 American Sociological Association Presidential address: For public sociology. *The British Journal of Sociology*, 56: 259–294.
Dahl, R. A. 1989. Democracy and Its Critics. New Heaven: Yale University Press.
Eliaeson, S., R. Kalleberg eds. 2008. *Academics as Public Intellectuals*. Newcastle Upon Tyne: Cambridge Scholars Publishers.
Elster, J. ed. 1998. *Deliberative Democracy*. Cambridge: Cambridge University Press.
Engelstad, Grenness, Kalleberg, Malnes. (2005) *Introduksjon til samfunnsfag. Vitenskapsteori, argumentasjon og faghistorie*. /Introduction to the social sciences. Theory of science, argumentation and history of science/Gyldendal.
Forland, A., A. Haaland. 1996. *Universitetet i Bergens historie*. /The history of the University of Bergen/ Bergen: Universitetet i Bergen.
Galtung, J., M. H. Ruge. 1965. 'The Structure of Foreign News.' *Journal of Peace Research*, vol. 2, no1, pp. 64–91.
Galtung, J. 2004. *Transcend and Transform. An Introduction to Conflict Work*. London: Pluto Press.
Galtung, J, A. Galtung. 2007. *A flying orange tells its tale*. Oslo: Kolofon Forlag.
Gleditsch, N. P. 1980. Johan Galtung: a bibliography of his scholarly and popular writings 1951–1980. Oslo: PRIO.
Grepstad, O. 1997. *Det litterære skattkammer. Sakprosaens teori og retorikk*. /The literary goldmine. The theory and rhetoric of factual prose/ Oslo: Det norske samlaget.
Habermas, J. 1962. *Strukturwandel der Öffentlichkeit*. Neuwied:Luchterhand.
Habermas, J. 1984. *The Theory of Communicative Action*. Boston: Beacon Press.
Habermas, J. 1996. *Between Facts and Norms. Contributions to a Discourse Theory of Law and Democracy*. Cambridge: The MIT Press.

Habermas, J. 1998. 'Civil Society and the Constitutional State', pp. 273- 287 in Sang-Jin Han ed., *Habermas and the Korean Debate*. Seoul: Seoul National University Press.

Habermas, J. 2007. 'How to save the quality press'. In *Süddeutsche Zeitung*, May 16th. This translation on the internet site 'Habermas Forum'.

Hagtvet, B. ed. 1992. *Politikk mellom økonomi og kultur: Stein Rokkan som politisk sosiolog og forskningsinspirator.* /Politics between economics and culture: Stein Rokkan as political sociologist and inspirator of research/ Oslo: Ad Notam, Gyldendal.

Holmaas, L. 2008. 'Norwegian academics and their contribution to international reconciliation and peace: The Institute for Comparative Research in Human Culture. In Eliaeson and Kalleberg, pp. 87–110.

Kalleberg, R. 1997. 'Sosiologi, forståelsesformer og samfunnsformer. Dag Østerberg som vitenskaps- og sosialfilosof' /Sociology, formations of understanding and societies. Østerberg as a philosopher of science and society/ pp. 26–51 in Bostad ed. *Filosofi på norsk II. Vår nære filosofihistorie*. Oslo: Pax forlag.

Kalleberg, R. 1998. 'Studenter i det sivile samfunn: et perspektiv på norske "studentopprørere"'. /Students in civil society: a pespective on Norwegian 'studentrebels'/Pp. 52–86 in G. Hjeltnes ed., *Universitetet og Studentene. Opprør og identitet*. Oslo: Forum for universitetshistorie, Universitetet i Oslo. Skriftserie no 4.

Kalleberg, R. 2000a. Universities: Complex Bundle Institutions and the Projects of Enlightenment. *Comparative Social Research*, pp. 219–255.

Kalleberg, R. 2000b. 'The most important task of sociology is to strengthen and defend rationality in public discourse'. On the sociology of Vilhelm Aubert. *Acta Sociologica*, no 4, 399–411.

Kalleberg, R. 2004. 'Forskningsformidling, knippeinstitusjoner og norsk som fagspråk' /Dissemination, bundle institutions and Norwegian as science language/ pp. 85–111 in F. D. Simonsen, ed.: *Språk i kunn-*

skapssamfunnet. Engelsk – elitenes nye latin? Oslo: Gyldendal Akademisk.

Kalleberg, R 2005. What is 'public sociology'? Why and how should it be made stronger? *The British Journal of Sociology*, 56, pp. 387–393.

Kalleberg, R. 2006. 'Meningsdannelse og verdiskaping'. / Opinion formation and value production/ *Kronikk* in *Morgenbladet* 10th of November.

Kalleberg, R. 2007. 'A Reconstruction of *The Ethos of Science*', pp. 137–160, *Journal of Classical Sociology*, no 2.

Kalleberg, R. 2008. 'Sociologists as public intellectuals during three centuries of the Norwegian project of enlightenment'. In Eliaeson and Kalleberg, pp. 17–48.

Kershaw, I. 2007. *Fateful Choices. Ten Decisions That Changed the World*, 1940 – 1941. New York: The Penguin Press.

Kramish, A. 1986. *The Griffin*. Boston: Houghton Mifflin Company.

KUF (1996): *Læreplanverket for den 10-årige grunnskolen*. (The curriculum for the 10-year compulsory school). English version on the net: http://www.udir.no/L97/L97_eng/index.html

Kyvik, S. 2004. *The roles of the academic researcher. An analysis of research and related activities in Norwegian universities*. NIFU/STEP.

Kyvik, S 2005. 'Popular Science Publishing and Contributions to Public Discourse among University Faculty', *Science Communication*, vol. 26.

Lindblad. S. 1990. *Vilhelm Aubert. En bibliografi.* /Vilhelm Aubert. A bibliography/Oslo: ISF Report no. 6.

Lynch, J., A. McGoldrick. 2007. 'Peace Journalism'. Pp. 248–264 in C. Webel and J. Galtung eds., *Handbook of Peace and Conflict Studies*. London: Routledge.

Moe, O. 2004. 'Gudmund Hernes som utdanningspolitiker: Kjent, men miskjent?' /G. Hernes as educational politician: Known but misunderstood?/ pp. 118–139 in P. Aasen, P. B. Foros, P. Kjøl eds., *Pedagogikk og politikk*. Oslo: Cappelen Akademisk Forlag.

Mjøset, L. 2000. 'Stein Rokkan´s Thick Comparisons'. *Acta Sociologica*, no 4

Myrdal, G. 1944. *An American Dilemma: The Negro Problem and Modern Democracy*. (With R. Sterner and A. Rose.) New York: Harper & Brothers.

NESH (The National Committee for Research Ethics in the Social Sciences and the Humanities) 2006. *Guidelines for research ethics in the social sciences, law and the humanities*. Oslo.

Neumann, I. B. 2007. 'Norsk sosiologi – samfunnsteoretisk avantgarde eller arrière garde?', /Norwegian sociology – social theoretical avantard or arrière garde?/ pp. 269–281, *Nytt Norsk Tidsskrift*, nr. 3.

NOU (Norwegian Official Report) 1982: 3. Maktutredningen. Sluttrapport. /The power study. Final report/ Oslo: Universitetsforlaget.

NOU (Norges Offentlige Utredninger) 1984. *Åpningstider og tilgjengelighet. Bidrag til en samlet åpningstidspolitikk*. No. 13. Oslo: Universitetsforlaget.

NOU 1988. *Med viten og vilje*. Oslo: Universitetsforlaget.

NOU (1999/2005:27). *'There shall be freedom of expression.' Proposed new Article 100 of the Norwegian Constitution. Report of commission appointed by Royal Decree on 26 August 1996*. Excerpts. Oslo: Ministry of Justice and the Police. The Norwegian National Commission for UNESCO.

Slagstad, R. 1998. *De nasjonale strateger*. Oslo: Pax Forlag.

Slagstad, R. 2005. *Utvagte polemikker*. /Selected polemics/ Oslo: Pax Forlag.

Sundbø, S. 1999. *Dag Østerberg. En kronologisk bibliografi over forfatterskapet 1955–1999*. Oslo: Nasjonalbiblioteket.

Sundbø, S. 2005. *Rune Slagstad. En kronologisk bibliografi over forfatterskapet 1962–2005*. Oslo: Nasjonalbiblioteket.

Sørbøe, J.I. 2002. *Hans Skjervheim: ein intellektuell biografi*. Oslo: Samlaget.

Zelitzer, B. 2004. *Taking Journalism Seriously. News and the Academy*. London: Sage Publications.

Østerberg, D. 1997. 'Min filosofiske situasjon i 1960-årene' / My philosophical situation in the 1960s/, pp. 14–25 in Bostad ed. *Filosofi på norsk II. Vår nære filosofihistorie*. Oslo: Pax forlag.

Equality or meritocracy? The choice before the postwar British Labour Party

Ben Jackson

Introduction

A lively debate has developed in recent years about the distributive objectives of the British Labour Party. Several commentators and political actors have observed that the question of what would constitute a just distribution of resources and social positions is of defining ideological significance for Labour. According to this view, political movements of the Left are demarcated from their ideological competitors by their commitment to an egalitarian model of social justice. The clear implication of this argument, of course, is that the governing philosophy of the early twenty-first century Labour Party is, at best, located on the borderline between the Left and the Right, and that this philosophy therefore represents a deviation from the view of social justice articulated by previous generations of Labour thinkers and politicians.[1]

There are many things that could be said about these arguments, but in this paper I want to pick out one aspect of

---

[1] For this line of argument, see e.g. B. Jackson and P. Segal, 'Why inequality matters', *Catalyst Working Paper* (London, 2004); B. Barry, *Why Social Justice Matters* (Cambridge, 2005); K. Hickson, 'Equality', in R. Plant, M. Beech, and K. Hickson (eds), *The Struggle for Labour's Soul: Understanding Labour's Political Thought Since 1945* (London, 2004), 120–36; P. Toynbee, 'This was the week that Labour's leaders left social democracy for dead', *Guardian*, 12.10.2007.

this discussion that seems to me to require a clearer analysis than it has so far received, namely the implicit historical comparison between the ideas of social justice defended by present day social democrats and their ideological ancestors.[2] For one important precondition of an accurate assessment of the alleged ideological backsliding of contemporary Labour Party theorists is surely an exposition of the position taken by earlier Labour thinkers on equality. If New Labour is to be classified as a deviant strain of social democracy, then we need to have a clear view of what we are comparing it with; we need to understand what 'pure' social democracy looked like. It is generally agreed that the political philosophy most suitable for the purposes of this historical comparison is the socialist revisionism that emerged as the dominant ideology of the Right of the Labour Party in the 1950s and 60s, associated with intellectually-inclined Labour politicians such as Hugh Gaitskell, Anthony Crosland, Roy Jenkins and Douglas Jay, as well as politically engaged intellectuals such as Michael Young, Arthur Lewis or the Socialist Union group.[3] If we take this revisionism as a crude but serviceable index of the political thought of British social democracy during the postwar 'golden age' of full employment and the welfare state, then we can come to a more definite verdict about the ideological transition between the Labourism of yesterday and the Labourism of today. For, if we know anything about the revisionists, it is that they believed that socialism was above all about equality, a claim that would seem to offer a fruitful point of contrast with their present day counterparts. As a number of commentators have observed, however, this raises a difficult question: since equality is a complex concept, laden with various different meanings, which variant of equality were the revisionists defending? As Stephen Fielding has put it in his recent book on the evolution of New Labour: 'Establishing what the revisionists

---

[2] I have discussed this issue at greater length in my book *Equality and the British Left: A Study in Progressive Political Thought, 1900–64* (Manchester, 2007); this paper draws on material previously published in chapter 6 of this book.

[3] On revisionism, see S. Haseler, *The Gaitskellites: Revisionism in the British Labour Party* (London, 1969).

meant by equality has become crucial to determining how far "New" Labour can claim continuity with the past.'[4]

Unfortunately, it has proved difficult to provide an uncontroversial answer to this question. One influential interpretation has been that the revisionists, and in particular Crosland, were meritocrats in the straightforward sense that they believed that individuals with similar talents deserved the same chance to develop and be rewarded for their skills.[5] However, other writers on this question have found rather different views of social justice at the heart of the revisionist project. Raymond Plant has drawn attention to the similarities between Crosland's egalitarianism and John Rawls's notion of 'democratic equality'.[6] Present-day debates about social-democratic ideology have even cultivated the impression that the revisionists desired a strict equality of outcome,[7] while other commentators have suggested that Crosland was fundamentally concerned with the distribution of social status, not with wealth, and explicitly changed the objective of socialist theory from economic to social equality.[8]

Matters are further complicated by conflicting claims about the extent to which there was a unified revisionist position on equality at all. Some historians have argued that the leading revisionists were in fact sharply divided over their distributive objectives, and have distinguished between egalitarian and meritocratic strands of revisionist thought. Unfortunately, there is no agreement about exactly who was in each camp. Ellison has argued that a contrast can be

---

[4] S. Fielding, *The Labour Party: Continuity and Change in the Making of 'New' Labour* (Basingstoke, 2003), 68.

[5] B. Barry, *Political Argument* (London, 1990 [1965]), 104; F. Parkin, *Class Inequality and Political Order* (London, 1972), 122–3; S. Lukes, 'Socialism and equality', in L. Kołakowski and S. Hampshire (eds), *The Socialist Idea* (London, 1977), 82–3; Fielding, *Labour Party*, 70.

[6] R. Plant, 'Democratic socialism and equality', in D. Lipsey and D. Leonard (eds), *The Socialist Agenda: Crosland's Legacy* (London, 1981), 135–55; his 'Social democracy', in D. Marquand and A. Seldon (eds), *The Ideas That Shaped Post-War Britain* (London, 1996), 165–94; his 'Crosland, equality and New Labour', in D. Leonard (ed.), *Crosland and New Labour* (Basingstoke, 1999), 19–34.

[7] See Jackson and Segal, 'Why inequality matters', 7–11, 21–38.

[8] M. Francis, 'Mr Gaitskell's Ganymede: re-assessing Crosland's *Future of Socialism*', *Contemporary British History*, 11 (1997), 58.

drawn between the more egalitarian position advocated by Crosland and the meritocratic outlook of other leading revisionists such as Gaitskell, Jenkins and Jay; he thus identifies 'a "majority" and "minority" perspective within Gaitskellism' on this question.[9] Other writers have shuffled the same names into slightly different ideological constellations. For instance, Bryan has also detected an internal split within revisionist thought, but differs from Ellison in characterising both Crosland and Jenkins as egalitarians, setting them apart from Jay and Gaitskell 'who did think merit or desert could justify rewards.'[10]

In the face of these contradictory interpretations, it is tempting to conclude that some of this confusion must stem from the revisionists themselves, and that they were either internally inconsistent or in straightforward disagreement with each other about the kind of equality they favoured. While tempting, this conclusion would be too quick. To get a fuller understanding of what the revisionists meant by 'equality', it is necessary to look more systematically at the specific historical context of the revisionist debate. While it might seem that these historical circumstances have been discussed at exhaustive length, in practice one important aspect of the context of revisionism has been passed over in silence by the existing secondary literature. As has been widely discussed, the revisionist turn in socialist thought emerged from a particular set of political circumstances: the astonishing legislative success of the 1945 government; the subsequent electoral failures of the Labour Party; the bitter divide between Gaitskellites and Bevanites over the leadership and strategy of the Party; and the perceived emergence of a so-called 'affluent society'. While these features of the social and political context of revisionism have been well documented,[11] the *intellectual* context of revisionist ideas has yet to be investigated in comparable detail. This can be

---

[9] N. Ellison, *Egalitarian Thought and Labour Politics: Retreating Visions* (London, 1994), 84–98, quote at 85.

[10] D. E. H. Bryan, 'The development of revisionist thought among British Labour intellectuals and politicians, 1931–64' (unpublished DPhil thesis, Oxford University, 1984), 231–5, quote at 232.

[11] See e.g. L. Black, *The Political Culture of the Left in Affluent Britain, 1951–64: Old Labour, New Britain?* (Basingstoke, 2003), 124–54.

done both synchronically and diachronically: by investigating the ideological opponents and allies that the revisionists engaged in debate with, and by identifying the political ancestors whose ideas they absorbed. What can we learn about revisionist egalitarianism if we use these techniques to examine its intellectual context?

Investigating social mobility

In terms of synchronic influences on revisionist ideology, a crucial source for revisionist egalitarianism was a novel body of academic research. This research, which appeared immensely promising to some of the most creative minds in the Labour Party at this time, was sociology, a discipline that was starting to gain widespread academic recognition in Britain in the 1950s and that was tackling a research agenda that appeared directly relevant to the difficult political questions preoccupying the revisionists.[12] The sociological genre that initially attracted most attention was the study of social stratification, an area of research that acquired much greater quantitative and theoretical sophistication in the postwar era. The emergence of this style of sociology provided an important new ideological resource for egalitarians and was analogous to the role that economics played in the 1930s. Just as the cutting-edge treatises on Keynesian economics had provided the Left with a powerful new argument for the redistribution of economic resources, mobility surveys that catalogued the grave inequality of life chances between individuals born into different classes gave fresh impetus to the Left's case for the radical reform of the social institutions that structured those inequalities. The inspiration for much of this work came from the United States, where a number of studies had been completed into rates of class mobility and the mechanisms by which individuals were grouped into

---

[12] See G. Hawthorn, *Enlightenment and Despair: A History of Social Theory* (Cambridge, 1987), 245–52, and the contrasting verdicts of P. Anderson, *English Questions* (London, 1992), 51–60, 205–7; and A. H. Halsey, *A History of Sociology in Britain* (Oxford, 2004), 70–112.

social classes,[13] although there was also an obvious overlap between this type of inquiry and the British tradition of detailed empirical investigations into poverty and inequality. Influenced by the American research, British sociologists began to tackle similar questions in a number of pioneering studies produced in the 1950s and 60s, most importantly in the research undertaken by David Glass and his colleagues at the London School of Economics (LSE), and the related work undertaken by A. H. Halsey and Jean Floud on the relationship between social class and educational attainment.[14] The sociologists made three points of particular importance for socialist revisionism.

First, they stressed the heightened salience of merit (measured by educational qualifications) as a distributive principle in postwar Britain. Since the 1944 Education Act was thought to have created a meritocratic school system based on academic selection rather than the ability to pay, it did not take much sociological insight to notice that there was a growing link between formal educational qualifications and occupational status. Nonetheless, professional sociologists were unusually authoritative disseminators of this observation. T. H. Marshall's famous essay *Citizenship and Social Class*, for example, drew attention to this change in social selection mechanisms and pointed out that a meritocratic distributive principle would in turn produce a fresh set of inequalities. 'The more confident the claim of education to be able to sift human material during the early years of life, the more is mobility concentrated within those years, and consequently limited thereafter.' In a pithy phrase that was subsequently much quoted in socialist circles, Marshall drew the moral that 'the ticket obtained on leaving school or college is for a life journey.' Marshall himself was sanguine

---

[13] See D. MacRae, 'Social stratification: a trend report', *Current Sociology*, 2 (1953–4), 21–7; S. M. Lipset and R. Bendix, *Social Mobility in Industrial Society* (Berkeley and Los Angeles, 1959); R. Bendix and S. M. Lipset (eds), *Class, Status and Power: Social Stratification in Comparative Perspective* (London, 1967).

[14] On the origins of British social stratification research, see R. A. Kent, *A History of British Empirical Sociology* (Aldershot, 1981), 124–86; J. Goldthorpe, *Social Mobility and Class Structure in Britain* (Oxford, 1987), 1–36.

about the inegalitarian effects of stratification on the basis of educational ability, believing that the advantages of this system 'in particular the elimination of inherited privilege, far outweigh its incidental defects.'[15] As Jean Floud put it, education had therefore become 'the primary agency of occupational and social selection.' Since the framework of the British education system had recently been altered in the interests of encouraging greater equality of opportunity, Floud speculated that the consequences of such reform, although unclear, might be 'considerable changes both in the social hierarchy of occupations and in the degree of mobility within and between occupations.'[16]

Second, the sociologists undermined the empirical basis of the belief that British society had historically offered a route to the top for the talented regardless of their social class and, in spite of Floud's initial optimism about the social fluidity that would be fostered by the 1944 Act, they also cast doubt on the widespread conviction that the post-1944 system of academic selection had settled the issue of equality of opportunity once and for all. The work on social mobility conducted by David Glass and his colleagues provided an effective and widely read summary of the substantial inequalities in opportunity that characterised Britain before the 1944 Act was passed. Their research demonstrated that there was a strong correlation between the social status of fathers and sons at the top of the class hierarchy, and that over successive generations there had been no change in the intensity of

---

[15] T. H. Marshall, *Citizenship and Social Class* (Cambridge, 1950), 62–8, quotes at 65, 67; also his 'Social selection in the welfare state', in Bendix and Lipset (eds), *Class, Status and Power*, 640–8. See the citation of Marshall's phrase about 'the ticket obtained on leaving school' in Socialist Union, *Twentieth Century Socialism* (Harmondsworth, 1956), 36; P. Willmott, 'The status seekers', *New Left Review*, No. 3, 1960, 71. Crosland also used a similar phrase, though he did not attribute it to Marshall: 'Comprehensive education' [1966], in his *Socialism Now and Other Essays* (London, 1974), 195.

[16] J. Floud, 'The educational experience of the adult population of England and Wales as at July 1949', in D. V. Glass (ed.), *Social Mobility in Britain* (London, 1954), 122–3; also A. H. Halsey, 'Inequalities in education', *New Reasoner*, Spring 1958, 102.

this correlation.[17] In spite of some mobility elsewhere within the class structure, the most prestigious professions were largely closed shops; they recruited from within, excluding talented members of the working class. Implicit within this study was also a pessimistic view of the likely impact of the 1944 reforms. The evidence on the effect of education on social mobility suggested that while working-class children who were selected to attend grammar schools were more likely to move up the class structure than those who went to other types of school, the overall pattern of association between fathers and sons still displayed the same basic characteristic, in that the children of fathers from lower status occupations still had a poorer chance of entering the higher status occupations than their grammar-school colleagues from more privileged backgrounds. In short, 'education as such appears to modify, but not to destroy, the characteristic association between the social status of fathers and sons.'[18]

Indeed, the early research into the effects of the 1944 Act, notably studies conducted by Halsey and his colleagues, drew attention to a disturbing fact: there remained a strong class bias in the allocation of children between grammar and secondary modern schools. The basic finding of this early fieldwork was that the class distribution of pupils at grammar schools was heavily skewed towards the middle class and what was known as the 'upper working class'.[19] Floud, Halsey and Martin argued that this could largely be attributed to the unequal distribution of measured intelligence between social classes.[20] Additionally, the performance of working-class children once they reached grammar schools was worse than that of their middle-class contemporaries,

---

[17] D. V. Glass and J. R. Hall, 'Social mobility in Great Britain: a study of inter-generation changes in status', in Glass (ed.), *Social Mobility*, 177–217, especially 216–7; also MacRae, 'Social stratification', 19–20.

[18] J. R. Hall and D. V. Glass, 'Education and social mobility', in Glass (ed.), *Social Mobility*, 307.

[19] A. H. Halsey and L. Gardner, 'Social mobility and achievement in four grammar schools', *British Journal of Sociology*, 4 (1953), 60–75; discussed by C. A. R. Crosland, *The Future of Socialism* (London, 1956), 259. See also B. Jackson and D. Marsden, *Education and the Working Class* (London, 1962), 51–3, 152–3.

[20] J. Floud, A. H. Halsey and F. M. Martin, *Social Class and Educational Opportunity* (London, 1956), 44–58.

and working-class pupils were more likely to drop out before reaching the sixth form.[21] Floud, Halsey and Martin concluded the first phase of their research into schools in Hertfordshire and Middlesbrough on an equivocal note: 'If by "ability" we mean "measured intelligence" and by "opportunity" access to grammar schools, then opportunity may be said to stand in close relationship with ability in both these areas today.' Accordingly, they characterised their central finding as 'the chances of children at a given level of ability entering grammar schools are no longer dependent on their social origins.'[22] However, their work explicitly questioned the premise that equality of opportunity could be construed in these narrow terms, and expressed grave doubts about the equity of distribution according to measured intelligence, given that it seemed likely that access to measured intelligence was itself dependent on a range of environmental rather than genetic variables.[23]

Third, these empirical findings led sociologists to comment on the normative plausibility of the ideal of equality of opportunity currently embodied in Britain's social institutions. As the sociologist Peter Willmott pointed out, it was not obvious that the growing link between educational qualifications and occupational status had a straightforward relationship with social mobility. The greater emphasis on formal education might not mean, as many suggested, that there was greater social mobility than before; nor did it mean that there was less, as some radicals argued. Rather, 'the evidence suggests that there has been little change in the *extent* of mobility in both countries [Britain and the USA]; the difference is almost certainly in the *means* of achieving mobility, which was formerly via the shop floor and is now characteristically through the 11-plus, grammar school and university.' One consequence of this, thought Willmott, was

---

[21] Central Advisory Council for Education, *Early Leaving* (London, 1954), 16–21, 34–48, 56–63; Jackson and Marsden, *Education*, 10–3.
[22] Floud, Halsey and Martin, *Social Class*, 139.
[23] A. H. Halsey, 'Genetics, social structure and intelligence', *British Journal of Sociology*, 9 (1958), 15–28; MacRae, 'Social stratification', 29–30; Jackson and Marsden, *Education*, 211–2.

'that society is becoming inflexible in new and dangerous ways.' In short, 'mobility has become institutionalised.'[24]

This worry about the 'institutionalisation' of mobility led a number of sociologists to point out that such a system might endow unjust social inequalities with greater legitimacy than previous social selection mechanisms, and create new hierarchies of social status with damaging effects on the self-respect and life chances of those at the bottom. One of the most influential social scientists of this period, Richard Titmuss, offered a particularly evocative description of this development:

> This is perhaps one of the outstanding social characteristics of the twentieth century; the fact that more and more people consciously experience at one or more stages in their lives the process of selection and rejection; for education, for work, for vocational training, for professional status, for promotion, for opportunities of access to pension schemes, for collective social benefits, for symbols of prestige and success, and in undergoing tests of mental and physical fitness, personality, skill and functional performance. In some senses at least, the arbiters of opportunity and of dependency have become, in their effects, more directly personal, more culturally demanding, more psychologically threatening.[25]

This warning was echoed by virtually all of the professional sociologists working in this area. For example, Glass had introduced his study with a cautionary message about the ambiguities of the particular understanding of equality of opportunity embodied in the 1944 Education Act. He was concerned about the potential for academic selection at an early age 'to reinforce the prestige of occupations already high in social status and to divide the population into streams which many may come to regard – indeed, already

---

[24] Willmott, 'The status seekers', 71; his 'Opportunities for all?', *Socialist Commentary*, April 1960, 32, Willmott's emphasis.

[25] R. M. Titmuss, 'The social division of welfare: some reflections on the search for equity' [1956], in his *Essays on the 'Welfare State'* (1963 [1958]), 43–4.

regard – as distinct as sheep and goats.'[26] The most celebrated expression of these worries came in Michael Young's 1958 work, *The Rise of the Meritocracy*. The specific concerns expressed by Young and others are explored later in this paper. For the moment, the important point to note is that debates about the justice of a meritocratic distribution gained greater political salience and empirical specificity as a result of this burgeoning sociological literature.

Tawneyite social democracy

In addition to the influence of academic sociology, a second aspect of the intellectual context of revisionism should be noted: the revisionists perceived themselves as located within an ideological lineage, a tradition of gradualist liberal socialism that had deep roots in British political history and culture.[27] As well as the synchronic influences just examined, then, there is also a diachronic question: who were the intellectual ancestors whose work helped to form the revisionists' thoughts on equality? Here it is worth singling out one particular text: R. H. Tawney's *Equality*. The way in which Tawney was appropriated and sanctified by the Labour Party as an in-house philosophical guru is a complicated story, and has rightly been subjected to some sceptical treatment by succeeding generations of scholars.[28] Nonetheless, giving due regard to these health warnings, Tawney's work on equality did exert a substantial influence on revisionist thought, both directly and through its dissemination into the Labour Party's conventional wisdom. Indeed, Tawney's egalitarianism was broadly representative of the British Left's thinking in the first third of the twentieth century, so this claim about his influence serves as a proxy for

---

[26] D. V. Glass, 'Introduction', in Glass (ed.), *Social Mobility*, 25–8, quote on 25–6; also MacRae, 'Social stratification', 30; Floud, Halsey and Martin, *Social Class*, xviii–xix.
[27] See e.g. Gaitskell's foreword to the 1954 edition of Evan Durbin's *Politics of Democratic Socialism* (London, 1954 [1940]), 7–14.
[28] E.g. A. Arblaster, 'Tawney in retrospect', *Society for the Study of Labour History Bulletin*, 54 (1989), 95–102; S. Collini, 'Moral mind: R. H. Tawney', in his *English Pasts* (Oxford, 1999), 177–94.

the continuing vitality of a wider social-democratic discourse about equality.[29]

The fourth edition of Tawney's *Equality* was published in 1952, with a new epilogue that detailed his favourable assessment of the 1945 government and exhorted further progress along the road to an egalitarian society.[30] A further edition was released in 1964, with an introduction by Richard Titmuss. Tawney's egalitarianism was continually cited and praised by each of the political and ideological factions on the Left,[31] and the Tawneyite critique of equality of opportunity was strongly in evidence throughout the revisionist writings of this period. Tawney's text had exposed the fragile coherence and limited plausibility of the traditional ideology of equality of opportunity on two counts. First, he argued that it was impossible to obtain an equal chance for individuals of like ability to develop and exercise their abilities in the presence of the kind of material inequalities that were generated by unregulated capitalism. According to Tawney's argument, as long as privileged individuals were capable of greatly advantaging their children in terms of education, financial assets and cultural resources, equality of opportunity would remain a sham. Second, he demonstrated that a single-minded focus on facilitating greater social mobility would be unjust, since it would accord prestige, financial reward and greater personal fulfilment to those who were fortunate enough to possess marketable skills. Opportunities to rise up the occupational hierarchy, argued Tawney, must be complemented by greater equality of condition in order to

---

[29] For a full account of this social democratic discourse about equality in the early twentieth century, see Jackson, *Equality and the British Left*, 17–90.

[30] R. H. Tawney, *Equality* (London, 1952 edition), 239–68.

[31] R. Miliband, 'Equality to date', *New Statesman*, 17.5.1952, 589–90; B. Wootton, 'Return to equality?', *Political Quarterly*, 23 (1952), 261–8; H. Gaitskell, *Recent Developments in British Socialist Thinking* (n.d. [c.1956]), 18–9; R. Williams, *Culture and Society, 1780–1950* (London, 1958), 220–6; R. M. Titmuss, 'Introduction', in R. H. Tawney, *Equality* (London, 1964), 9–11. Tawney also influenced the sociologists: see A. H. Halsey and N. Dennis, *English Ethical Socialism: Thomas More to R. H. Tawney* (Oxford, 1988), vii–xiv, 149–238.

ensure that the majority, and not just the exceptional few, have the opportunity to live fulfilling lives.[32]

In summary, both the findings of the sociologists and the tradition of socialist theory the revisionists located themselves within pointed in the same direction: towards a distributive theory that acknowledged a meritocratic distribution as an important improvement on existing inequalities, but also emphasised that this objective was not exhaustive as far as social justice was concerned. Clearly, though, setting out the intellectual environment surrounding the revisionists is only the first stage in understanding their ideas, since it is then necessary to examine how these environmental influences shaped the arguments made by the revisionists themselves. The next section aims to do just that.

Egalitarians or meritocrats?

There are a number of well-known connections between the revisionists and both the sociological debates and social-democratic tradition examined in the previous sections. Crosland was an assiduous reader of sociological research, and his writings are replete with references to the sociological literature summarised above.[33] Indeed, when Crosland served as Secretary of State for Education from 1965–67, Halsey served as his special advisor.[34] Michael Young was a friend and intellectual sparring partner of Crosland. As Head of the Labour Party's Research Department until 1950 he had access to the inner circles of the Party, and after he left he was a regular fixture at the numerous conferences and seminars convened throughout the 1950s to rethink socialism. Young's new career as a professional sociologist

---

[32] Tawney, *Equality* (1952 edition), 108–13; his 'British socialism today', *Socialist Commentary*, June 1952, 129–30. See also G. D. H. Cole's warning about the 'new class structure' created by the 11-plus: *Is this Socialism?* (London, 1954), 16.

[33] Crosland, *Future*, 231–2; S. Crosland, *Tony Crosland* (London, 1982), 54, 66; C. Torrie, 'Ideas, policy and ideology: the British Labour Party in opposition, 1951–59' (unpublished DPhil thesis, Oxford University, 1997), 245–6; K. Jeffreys, *Anthony Crosland* (London, 1999), 57.

[34] See A. H. Halsey, *No Discouragement: An Autobiography* (Basingstoke, 1996), 121–37; and his 'Education and ethical socialism', in G. Dench, T. Flower and K. Gavron (eds), *Young at Eighty* (Manchester, 1995), 129–34.

meant that he was a vital link between the work of academic sociologists and the revisionist politicians who were setting the intellectual agenda within the Labour Party. As well as joining Socialist Union (and serving on the editorial committee of their journal *Socialist Commentary*), he regularly exchanged views about politics and sociology with Crosland.[35] Many sociologists frequently wrote for directly political audiences in journals such as the *New Statesman* and *Socialist Commentary*, and a few, for example Peter Willmott and the Oxford industrial-relations scholar Alan Fox, actively contributed to the work of groups such as Socialist Union. Through these links, the findings of social stratification research became widely discussed on the Left. Similar connections existed between the revisionist camp and Tawney: Gaitskell was eventually to provide a generous tribute to Tawney at his funeral, and Rita Hinden edited a book of Tawney's essays, *The Radical Tradition*.[36] The writings of Socialist Union were more or less explicitly based on Tawneyite principles, and Tawney himself corresponded with Hinden about drafts of Socialist Union publications.[37]

More importantly, it is possible to show not just the mechanisms by which egalitarian ideas were transmitted, but also the adoption of these ideas by the revisionists in their political thought. Revisionists began by allaying any fears that they might advocate a strict egalitarianism. Gaitskell emphasised that this omnipresent, anti-egalitarian allegation was untrue: 'Let us have no more nonsense

---

[35] Crosland, *Tony Crosland*, 46; A. Briggs, *Michael Young: Social Entrepreneur* (London, 2001), 66–109, 221–3. For Young's membership of Socialist Union, see 'Foundation meeting of Socialist Union, 31 March 1951', typescript, Socialist Union Papers, Modern Records Centre, Warwick University, MSS.173/12, 1; and Young's membership form, MSS.173/15. On the links between Socialist Union and senior Labour Party figures, see L. Black, 'Social democracy as a way of life: fellowship and the Socialist Union, 1951–9', *Twentieth Century British History*, 10 (1999), 499–539.

[36] R. Hinden, 'Editor's preface' and H. Gaitskell, 'Postscript – an appreciation', both in R. H. Tawney, *The Radical Tradition* (London, 1966 [1964]), 7–9, 220–3. On Tawney's influence on Gaitskell, see P. Williams, *Hugh Gaitskell* (London, 1979), 21, 42, 71–2.

[37] E.g. R. H. Tawney to R. Hinden, 9.3.1952, Socialist Union Papers, Modern Records Centre, Warwick University, MSS.173/11.

about us being in favour of an exact and precise equality of income with no differentials at all.'[38] Socialists did, however, 'start from a presumption in favour of equality', asking: 'What are the various factors justifying differentials?'[39] An immediate challenge to the revisionist position was to offer a more precise characterisation of how such differentials could be justified: did they entail an acceptance of the justice of social inequalities so long as they were grounded on individual merit, or were they simply a concession to the necessity of incentives for efficiency purposes? In short, were the revisionists meritocrats?

The latter position was certainly the interpretation of revisionist socialism that their opponents on the Left sought to promote, and some other commentators agreed with this assessment. For example, A. J. Ayer classified Crosland's egalitarianism in the following terms:

> [Crosland] is not, indeed, an out and out egalitarian. He sees that power and authority cannot be equally distributed, and he allows that those who have greater responsibilities, and those who have the talents to render greater services, in one way or another, should be more greatly rewarded. What he is chiefly concerned with is equality of opportunity. This is partly defensible on grounds of national interest ... But mainly, for Mr Crosland, it is a matter of justice. Not everybody can enjoy the bigger plums; there are not and never can be enough to go round, but it is right that everybody should be given a fair chance to pick them.[40]

Norman Birnbaum, one of the editors of the influential 'New Left' journal *Universities and Left Review*, took a more critical view. The sociologist Daniel Bell had in fact reported to

---

[38] H. Gaitskell, speech, 3.10.1956, in *Labour Party Annual Conference Report* 1956, 130.
[39] 'Synopsis for a research project on equality', Labour Party Research Department Archive (microfiche), Bodleian Library, Oxford, RE5/November 1955, 3.
[40] A. J. Ayer, 'Forward from the welfare state', *Encounter*, December 1956, 77; see also B. Crick, 'Socialist literature in the 1950s', *Political Quarterly*, 31 (1960), 368.

Crosland after meeting the editors of this journal that 'you will be amused to know that they consider the chief enemy to be "Croslandism"'.[41] This was borne out as Birnbaum took Crosland to task for his anaemic conception of equality:

> Mr Crosland would like Britain to become more egalitarian – but his conception of equality is one of equal right to enter this unequal contest. He proposes, for instance, to broaden educational opportunity so that the possibility of easy ascent into the elite will diminish resentment at the existence of an elite. But he does not suggest eliminating the elite or seriously diminishing its advantages.[42]

Other writers aligned with the emerging 'New Left' also criticised the 'mediocre meritocracy' and the 'competitive ethos' allegedly envisaged by the revisionists as their social ideal, an objective that they argued simply 'disarmed the labour movement', robbing it of its basic critique of capitalism.[43] Birnbaum suggested elsewhere that Labour had restricted itself to attacking 'the Conservatives for denying equality of opportunity', when in fact what was required was 'a new conception of opportunity for another sort of society.'[44]

This perception of *The Future of Socialism*, and of revisionism more generally, was mistaken. The revisionists had far more substantial ideas about such 'a new conception of opportunity' than the New Left gave them credit for. Crosland himself responded to Birnbaum's criticism with the rejoinder: 'This shows, what I have long suspected, that one should not waste one's time writing books; for no one reads them.'[45] As Crosland then pointed out, he *was* keen to diminish the favoured position of the elite and was not just interested in

---

[41] D. Bell to C. A. R. Crosland, n.d. [c. 1957–60], Crosland Papers, British Library of Political and Economic Science, London, 10/1/2a. On the New Left's preoccupation with Crosland, see also M. Kenny, *The First New Left: British Intellectuals After Stalin* (London, 1995), 65, 126–9.

[42] N. Birnbaum, 'Ideals or reality?', *Socialist Commentary*, September 1959, 6.

[43] S. Hall, 'The supply of demand', in E. P. Thompson (ed.), *Out of Apathy* (London, 1960), 96; E. P. Thompson, 'A psessay in ephology', *New Reasoner*, autumn 1959, 6.

[44] N. Birnbaum, 'Foreword', in Thompson (ed.), *Out of Apathy*, x.

[45] C. A. R. Crosland, 'A reply', *Socialist Commentary*, September 1959, 9.

creating a more meritocratic society. This defence can be extended to other revisionists. When Socialist Union observed that equality of opportunity could be 'taken to mean no more than that everyone should have an equal start in life', they stressed that this 'liberal conception of equality' was 'part of what socialists want too, but only part.'[46] The idea of granting every citizen an equal chance to compete within a given hierarchical order of positions and rewards was, in Crosland's phrase, 'not, from a socialist point of view, sufficient', and therefore could not satisfy the revisionists.[47] In short, they advocated a far more expansive and pluralistic conception of equality of opportunity than that embodied by the conventional understanding of that term. Virtually all of the major revisionists of this period made the same point, including Gaitskell, Jay, Jenkins, Young and the members of Socialist Union. Despite differences of emphasis, the most important feature of their political outlook was precisely a critique of the conventional view that construed equality of opportunity as demanding access to social positions and material rewards on the basis of the attainment of certain educational qualifications. The revisionists joined with sociologists such as Glass, Halsey and Titmuss in expressing anxiety about the fairness and desirability of a society structured along such reductively meritocratic lines.

It is true that the revisionists saw meritocratic equality of opportunity as one dimension of social justice. This is probably where critics from the New Left managed to glean some textual justification for their categorisation of the revisionist position as meritocratic, since the revisionists stressed that the allocation of social positions on grounds of ability was of great importance, and that there was some way to go before Britain would even approach this standard. Partly, they saw this objective as important for reasons of economic efficiency, to ensure that 'talents and capabilities,

---

[46] Socialist Union, *Twentieth Century Socialism*, 25; also R. Jenkins, 'Equality' in R. H. S. Crossman (ed.), *New Fabian Essays* (London, 1952), 87.
[47] Crosland, *Future*, 237. See also M. Young, interviewed by P. Hennessy, 'The 1945 general election and the post-war period remembered', *Contemporary Record*, 9 (1995), 96.

instead of being wasted, will be utilised to their utmost.'[48] However, it was also felt to be a significant injustice that class background influenced the extent to which individuals could develop and exercise their abilities. As Jay noted, 'it is a sheer denial of basic human rights to deprive anybody of the chance to use and cultivate the capacities with which they are born', an injustice that was particularly profound given that one section of society was denied 'opportunities of development which are in fact offered to others at a price.'[49] But while this was certainly an important theme in revisionist writings, it should be recognised that it did not exhaust their view of social justice. The critics of revisionism who focused only on the rhetoric about encouraging greater social mobility and a fair start in life offered only a partial account of the revisionists' conception of socialist ends.

This can be substantiated by noting two more egalitarian principles of social justice defended by the revisionists. First, they argued in favour of a radical principle of equal opportunity. While the revisionists recognised that efficiency and fairness suggested that jobs should be allocated according to ability, they were also convinced that the distribution of 'merit' was a product of environmental influences rather than genetic inequalities. Although sociologists had demonstrated that there was an unequal distribution of measured intelligence between social classes, the revisionists agreed with progressive sociologists such as Halsey that this could largely be accounted for by the unequal environmental conditions that individuals from different social classes were exposed to. Accordingly, it was argued that the distribution of ability could itself be equalised through the use of education and social policy.[50] This commitment picked up on the argument classically expounded by Tawney: a genuine attempt to facilitate social mobility would itself demand substantive

---

[48] 'Preliminary memorandum on equality', Labour Party Research Department Archive (microfiche), Bodleian Library, Oxford, RE36/March 1956, 2; also Crosland, *Future*, 214–5.
[49] D. Jay, *Socialism in the New Society* (London, 1962), 243.
[50] E.g. C. A. R. Crosland, 'The public schools and English education', in his *The Conservative Enemy* (London, 1962), 167–82; W. A. Lewis, *Principles of Economic Planning* (1969 [1949]), 36–7; R. Marris, 'How unfair are incomes?', *Twentieth Century*, May 1955, 411, 413.

equality of economic condition. Implementing this principle of equal opportunity, it was argued, would require radical reforms to the distribution of resources and opportunities in society, especially the organisation of the education system.

Second, it was clear that even once class biases in the distribution of measured intelligence had been corrected, there would still be wide variations in the capacities of individuals. While the 'monopoly' element in the higher salaries commanded by the talented would be eliminated, a society that continued to proportion rewards to productive capacities would still be characterised by significant inequalities of wealth and social status. The revisionist thinkers who wrote at the greatest length about this question anticipated this implication, and concluded that there did not seem to be any obvious moral reason to distribute material resources, or social status, on the basis of productive ability.

Indeed, although there are always hazards associated with retrospectively attributing causal influence to one individual within a group of thinkers, there is a strong case that the contribution of Michael Young to this aspect of revisionist thinking has been underestimated. While the egalitarianism of revisionist politicians, and in particular Crosland, has received considerable attention, the role of Young in transmitting both Tawneyite ideals and sociological evidence to the more famous and politically powerful revisionist thinkers has not been sufficiently emphasised. Young's major work on this theme, *The Rise of the Meritocracy*, did not appear until 1958, after the revisionist debate was well under way. However, it is clear from archival and textual evidence that Young had in fact been elaborating his arguments about 'meritocracy' amongst progressive elites from the late 1940s onwards.

Famously, Young has been credited with introducing the word 'meritocracy' into the English language. Although he intended the word to have a negative connotation, in subsequent political debate it increasingly came to be used to indicate a highly desirable social objective. As a prescient reviewer observed at the time, Young had 'supplied a shibboleth to test the tongue of every aspirant to power in contemporary Britain.'[51] Intriguingly, there is at least one earlier

---

[51] C. Curran, 'The fable of 2034 AD', *Encounter*, February 1959, 68.

published instance of the word being used: in a 1956 article by Alan Fox in *Socialist Commentary*, where Fox made the point that a society stratified through equality of opportunity would be a '"meritocracy"; the society in which the gifted, the smart, the energetic, the ambitious and the ruthless are carefully sifted out and helped towards their destined positions of dominance, where they proceed not only to enjoy the fulfilment of exercising their natural endowments but also to receive a fat bonus thrown in for good measure.'[52] It is unclear whether Fox coined this term himself or whether he had heard it at first hand from Young. It is likely to be the latter, since Young's first draft of the text that later became *The Rise of the Meritocracy* was produced in the early 1950s as a possible contribution to the *New Fabian Essays*,[53] and Young had elaborated his nascent critique of meritocracy in other early works, notably in a private research paper he wrote for the Labour Party NEC at the end of his tenure as Head of Research in 1951, entitled *For Richer, For Poorer*, and in his PhD thesis, supervised by Richard Titmuss and awarded by the LSE in 1955.[54]

In any case, Young played a crucial role in disseminating the insight that a meritocratic society would be extremely unfair and unattractive, since if taken to its logical conclusion, it would concentrate material resources and social status on the section of the community who were fortunate enough to possess one particular kind of ability, namely marketable talents. The result, speculated Young, would be the creation of a fresh class hierarchy, just as pernicious as the class divisions that characterised Britain in the 1950s, but without the consoling message that those in the lower classes were trapped in their subordinate position by the unfairness of the system. On the contrary, in terms of the dominant social

---

[52] A. Fox, 'Class and equality', *Socialist Commentary*, May 1956, 13. Fox later reviewed *Rise of the Meritocracy*: 'Top people', *Socialist Commentary*, December 1958, 20–2. Interestingly, although *The Future of Socialism* was also published in 1956, and was the subject of private discussion between Young and Crosland, it does not use the word 'meritocracy', although Crosland analysed the shortcomings of the idea in all but name, referring to the dangers of 'an aristocracy of talent': *Future*, 235–7, quote at 235.
[53] Young, interviewed by Hennessy, '1945 general election', 96.
[54] See Briggs, *Michael Young*, 155–7.

morality, they would know that their inferior status was entirely their own fault. The narrator of Young's book conveyed the unjustified sense of superiority that would characterise the upper echelons of such a society, and their condescension and inhumanity towards the 'meritless': 'the eminent know that success is just reward for their own capacity, for their own efforts, and for their own undeniable achievement. They deserve to belong to a superior class.' Those at the bottom 'know they have had every chance' and, if they have failed to make the grade, 'are they not bound to recognise that they have an inferior status – not as in the past because they were denied opportunity; but because they *are* inferior?'[55]

A central theme of the book was the way in which socialists and other progressives had unwittingly prepared the way for the meritocracy by campaigning for equality of opportunity and undermining the moral legitimacy of inherited wealth and other mechanisms that transmitted intergenerational advantage. The socialists had instilled self-respect and ambition in the working class, and had offered such persuasive arguments against parental partiality that it was no longer conceivable for the wealthy to argue openly for inherited wealth or nepotistic appointments. In the end, 'the wealthy could not fight because their morale was sapped by socialist teaching.'[56] The ironic praise for these great achievements of the labour movement was both Young's subtle expression of disquiet about the future direction of Labour policy after the triumphs of the 1945 government, and a philosophical meditation on the kind of equality that socialists ought to aim at. Although he was not particularly prescriptive in *The Rise of the Meritocracy*, the warning he offered about impoverished thinking about 'equality of opportunity' was clear. As the narrator observed, the introduction of merit as a social selection mechanism 'made nonsense' of 'loose talk of the equality of man':

> Men, after all, are notable not for the equality, but for the inequality, of their endowment. Once all the geniuses are

---

[55] M. Young, *The Rise of the Meritocracy: An Essay on Education and Equality* (London, 1961 [1958]), 106–8, Young's emphasis.
[56] Young, *Rise*, 129–31, quote at 130.

amongst the elite, and all the morons amongst the workers, what meaning can equality have? ... What is the purpose of abolishing inequalities in nurture except to reveal and make more pronounced the inescapable inequalities of nature?[57]

Young's book was widely read, reviewed and discussed after its publication in 1958.[58] As we have seen, the central arguments of the book were in any case accessible to a number of important socialist intellectuals before 1958, thanks to Young's personal connections to, and indefatigable participation in, the many debates about socialist ideology during the 1950s. There is direct evidence of Young's influence in the case of Crosland's *Future of Socialism*.

Contrary to the interpretation of the New Left and other reviewers, Crosland did state that the meritocratic ideal was unjust: 'Admittedly, from the point of view of social justice, an aristocracy of talent is an obvious improvement on a hereditary aristocracy, since no one is in fact denied an equal chance. Yet I do not believe, as a personal value judgement, that it can be described as a "just" society.'[59] Crosland's reason for this was two-fold. One was that it seemed unfair to reward individuals for having greater intelligence than others, given 'that superior intelligence is largely due to parental status, through a combination of heredity and beneficial upbringing: and that no one deserves either so generous a reward or so severe a penalty for a quality implanted from outside, for which he himself can claim only a limited responsibility'. More fundamentally, however, Crosland argued that no matter whether a particular individual trait was 'inbred or not':

> Why should this one trait, or even a group of traits, alone determine success or failure, riches or poverty, a high or

---

[57] Young, *Rise*, 115.
[58] E.g. R. Williams, 'Democracy or meritocracy?', *Manchester Guardian*, 30.10.1958, 10; R. Hoggart, 'IQ plus effort = merit', *Observer*, 2.11.1958, 21; P. Shore, 'More than opportunity', *New Statesman*, 29.11.1958, 766. See P. Barker, 'The ups and downs of the meritocracy', in Dench, Flower and Gavron (eds), *Young at Eighty*, 153–62; Briggs, *Michael Young*, 160–82.
[59] Crosland, *Future*, 235.

low prestige? Why should no marks be given for saintliness, generosity, compassion, humour, beauty, assiduity, continence, or artistic ability? ... It is the injustice of isolating, as a basis for extreme inequality, certain selected ones out of the multiple strands that go to make up the human personality, which constitutes the fundamental ethical case against any elite or aristocracy.[60]

Obviously, Crosland conceded that there were practical reasons for continuing to offer higher rewards to those with greater ability, but 'if this requires such large differential privileges as to create a distinct elite, differently educated and socially select, it must be regarded as an unpleasant concession to economic efficiency, and not as being intrinsically just'.[61] All of which offered an analysis that was broadly in line with Young's, and indeed Crosland acknowledged in a footnote to these passages that 'my views on this point owe much to discussions with Mr Michael Young.' Young's comments on the draft of the *Future of Socialism* support this claim.[62]

The injustice of a formal equality of opportunity was also seen by Socialist Union. Rather than 'an equal start with the race left to the swiftest,' Socialist Union argued, 'what socialists want is an equal chance for everyone, taking their lives as a whole. They are concerned with the whole bundle of opportunities which society distributes throughout a lifetime.'[63] While socialists had previously concentrated on the importance of tackling class distinctions, and the role of class background in preventing working-class individuals from developing their talents, this did not exhaust the socialist concern about inequality:

> Even if all class distinctions were wiped out, the inequalities inherent in man would remain. Society would still face the task of honouring the claim of every man to an

---

[60] Crosland, *Future*, 236.
[61] Crosland, *Future*, 236.
[62] Crosland, *Future*, 235, fn. 1; M. Young to C. A. R. Crosland, 30.1.1956, Crosland Papers, British Library of Political and Economic Science, London, 13/8/5–6.
[63] Socialist Union, *Twentieth Century Socialism*, 25.

equal chance in life. There would still be the weak and the strong, the bright and the backward, the lucky and the unlucky. These inequalities can never be eliminated but they can be prevented from becoming a source of social discrimination.[64]

As Arthur Lewis approvingly remarked, this was socialism as 'a philosophy for underdogs, championing their rights against those of the top dogs', whether the latter were 'born in the purples, or have made their way up by brains, work or local authority awards.'[65] There are numerous other examples of this criticism of meritocracy in revisionist or other mainstream Labour Party writings of this period.[66]

Since the revisionists rejected both a strict equality of income and a meritocracy, it was necessary to formulate an alternative criterion that could specify the range of permissible inequalities. In line with earlier egalitarians such as Tawney, the revisionists aimed to reduce inequality to the minimum level necessary to stimulate productive contributions. Lewis argued that socialists 'believe that wide differences of income and property are bad, and we desire to limit differences of income to the minimum required to stimulate and reward initiative, effort and responsibility.'[67] It should be stressed that not all of the pronouncements of the revisionists on this question achieved a level of consistency that

---

[64] Socialist Union, *Twentieth Century Socialism*, 26. See also P. Willmott, 'Attitudes towards class', typescript, March 1956, Socialist Union Papers, Modern Records Centre, Warwick University, MSS.173/13.

[65] W. A. Lewis, 'Underdog-ism', *Observer*, 22.7.1956, 8. This reference to 'underdogs' was reminiscent of Cole's famous definition of the ILP's socialism as 'a broad human movement on behalf of the bottom dog': G. D. H. Cole, *A Short History of the British Working Class Movement Volume 3* (London, 1937), 22.

[66] E.g. Jenkins, 'Equality', 85; Fabian Society Local Societies Committee, *About Equality* (London, December 1954), 2, copy in Fabian Society Papers, British Library of Political and Economic Science, London, F47/4, Item 1; 'Preliminary memorandum on equality', Labour Party Research Department Archive (microfiche), Bodleian Library, Oxford, RE36/March 1956, 2–3 (compare with Young, *Rise*, 169); R. Marris, 'An economist's challenge', *Twentieth Century*, February 1955, 166; Jay, *Socialism*, 15–7; B. Magee, *The New Radicalism* (London, 1962), 61–3.

[67] W. A. Lewis, 'A socialist economic policy', *Socialist Commentary*, June 1955, 171.

would satisfy the rigorous scrutiny of a political philosopher. In particular, there was an occasional tendency for writers to blur together meritocratic and incentive-based arguments for inequalities of material reward. Gaitskell himself was prone to do this:

> While we do not say that all should receive the same income, we hold that the differences should be related to generally accepted criteria of merit – such as the nature of the work – more being paid for dirty, harder, more skilled, better performed, more responsible jobs. We say too that these differences should not be greater than are necessary to provide adequate incentives in the interest of economic progress.[68]

In a similar vein, Jay argued: 'The skilful or diligent or responsible worker is felt to deserve more; but this perfectly valid moral judgement does not tell us how much more. The only rational answer to the question "how much more?" is, therefore, this: that amount more which will ensure that their talents are exercised and that society benefits from them.'[69] It was uncertain whether these occasional gestures towards the idea that more skilled work deserved a greater reward signalled an endorsement of differential rewards on this basis, perhaps as a concession to popular opinion about the justice of desert, or whether these remarks were intended as an incentive-based justification for inequality, or even one grounded on the idea of compensatory equalisation.

Since absolute logical precision and consistency were not priorities in the kind of political argument the revisionists were constructing, it would be unrealistic to expect an exhaustive treatment of these intricate conceptual distinctions. However, if we take into account the contextual and textual evidence discussed earlier, especially the scepticism about the use of merit as a distributive ideal, there are strong grounds for taking incentives to be the basis for

---

[68] H. Gaitskell, 'Socialism and nationalisation', *Fabian Tract No. 300* (London, 1956), 3.
[69] Jay, *Socialism*, 8–9. See also the similar ambiguity in Labour Party, *Towards Equality: Labour's Policy for Social Justice* (London, 1956), 14.

the revisionist justification of differentials. As an internal Labour discussion paper on equality argued, 'socialists recognise the validity of income differences, not as a recognition of differences in merit, but for the practical purpose of providing incentives to persons performing the more skilled and responsible, or the heavier and less congenial work of society.'[70] It was necessary, thought Crosland, to ground inequalities on the idea of rent of ability, understood as necessary incentive payments to secure the performance of important economic functions; 'that is, the additional reward which exceptional ability can in practice command from the community.'[71] The revisionist aim is therefore best understood as 'the minimum practicable inequality', this commitment carrying with it the clear implication 'that inequality is not justified beyond the point necessary to ensure that the productive abilities of the community are reasonably fully used.'[72] This position was consonant with that adopted by earlier egalitarians and, as both Crosland and Young later noted, was similar to the 'democratic equality' advocated by John Rawls in his *Theory of Justice*.[73]

Although the revisionist view of social justice therefore allowed some material inequality, it was a broadly egalitarian position, and there is little evidence that the ideological rivals of the revisionists from the Left endorsed distributive principles that were somehow more egalitarian. Indeed, as

---

[70] 'Preliminary memorandum on equality', Labour Party Research Department Archive (microfiche), Bodleian Library, Oxford, RE36/March 1956, 4. Socialist Union indicated that inequalities freely chosen by individuals were also acceptable in their *Twentieth Century Socialism*, 28.
[71] Crosland, *Future*, 212.
[72] Jay, *Socialism*, 8.
[73] In the 1970s Crosland and Young explicitly aligned their view of social justice with Rawls's: M. Young, 'Is equality a dream?', First Rita Hinden Memorial Lecture, supplement to *Socialist Commentary*, January 1973, 4; Crosland, *Socialism Now*, 15–6; M. Young, 'Introduction', in *Rise of the Meritocracy* (New Brunswick, NJ, 1994 [1958]), quoted in R. Dore, 'Man of merit', in Dench, Flower and Gavron (eds), *Young at Eighty*, 173. See also S. Hampshire, 'A new philosophy of the just society', *New York Review of Books*, 24.2.1972, 36–7. Rawls himself had referred to three important books by British egalitarians: Tawney's *Equality*, Young's *Rise of the Meritocracy* and James Meade's *Efficiency, Equality and the Distribution of Property*: J. Rawls, *A Theory of Justice* (Oxford, 1999 [1971]), 63, fn.11; 91, fn. 21; 241–2, fn. 12, fn. 13; 245, fn. 15.

revisionist writers repeatedly made clear, this theoretical commitment entailed an end to selective schooling; a concerted attempt to end private education; substantial redistribution of wealth through heavy taxation of inherited wealth and capital ownership; and a cap on the extent of earned income inequality. Of course, this is only an analysis of what the revisionists *said* they wanted to do, as opposed to what they actually did once they got into government, but for the purposes of a comparison with present-day social-democratic ideology this would seem to be the relevant yardstick. Although it is beyond the scope of this paper to discuss in any detail how the revisionist view compares with the 'equality of opportunity' advocated by New Labour, it should at least be clear from my analysis that, at an ideological level, present-day modernisers of social democracy have a hard act to follow.

Academics as intellectuals: Studying Norwegian academics and intellectuals in the public sphere

Jan Eivind Myhre

The American cultural historian Christopher Lasch once uttered that he 'wanted to be an intellectual, not an academic.'[1] By that he meant that he wanted to influence society in the best intellectual tradition, as a participant in the public exchange of ideas. As an academic he would be trapped in an ivory tower, communicating mainly with colleagues. It would however be difficult to imagine Lasch as an intellectual communicator without his academic background. His books are academically based works with an important political, social and cultural critique.[2] Lasch wanted to make the point that in the US, the role of the academic and that of the intellectual are different and separate.[3] According to another American, the sociologist Craig Calhoun, Norway is an extreme case in that academic research is well connected to public policy. The sociologist (in this case) acts as a public intellectual.[4] Ragnvald Kalleberg's guess is that Norwegian

---

[1] Christopher Lasch in an interview in 1994, according to S. Collini, *Absent Minds. Intellectuals in Britain* (Oxford 2006), p. 234.
[2] e. g. *The Culture of Narcissism* (N. Y. 1978), *Heaven in a Heartless World* (N. Y. 1977), *The Revolt of the Elites and the Betrayal of Democracy* (N. Y. 1995).
[3] Russell Jacoby, *The Last Intellectuals. American culture in the age of academe* (N. Y. 1987) argues that some decades ago, this was not necessarily the case.
[4] C. Calhoun, 'Academics as Public Intellectuals', Lecture, Institute of Sociology, University of Oslo, 12 June 2007.

academics are among the most prolific in the world in disseminating their knowledge. This paper will investigate the past and present of the role of Norwegian academics as intellectuals, and directly or indirectly, point to the many questions that remain for future scholars to probe.

A master narrative: decline of academics as intellectuals

Making sweeping statements about the role, status and development of academics as intellectuals in Norway in the modern period, i.e. the last two hundred years, is in some ways an easy task because such statements already exist: sometimes for everybody to read; sometimes just alluded to or easy to infer from various historical accounts. It is particularly easy if we are a bit sloppy with our terms, and do not state clearly what we mean by intellectuals or academics and not say what the relations might be between the two.

One such sweeping statement, or master narrative, would be telling a story of decline, namely the demise of the educated class or classes. The story is not mainly about higher education becoming less exclusive, which is of course true: it is the story of a country governed in the nineteenth century by a small elite of university-educated senior civil servants, known as *embetsmenn* (German: *Beamten*), who dominated politics as well as the emerging civil society.[5] '*Intelligentsen*' (the intelligence) was the nickname of a group of young academics from the 1830s, who were soon to occupy the highest political and academic positions in the country. The concept of the 'professor politician' became widely recognized later in the century, and this indicates that the pinnacle of higher education, the university professor, was a major figure in national politics as well as in the public sphere. *Education* and *breeding* (formation or liberal education) determined one's social standing (these concepts may

---

[5] The officers, not educated at the university, were also senior civil servants. However, they did not usually have a prominent position in politics or the public sphere. An *embetsmann* was appointed by the King, i.e. the cabinet presided over by the King.

be somewhat clearer in Norwegian or German: *Utdannelse* and *dannelse, Ausbildung* and *Bildung*).

Academically educated people in the nineteenth century, whether within or outside of the university, were great disseminators. They popularized their knowledge in a great number of works about a range of subjects: from theology via history and law to natural history. However, to call the vast majority of them intellectuals would not be precise. Their aim in writing books was mainly practical, not political or philosophical. And these highly educated authors mainly represented the authorities rather than challenging them. Nonetheless, there were always independent and oppositional academics, and they grew more numerous towards the end of the century.

Although academics as intellectuals were certainly visible and important throughout the twentieth century as well, the public stage on which they acted had changed considerably. Despite the fact that such academics and intellectuals certainly were overlapping groups, from the late nineteenth century onwards one must distinguish between them, both analytically and empirically. However, many people often confused the two groups or thought them to be identical, in part because the related concepts of intellect, intellectual, intellectuals and intelligence were lumped together, resulting in Norwegian anti-intellectualism and anti-academic attitudes going hand in hand. The concept of the intellectual strongly connotes to something oppositional, as with the *intelligentsen* back in the 1830s. But the rise of this group to a position of power eroded its position as intellectuals, and in the long run even undermined intellectuals in general.

Intellectuals and academics: similarities, differences and connections

For most of the nineteenth century, the literary sphere and the sphere of the press was largely an academic one. Novelists, playwrights, poets and non-fiction authors, newspaper editors and contributors were mainly university educated people, in fact to a remarkable degree these were people employed by Norway's only university, founded in

1811.⁶ From late in the nineteenth century, especially from the 1870s onwards, the literary and academic spheres parted. The reasons for this are important, shed considerable light on developments in the twentieth century, and are to be found both within and outside of the university.

In the decades around 1900, around the turn of the century, the university was undergoing a process of professionalization in the sense that research was more greatly emphasized, also basic research, and the university was granted extensive freedom from the government to do this. Consequently, the professor as scientist and scholar acquired a certain distance from aspects of surrounding society.⁷ For example, they became far less directly involved in politics and fiction-writing and instead became more involved in what one may label pre-politics by furnishing politicians with expert reports, not least in the political and professional processes leading to a welfare state. However, quite a few university people as well as other academics still participated in public debates.

Outside of academe, non-academic intellectuals appeared, particularly in journalism and the literary sphere. The combination of widespread literacy and the rotary press led to there being many more newspapers and more copies sold, thereby creating a sizeable journalistic profession. New generations of writers appeared who often took part in public debates. Some of them had been at the university for a short time, but the bulk of the new generations of authors, making their début in the decades around the turn of the century, were modestly educated. Occasionally, writers vividly coloured the public debates. The historian Ernst Sars in 1903 coined the phrase *poetokrati* (poetocracy: the rule of poets) to characterize their influence, a term with an enduring influence in Norway, although Sars was mainly alluding to one person in particular, the national poet and playwright

---

⁶ The Royal Frederik's University, since 1939 named the University of Oslo, began teaching in 1813, the first students graduating in 1815. Prior to this, Norwegians were mainly educated in Copenhagen, the country's capital before 1814.

⁷ U. Torgersen, 'Universitetet og politikken', *Tidsskrift for samfunnsforskning*, 2, 1961.

Bjørnstjerne Bjørnson.[8] In many senses an archetypical public intellectual, he was even a Norwegian *Dreyfusard*, with easy access to major French and German newspapers, not to mention Norwegian ones.[9] Norway was not yet oriented towards the English-speaking world in intellectual matters.

Another important novel group of intellectuals consisted of primary school teachers, not unlike the situation in Ireland. They were prominent local intellectuals and often leaders of national organizations of various sorts. Above all, however, the teachers often emerged as leaders of the liberal political opposition in Norway from the late nineteenth century onwards. Its geographic strongholds were the rural districts, its social base farmers and town liberals, its cultural base what may be referred to as the countercultures (Norwegian rural language and other cultural traits, lay Christianity, teetotalism), its ideology liberal nationalism. The old regime of senior civil servants was one of its main opponents, one of whose strongholds was the university. The old political regime fell to the liberals in 1884, but cultural struggles continued, even after some representatives of the countercultures had gained university chairs.[10]

Anti-intellectualism and anti-academism

The national countercultures and the political opposition created a corner of their own in the public sphere from which they tried to conquer the existing one. Although in one sense populated by intellectuals, the countercultures harboured their fair share of anti-intellectualism and anti-academic attitudes. Twentieth-century history may in fact be interpreted as the revenge of various oppositional groups on the arrogant civil-servant academics of the previous century. Part

---

[8] G. Skirbekk, 'Forord', *Er ideologiane døde?* (Oslo 1968); G. Skirbekk, 'Spådommen om "poetokratiets død" – ein feilaktig prognose?' *Nytt Norsk Tidsskrift*, 3–4, 2004; G. Gulliksen, 'Poetokratiet gjenoppstår som litteraturhat', *Samtiden*, 3, 2003. Bjørnson was awarded the Nobel prize for literature in 1903.
[9] B. Hagtvet, *'Hvor gjerne vilde jeg have været I Deres sted...'. Bjørnstjerne Bjørnson, de intellektuelle og Dreyfus-saken* (Oslo 1998).
[10] E. Rodvang. *Sosial åpning – kulturell erobring : målsak og målmenn ved det Kongelige Frederiks Universitet* (Oslo 2002).

of this took the form of anti-intellectualism. In addition to the anti-intellectualism of the countercultures, there are certainly elements of it in the labour movement. Neither of the two movements were one-sidedly anti-intellectual, however: quite a few academics and intellectuals joined the labour movement, and quite a few people from the countercultures entered the academic world without leaving their countercultural attitudes behind. In fact, they wanted to create an alternative liberal education. The university, increasingly emphasizing scientific and scholarly achievements, was in some cultural senses a rather anarchic institution, and could well exist with cultural differences. In this encounter, both sides changed permanently, and the countercultures, in particular the more national ones, can hardly be said to have bequeathed a lasting legacy of anti-intellectualism or strongly anti-academic sentiments. In the labour movement, however, the two parallel movements do still exist, especially within the trade unions.

If these two traditions of being anti-academe and anti-intellectual have not been particularly visible in the last few decades, this is also because anti-intellectualism and anti-academic outlooks have been taken over by two other groups. One is the populist side of the political right, claiming, rather correctly, that intellectuals and academics are often on the left, and voicing an aggression from below against experts, cultural elitists, *besserwissers* of all kinds (see below). Carl I. Hagen, the leader until 2006 of the Progress Party (*Fremskrittspartiet*) which expressed such opinions used to denounce politicians, socialists and bureaucrats as the new upper class, at least until the party itself gained some power.[11] The other anti-group is a mixed one and difficult to label, but is composed of representatives from what one may call the consumer- and market-oriented sector of society, people in media, entertainment and advertising. Among the complaints filed are that intellectuals and academics live in ivory towers, shielded from reality, and that academics are condescending or politically correct.

---

[11] From 1978 on, according to A. Johansen & J. E. Kjeldsen, *Virksomme ord. Politiske taler 1814–2005* (Oslo 2005), p. 642.

The result of this is that contemporary society can be interpreted as very much the opposite of its nineteenth-century counterpart in evaluating academic knowledge, at least on the surface. Several studies have shown that of all Western countries, Norway is where higher education renders the smallest financial rewards.[12] In a recent poll of university and college employees, 47 per cent disagreed with a statement saying that academic occupations were well respected in Norway. 58 per cent agreed that Norway is a society with strong elements of anti-intellectualism.[13] A recent study of the cultural values of academically educated people revealed ambivalent and not infrequently negative attitudes towards *intellektuelle*: they are viewed as snobbish, elitist and as distancing themselves from the real world. These people held that having a higher education, even the highest, does not in itself qualify one to be an intellectual. It would seem, however, that such unenthusiastic attitudes are mainly linked to cultural traits (such as musical or literary tastes) and not particularly to thoughts and ideas. Some of the people with a higher education view those who stayed on in academe as being remote from reality.[14] However, it is in groups without higher education that we normally find that the anti-intellectual and the anti-academic are more or less the same phenomenon

Is this yet another story about the demise of intellectuals, the insignificance of scholarship or academics or the decline of the university? This of course would depend on the questions one asks and the evidence one collects and would certainly need to be proven. Claims to the contrary of what has been said above have certainly been made. For example, the number of professors, other educated people, written articles, columns or letters in newspapers and journals is unprecedented. Concerning professors, in the field of history only, to give an example, their numbers have increased from six in the 1950s to over 70 half a century

---

[12] Seen from different angle, Norwegians with little education are relatively well paid.
[13] *Forskerforum* 1, 2006, p. 9.
[14] O. Skarpenes, 'Den "legitime kulturens" moralske forankring', *Tidsskrift for samfunnsforskning*, 4, 2007, pp. 553–554.

later.[15] International studies (Eurobarometer) show that Norwegians in general hold science and scientists (*vitenskapsmenn*) in high regard.[16] Some even participate in debates on the television or in talk shows. Is it so that scientists are ok, academics might be ok, but intellectuals are not? In what follows, I will try to systematize some aspects of academics as intellectuals.

The contemporary Norwegian intellectual

First of all, there is something more to be said about the terms 'academic' and 'intellectual', which I have so far employed rather indiscriminately. As mentioned above, in the twentieth century intellectuals with a modest formal education clearly have existed, such as the 'poetocrats' and a rather large group of journalist intellectuals. The working class as well as farmers have produced and still bring forth what Gramsci called organic intellectuals, self-taught learned men (and some women) with something to say. By virtue of the enormous expansion in general education since the 1960s, however, the intellectual is more likely than before to be a person with higher education.

The problem with the term 'intellectual' is not that he or she does not exist in Norway, but that intellectuals are rather difficult to study as a group which has certain characteristics such as social background, not to mention what intellectuals actually do, write or say.[17] It is notoriously hard to agree upon who the intellectuals actually are. The national newspaper *Dagbladet* is a tabloid paper, which at the same time tries to retain an old tradition of speaking to the educated strata of society. In 2005 it published a list of the ten most prominent intellectuals in the country; predictably,

---

[15] S. Corell and J. E. Myhre, 'The institutions of Norwegian historiography', in I. Porciani and L. Raphael (eds), *Atlas of the Institutions of European Historiographies 1800 to the Present* (forthcoming 2009). On the other hand, with the immense increase in number, the title of professor has become devalued.
[16] S. Sjøberg and C. Schreiner, 'Holdninger til og forestillinger om vitenskap og teknologi i Norge. En framstilling basert på data fra Eurobarometer og ROSE', manuscript, University of Oslo 2006.
[17] See also my introductory article above.

the selection caused disagreement and even disgust, and not just because a considerable proportion of those chosen could be associated with the very same newspaper. Of interest to us here, however, is that nine of the ten were academically educated and five were university scholars.[18]

Absent from the list, by the way, was the internationally renowned philosopher of social science Jon Elster, who for years has spent most of his time in Chicago and at Columbia and is now at College de France. In 1990 he was interviewed by the Norwegian Broadcasting Corporation on his fiftieth birthday, an interview memorable for two of his answers.[19] When asked if he was an intellectual, Elster replied: 'If there ever was an intellectual, that one would have to be me'. The second question was whether he had any hobbies, to which the answer was: 'I like messing about' (*drive dank*), an interesting answer from someone who has published about one and a half books annually for 40 years. The archetypical intellectual in this case is a world-class scholar.

The analytical separation of the roles of academics and intellectuals has a lot to say in its favour. Intellectuals are often regarded generalists. They set agendas, their voices are the ones most clearly heard. Quite a few of them are academically educated. The step from being just another academic to being an intellectual is a shift from being an expert, a contributor, in a certain restricted field, to expressing an opinion about wider social issues. I think, however, that the line between the two is difficult to draw, and this is becoming more difficult over time.

Academics

Who, then, are the academics, and what is their relation to intellectuals? The noun *akademiker* (an academic) is not unambiguous in Norway if we look at it historically.[20] Up

---

[18] *Dagbladet* 2005. The ten were: Rune Slagstad, Thomas Hylland Eriksen, Cathrine Holst, Unni Wikan, Brynjulf Braanen, Tor Erling Staff, Nina Witoszek, Espen Søbye, Eva Joly and Kjartan Fløgstad.
[19] Quoted according to memory.
[20] Probably up to sometime in the first half of the twentieth century, an 'academic' (*akademiker*) was someone who had finished *gymnasium* and was, in principle, ready to enter university.

until sometime in the first half of the twentieth century, an *akademiker* was someone who had finished the *gymnasium*, and was, in principle, ready to enter the university. Until around 1900, nearly all *gymnasium* graduates actually did so, but during the first two generations of the twentieth century this was no longer the case. Many stopped after the *eksamen artium* (*gymnasium* examinations) while others continued their education at colleges or other schools. However, in the 1950s the term academic, although rendered everybody who had finished *gymnasium*, was still rather exclusive, as only about ten per cent of the cohort passed the *eksamen artium*, slightly more men than women. From the late 1950s, however, a strong increase occurred, and upon entering the twenty-first century, the majority of young men and women are in principle qualified to enter the university.

This is probably the reason why the term *akademiker* has shifted from designating a person entering the university to someone who has graduated from it. Another usage, yet more exclusive, reserves the term for university and college employees, professors, lecturers and instructors.[21] The second of the three usages is the one that is employed by the unions representing their interests. These unions, such as *Forskerforbundet* (The Researchers' Union) or *Akademikerne* (The Academics), represent people who earn a living from their university education. True, not all knowledgeable people have a higher education yet still might be called academics. But the vast majority of academics, and probably an increasing share, do have university degrees.

Academics are to be found within and outside of universities and related research institutions and both groups will be dealt with here. As public intellectuals, they thus appear in slightly different guises. A professor, lecturer or a researcher may be taken to be speaking *ex cathedra* (in Spanish, a university professor is called *cathedratico*), even when his or her utterance does not relate precisely to his or her expert knowledge. However, the difference between a

---

[21] In some countries like Finland, but not in Norway, an academic, or rather an academician, means a member of an academy of science and letters.

university professor and a high-school teacher is one of degree only.

Academics, in other words, are relatively easy to define, whether we do so sociologically or social-historically. Although the meaning of the term *akademiker* changes with time, it is relatively easy to identify empirically at various stages. One does not have to work with the same definition of academics all the time, implying that we may deal with various groups. At one point one may study all university graduates above a certain level, on another occasion one may deal with university scholars, the inhabitants of academe. Dealing with a rather clearly identifiable group, empirically speaking, is certainly an advantage when relating these people to the much more evasive and contested notion of the intellectual. To what extent do academics act as intellectuals? What is it in the role, or role set, of academics which furthers or hampers activity as intellectuals?

Role of academics in society

The most obvious fact about academics in contemporary society is their vastly increased number compared to only a generation ago, not to mention a century back. In terms of the thriving public atmosphere in Norway around the turn of the century in 1900 one is tempted to say that there were more intellectuals than academics, although that was hardly the case. Around 1900 there were only about 5000 people in academic professions and only 1500 university students from a population of just over two million.[22] By 1970 there were 47,000 people with the highest university education: in 2000 this figure had risen to 206,000 people in academic professions, meaning graduates with more than four years of university education.[23] Whichever way one defines intellectuals, they make up only a tiny share of the number of academics. The number of university scholars grew from just over one

---

[22] Excluding officers (approx. 900), civil engineers and architects. Architects were educated abroad, since there was no Norwegian higher polytechnical education until 1910.
[23] Including the education of civil engineers and at the Norwegian School of Business (NHH) and the College of Agriculture (NLH), but excluding colleges for teachers, nurses etc.

hundred in 1900 to 3262 in 1970 (704 of whom were professors) and about 15,000 in 2006 (about 2700 professors).

Apart from in terms of their sheer numbers, how can one assess the role and position of academics and intellectuals in society, and particularly in the public sphere? One possible way is to look at the presentation of individuals in *Hvem er Hvem* (HH (*Who is Who*)), published at irregular intervals from 1912 to 1994 and the annual reference book on current affairs *Hvem-Hva-Hvor* (H-H-H (*Who-What-Where*)) between 1948 and 2004.[24] The latter presented current names and a list of the deceased the previous year. In HH academics are quite noticeable in the first editions, but wane in the later editions. In the Norwegian biographical dictionary, published from 1923 onwards, practically all university professors from the nineteenth century are included. This is certainly far from the case with the latest edition, published around the turn of the century. In H-H-H politicians are present from the 1940s to the 2000s, whereas scholars and to some extent intellectuals became less visible to allow space for representatives of major interest organizations, journalists, sports stars and celebrities.

In postwar Norwegian society, university employees make up a small, but growing number of academics, whose formal societal task it is, not only to teach and research, but to disseminate (*formidle*) their knowledge to a broader public, an assignment not very far from the task normally assigned to an intellectual. Although a fairly recent part of the job description of Norwegian university academics, many have long taken seriously the task of disseminating research results to a wider public.[25] This is particularly true of scholars in the humanities and social sciences, but also to some extent of scientists. In the first decades of the Norwegian Broadcasting Corporation, up until the 1960s, academics were often on the air as a part of a large enterprise to promote popular

---

[24] The investigation is carried out by Elin Myhre.
[25] Dissemination was included in the statutes of the newly established University of Bergen immediately after World War II. It was later included in the general University Act of 1975, as a duty of the institution, but not of the individual scholar. See Kalleberg's article earlier in this collection and also his 'The Role of "Intellectual" in the Academic Role-Set', *LOS-senter, Notat 0101*, (LOS-senteret, Bergen 2001).

public education (*folkeopplysning*). A young mathematician recounts how he in 1957 was given a microphone and 30 minutes to speak about what interested him (in this case logical paradoxes), on the radio, a state monopoly.[26] The importance to scholars of this task of dissemination is underlined by the fact that the scholars who publish the most research papers, also publish more frequently for a wider audience.[27]

If one looks at the arenas of the public sphere, one will find that they were long dominated by, in fact created by, the academic stratum of society. Up until the 1960s, the speaker's platform at the student union in Oslo (*Studentersamfundet*) was regarded as one of the most important arenas in the country. Today it is insignificant. There are still some rather academically dominated arenas, which nevertheless claim the status of a general public sphere (space), notably some monthly or bi-monthly journals dealing with general political and cultural issues (*Nytt Norsk Tidsskrift, Samtiden, Syn & Segn*). In addition there are weekly papers with a decidedly academic flavour (*Morgenbladet, Klassekampen, Dag og Tid*). These partly make up for the fact that Norway hardly has the market for a serious daily newspaper of *The Guardian* or *El Pais* type. However, there are few and insignificant purely tabloid papers, as most daily newspapers balance between the serious and the tabloid in their content. In the spring of 2006 one of them, *Dagbladet*, published a translation of Timothy Garton Ash's review of Collini's book *Absent Minds. On Intellectuals in Britain* (*Hvem er de intellektuelle?*).[28] The media structure of Norway is one of a small country, or rather a small language. However, it is also characterized by the fact that most educated Norwegians read English well, and newspapers like *Die Zeit, Le Monde* and *El Pais* also sell rather well in Norway.

The important question, however, is the role of academics in what one might call the *generalized* public sphere, the one reaching large audiences and dealing with major societal issues. The concept of the public sphere has been a topic of

---

[26] Jens Erik Fenstad, personal communication 19 June 2003.
[27] S. Kyvik, 'Publisering for allmenheten', in M. Gulbrandsen and J.-C. Smeby (eds), *Forskning ved universitetene* Oslo 2005).
[28] *Dagbladet* 30 April 2006.

scholarly debate for at least 40 years, since the publication of Habermas' classic on the rise of it from 1962, introduced to Norway as early as the late 1960s (by Ragnvald Kalleberg, amongst others, and translated in 1971). One of the issues is whether the public sphere consists of one major sphere or many sub-spheres. Not that anyone would doubt that there, in a sense, are many public spheres, created and used by political, social or cultural subgroups. There is a women's sphere, a sports sphere, one for gay people, not to mention several academic, scholarly and scientific spheres. In speaking of a public sphere, the Norwegian or German terms, *offentlighet* and *Öffentlichkeit*, do not have the spacial connotations of the English term, although it is possible to speak of a public sphere (*offentlig sfære*) or public space (*offentlig rom*) in Norwegian as well. It is likely that academics, in particular university academics, over time come in the main to occupy only limited parts of the public sphere(s).

One of the interesting questions to ask concerning academics in the public sphere touches on the workings and changes of *democracy* in the last few decades. If democracy requires a rational and enlightened public debate, and academics therefore ought to be important participants, then changes in democracy may be studied through the participation of academics. This does not commence with the premise that the more academics, the better for democracy, or that the more centrally located they are, the better. The rise of a meritocracy can be a dangerous thing. And academics certainly do not behave in the same way; they are also shaped by circumstances, and the main circumstance is the structure of the public sphere. This means that studies of academics and studies of changes in the public sphere will have to go hand in hand. To show this, there are several strategies one can follow.

To what degree have academics been looked upon as intellectuals, and which academics have been treated as such? In the first decade after World War II, the leading Norwegian philosopher Arne Næss and his followers wanted all the crucial societal questions to be answered by empirical social research, relevant to the development of democracy.[29] Næss and his group also wanted to be at the vanguard of a rational debate. His book, *En del elementære logiske emner (Some Elementary Logical Topics)* was published in a number of editions from 1941 onwards. It was obligatory reading for new university students and aimed primarily at raising the level of public debate. In 1968 a young philosopher outside of the Næss group, Gunnar Skirbekk, signalled the end of poetocracy in Norway.[30] He heralded the coming of philosophers and social scientists as the pivotal group for thinking about social, economic and political development in the public sphere. Simultaneously, a group of young conservative students – jurists, social scientists and historians – looked upon their intellectual activity as 'pre-political'. Their task as academics was to lay the premises for politics rather than doing politics.[31] All of these groups and individuals, most of them academically brilliant, also saw it as their task to participate in the debate in the public sphere. Such participation is certainly one of the things possible to study systematically. It probably even lends itself to quantification, without my in any sense claiming quantifiable and systematic studies to be identical.

In the short run, Skirbekk was not quite mistaken in heralding the age of philosophers and especially social scientists. In the 1960s and 1970s, characterized as the golden age of Norwegian social research, sociologists and neighbouring disciplines played a vital role in researching, building and publicly discussing the conditions of a burgeoning welfare state. In the longer run, however, social scientists became more a part of a circular system within the governmental administration itself, and much less a group of public intellectuals commenting on public affairs from an independent angle.[32]

---

[29] F. Thue, *In Quest of a Democratic Social Order. The Americanization of Norwegian Social Scholarship*, (Oslo 2006).
[30] Skirbekk, 'Forord'.
[31] J. W. Løvhaug, *Politikk som idékamp: et intellektuelt gruppeportrett av Minerva-kretsen 1957–1972* (Oslo 2007).
[32] 'Samfunnsforskning som intellektuell pappsløyd'. Interview with Ottar Brox and Fredrik Thue, *Forskerforum* 2, 2003. See also Kalleberg's article in this volume.

Complaints about the increasing tabloidization of journalism induced the liberal daily newspaper *Dagbladet* to launch in 2002 an increased emphasis on informed public debate on its pages. A review of the attempt half a year later found that academically educated people dominated the scene. Quite a few, however, were experts representing institutions involved in debates, such as the school system or child welfare (41 per cent of all contributions). Among the formally independent contributors quite a few (36 per cent) had special interests (*særinteresser*) to care for and were therefore not independent after all. Many writers were academics, but the reviewer concluded that *Dagbladet* – once the favourite organ of academic intellectuals – lacked the necessary network in academe.[33]

Although university academics are still visible, other academics (or semi-academics) have come to offer considerable competition in the public sphere. A relatively new group of educated people in the broader cultural bureaucratic sphere between the universities and the editorial boards has grown considerably, and consists of publishers, research bureaucrats, journalists, commissioned researchers, leaders and employees of cultural organizations and the like. Their interception in the public discourse is sometimes, but not always, coloured by their institutional affiliation.[34]

Academics tend to move between societal spheres and institutions so their roles change as well as their freedom (and ability) to act as public intellectuals. Different institutions expect different work – and different kinds of loyalty – from their employees. The advantage of university academics, who are state employees in Norway, is a considerable degree of freedom to speak freely in the public sphere, notwithstanding contemporary attempts from the government to channel research into largely utilitarian programmes.

---

[33] H. F. Tretvoll, 'Debattdrømmen brast', *Dagbladet* 9 May 2003; H. F. Tretvoll, 'Drømmen om den gode Dagblad-debatten', *Samtiden* 2, 2003.
[34] Ø. Østerud, 'Maktutredningen og det intellektuelle hegemoniet', *Nytt Norsk Tidsskrift* 2, 2002, pp. 23–25.

Types of academic intellectuals

Academics in the public sphere appear in many guises. *Dagbladet* in 2005 characterized their top ten intellectuals with terms like 'popular intellectual' (Unni Wikan), 'hyper-academic intellectual' (Cathrine Holst), 'intellectual badger' (Espen Søbye), 'provocative intellectual' (Tor Erling Staff), 'playful intellectual' (Nina Witoszek), 'saber-rattling intellectual in favour of a civilized war' (Rune Slagstad). Others see it as their task to drag readers out of their smug complacency (Thomas Hylland Eriksen). The only one of the ten who did not have the highest academic education was an editor of a small left-wing newspaper (Bjørgulf Braanen). This is particularly interesting in the light of a recent large report (book series) commissioned by parliament about the distribution of power in Norway.[35] In one of the books, the power elite was divided into ten sectors or spheres. The only two spheres not dominated by academically educated people were the trade unions and the press. Whereas 53 per cent of the whole Norwegian elite had five years or more university education, the corresponding figure for the media was only 15 per cent.[36]

Of the remaining nine no less than five were university professors. Interestingly, at least three of those may be considered outsiders in terms of their trajectories into academe. Wikan had hardly any academic qualifications to her name before her gaining her doctorate. Slagstad has worked in politics and the media and still divides his time between universities and public arenas. Scholarly speaking, he blends philosophy, history, law and sociology. Witoszek is a scholar of culture with a multi-cultural background and also writes fiction.

How do academics enter into the public sphere? They often participate as 'experts', a role normally thought to imply a certain objectivity and therefore truthfulness. Many experts called upon in the media deal with science or technology, like

---

[35] *Maktutredningen*, led by professor Øyvind Østerud.
[36] T. Gulbrandsen et al, *Norske makteliter* (Oslo 2002), p. 54. The sectors were, with the share in per cent of members with five or more years higher education in brackets: church (94), research and higher education (89), police and justice (88), defence (86), central administration (73), business (42), organizations (38), culture (34), politics (21) and media (15). The Norwegian power elite, as defined by *Maktutredningen*, consisted of 1725 people.

medicine or aviation. As such they are hardly intellectuals. However, it is becoming increasingly common for experts, often incited by journalists, to step a little further or beyond their expertise. The medical professor comments on budgets, health politics, ethics and the social repercussions. But the field of medicine has links to yet other fields: abortion, for example, leads to questions of gender, of family problems and religious issues. At one point, a medical doctor may bring the whole field of medicine into the public sphere and become an intellectual with things to say on a number of societal issues. Norwegian examples that spring to mind include Per Fugelli in medicine, Bernt Hagtvet in political science and, perhaps, Dag O. Hessen in biology. The 'provocative' intellectual Staff is a lawyer whose agenda is mainly legal, but this often takes him into a number of moral questions.

Jean-Paul Sartre famously defined an intellectual as someone who interfered with something that was none of his concern. Nonetheless, an intellectual was qualified because he was considered wise and knowledgeable. In a society in which higher education is widespread, public sages are most likely academics of some sort. The conservative students I referred to above wanted to spread their ideas of 'pre-politics' to a wider public, and succeeded moderately in the 1950s when the media was less developed. Decades later the media often prefer to present what someone has labelled 'hired brains'. The historian David Cannadine is a British example, the social anthropologist Thomas Hylland Eriksen a Norwegian equivalent. These two experts obviously cross into the domain of intellectuals. This means, normally, that they make statements about nearly everything, far beyond their area of speciality.

When an academic in this way acts as a *uomo universale*, a universal man, he becomes vulnerable to critique, the reason being of course that he stretches beyond his field of competence. The normal academic-as-intellectual, therefore, is an expert who generalizes within his own field, enough for his statements to be of common interest, but not so far as to make him a dilettante. I would say that most academics who are intellectuals are of this variety. Where exactly the limits of expertise go, is of course impossible to tell. This will always be contested and varies between individuals. At the other end of the scale, however, it is safe to say that most Norwegian academics speaking in public appear only as experts and do not play a role as intellectuals.

Through which channels do academics write and speak publicly? Strictly professional academic publications are not relevant here, although some might occasionally cause a wider stir, for example when an author takes his material from the academic book or journal to a publication with a wider audience, or when a journalist makes a discovery in academe. The channels are mainly of three kinds: broadcasting; newspapers, magazines and journals; and the Internet. The state television NRK (three channels) and the privately owned TV2 regularly make use of academics as commentators or in debates, without letting the academic aspects ever get the upper hand. The leeway here is somewhat greater on NRK radio, although the media logic works totally different here nowadays in the radio-as-microphone example above. It is telling that our provocative intellectual, the lawyer Staff, is the one most frequently to be seen on the screen.

Norwegian daily newspapers are a blend of the tabloid and the serious, possibly due to the fact that the country is small. This means there is some room – sometimes very little and never very much – for informed debate in which academics, either within or outside of academe, regularly participate. The badgering intellectual Søbye is a regular reviewer for *Dagbladet*. Smaller weekly papers have in past decades become important arenas for informed debate, *Morgenbladet*, *Klassekampen* and *Dag og Tid* being the most important. There are relatively few journals writing about politics, education and culture, but they sometimes set important agendas: *Nytt Norsk Tidsskrift* is quite scholarly (not without reason is Holst one of the editors), *Samtiden* and *Dag og Tid* a bit more accessible. The number of purely political journals has been reduced since the radical seventies.

If many academics are reluctant to act as more than experts – that is as intellectuals – it is also because they are afraid to lose their foothold in objective knowledge, although that word is no longer that much used. Their objectivity, however, was also grounded in a position of impartiality. Looking at nineteenth-century Norway, the civil servants, more or less identical to academics, people with higher education, long claimed a special position in politics and therefore in the public sphere. Their argument for this was that they stood outside of, or were aloof from, interests, i.e. material interests. They could thus not be suspected of defending their own interests in the way merchants, artisans, industrialists or farmers did. They were the only ones capable of seeing things independently, and thus had the general well-being of the people in mind. Their superior education, of course, was considered an additional advantage.

What is the relation of university academics to intellectual independence in contemporary society? An initial reaction would be to claim that university academics are relatively free to speak their mind. This independence, or freedom if you like, has of course varied between countries and periods, although it is fairly obvious that the position of university academics in Norway (and in Britain too) has been among the freest in the twentieth century. So what is stopping many professors and others from becoming intellectuals?

Academic to intellectual – a step unnecessary, unwanted, difficult?

Quite a few academics, within or outside of the universities, find many reasons to shy away from the public sphere, or at least some of it. But academic minds are in no way totally absent: academics are very well represented in the media, particularly in the press, even in the semi-tabloid newspapers. What is it about academic education or the culture in academe which furthers or obstructs participation in the public sphere? The four themes of rationality, professionalization, media and elitism, all interconnected topics, seem relevant here.

Although reason is a faculty cherished by most quarters in most circumstances, academics normally claim expertise in the use of reason. To be rational, and to be allowed to be rational, is especially important to scientists and other scholars. Some think that participating in the public sphere means compromising one's rationality (or related concepts like complexity or professionality) because of the need to popularize their scholarship.

From the point of view of the people governing the public sphere, like editors, there is an ambiguity to science and scientists (scholars). On the one hand, science represents positive values like truth, reason and openness, scientific knowledge is in principle open to all. On the other hand, science is also associated with technocracy (dehumanizing) and the rule of experts (closure). Technocrats tend to talk to each other. In the context of a public sphere, these are quite negative associations.[37]

Professionalization is a many-faceted process. It is, among other things, an academic process. Professionals are academically educated people – expert labour – trying to control their profession in various ways. This means that they do not always speak on behalf of the 'truth', but also have their own professional axes to grind. The step from a professional to an intellectual is therefore in some ways a large one. Being in a union – a profession is also a union – is unthinkable for the intellectual *qua* intellectual. University scholars have weaker unions and are sociologically speaking far less professional than archtypical professionals like medical doctors. This is due to the academic ideal of searching for truth in an environment where disagreement is cultivated. In principle, this means that university academics are more at liberty, and are encouraged, to speak freely. This idealized picture, however, is slowly changing and there are two telling symptoms: researchers' unions have become more widespread and important than before; traditional academic freedom is regarded by many as under siege (why else would they appoint a commission to look into the matter?).[38]

Professionalization in a slightly different meaning, the attitude towards science or scholarship, has also proven to be an inhibiting factor. With the increasing specialization of knowledge, considerations of disciplinary boundaries are present, and there is the social norm of not stretching your knowledge too far for fear of reactions from colleagues. These

---

[37] 'Bill. Merk: "Ekspert"', *Forskerforum*, 7, 2007, pp. 19–21.
[38] *NOU 2006: 19. Akademisk frihet. Individuelle rettigheter og institusjonelle styringsbehov*. Sometimes referred to as 'Underdal-utvalget' (the Underdal Commission) after its chairman.

are restrictions far from the ideals of how a public intellectual behaves.

In addition comes the fact that work routines and the increasing governmental control of the universities do not leave much time for exposing oneself in the public sphere. One may thus speak of a *bureaucratization* as well as a professionalization. So, even though dissemination of knowledge is formally one of the duties of Norwegian professors and lecturers, they restrict themselves to being at most occasional intellectuals (if that is possible) or full time experts, with lots of them being virtually invisible.

In some quarters, the archetypical academic – within or outside of the universities – is an expert in a rather narrow field, though not all professionals or scholars regard themselves or their fields in this way; in some areas, writing syntheses or mastering wide areas of knowledge is certainly valued. This applies perhaps mostly to some social sciences or humanities, like history, but also to parts of the sciences. In the 1960s 'general medicine' (*allmennmedisin*, the general practitioner's encounter with the patient) was made an academic medical specialization. Some scholars are highly regarded for crossing even the boundaries between the two cultures of natural science and the humanities/social sciences.

The biologist Dag O. Hessen (one of the few science writers) and the social anthropologist Thomas Hylland Eriksen are an example of this: individually and together, they have explored basic questions of nature, human nature and humanity in a wide and accessible context. Nonetheless, I think very few academics nowadays would consider themselves universal in outlook or actually act as an *uomo universale*. That role, a classical role of an intellectual, seems, at least historically, to belong to writers, journalists or perhaps some academics of the past. We have already considered some academic reasons for this condition. The change in the public sphere, or to be specific, the media, provide us with another explanation.

I will not dwell long on the changes in the media situation and the increasing preference for elements such as pictures over words, entertainment over serious matters, short sentences over long ones. In Norway, this development gained pace in the 70s and 80s, as newspapers became independent of political parties or ideological matters (instead becoming dependent on commercial factors), and other media were opened up to competition. There is an interesting new logic here: when the press voiced the viewpoints of the various political parties, scholars and other academics might be called upon to support their standpoints. With the professional norms of journalism the press acted on behalf of the people, and saw it as their main role to criticize elites, often including educational ones.[39] The fact that so few journalists had the highest university education contributed to this.

With this new situation in the public sphere, the traditional role and norms of academic behaviour have several kinds of problems. The first is the one mentioned above, the new media situation providing little space for democratic deliberation, and much more space for the superficial and the irrational, the antithesis of academic pursuit. The academic group of scholars growing and flourishing in this situation, of course, are the ones in the departments of media and communication.

Another problem is connected to the *rules* of deliberation in the public sphere, seen through what one may call the *modern* paradigm. I am not thinking especially of the rules of the Enlightenment's public sphere: anybody can participate, no topic is above discussion, it is the quality of the arguments that counts.[40] Rather I am thinking of a number of 'perversions of the public debate' (Ottar Brox's phrase), which at least in part owe their existence to the structure of the modern media.[41] According to Brox, debates increasingly assume the form of *court trials*, where disagreement is overemphasized while doxic agreement disappears. Viewpoints are lumped together in bundles, even when they do not belong together. There is the problem of conceptual coercion; misleading but unavoidable concepts are introduced. A reliance on *aesthetically* satisfying models of society is easy to discern; *self-presentation* often overshadows factual presentation. The

---

[39] Gulbrandsen et al, *Norske makteliter*, p. 17.
[40] For example as presented by J. van Horn Melton, *The Rise of the Public in Enlightenment Europe* (Cambridge 2001).
[41] O. Brox, *Vår kollektive dårskap. Hvordan perverteres den norske offentlige samtalen?* (Oslo 2003).

overemphasis on individual actors (celebrities or not) and their intentions leads to the overlooking of *unintentional* consequences and other structural factors.

A final point to be made concerning the participation of academics in the public sphere, as intellectuals, is the possible mutual distrust between the educated and the non-educated echelons of society. Considered broadly, this phenomenon has quite a few other names as well and goes in both directions. One speaks about the fear of the masses, snobbism, the contempt for the masses, the rise of the meritocracy, populism, high-brow versus low-brow.[42] In Norway this phenomenon has been surprisingly little studied, although the field seems to be drawing more interest.[43] This recent interest seems to spring from the success of right-wing populist politics over the last couple of decades, which seems to be gaining strength from a sceptical attitude towards authorities of various kinds, particularly in culture and science. A hallmark of Norwegian right-wing populism is targeting cultural and educational elites rather than economic ones.

Antagonisms between high and low, between people in power and people outside of power are certainly nothing new in the last 200 years of Norwegian history. However, the rural countercultures largely sought power by launching an alternative liberal education and by trying to conquer academe from within. From the 1960s, when academic education became within reach of large segments of the population, a certain reconciliation between the academic world and the large popular movements dating from the nineteenth century took place.[44] This included the labour movement, which never

---

[42] See for example J Ortega y Gasset, *The Revolt of the Masses* (N. Y. 1930); J. Carey, *The Intellectuals and the Masses* (London 1992); P. Sloterdijk, *Masseforakt – kampen mellom høy og lav kultur i moderne samfunn* (Oslo 2005); M. Young, *The rise of the meritocracy 1870–2033: an essay on education and equality* (London 1958); Lasch, *The Revolt of the Elites*; Collini, *Absent Minds*.

[43] O. Krange/K. Skogen, 'Kodebok for den intellektuelle middelklassen', *Nytt Norsk Tidsskrift*, 3, 2007; Skarpenes, 'Den "legitime kulturens" moralske forankring'; T. Bjørklund, 'Fremskrittpartiets suksess og kulturell standardisering', *Nytt Norsk Tidsskrift*, 2, 2007; M. Marsdal, *Frp-koden. Hemmeligheten bak Fremskrittpartiets suksess* (Oslo 2007); H. Nilsen & Chr. Anton Smedshaug (eds), *Folkepartiet?* (Oslo 2007).

[44] Skirbekk 2006 (2007)

wanted to become academic in itself, but which always, like the countercultures, respected science (above all) and other forms of scholarship (with reservations). Although there are certainly sceptical attitudes towards academe from these old quarters, the most visible opposition comes from elsewhere, and is largely conveyed by the media.

It is possible to discern at least three different ways of distrusting academics. And in describing these three, suggestions for explanations follow almost automatically. The first phenomenon is a mistrust of and resistance to many kind of rules and regulations in the modern (welfare) society, from traffic rules, via detailed rules on how to treat animals domestic or wild, to laws or mere suggestions concerning smoking and what to eat and drink. Even locally, maintaining such rules and norms is associated with academics, who in many quarters come to be despised.

Secondly, academics tend not to look upon money as a sign of success and accomplishment. When a university scholar of literature reviewed a best-selling novel unfavourably, it caused a great stir of protest from the author herself and other best-selling writers. More commotion took place when it became known that another best-selling novelist had been refused membership of the Norwegian Authors' Union on grounds of quality. This was portrayed as an insult to her (presumably) rather common readers.[45] Both are classic cases of resistance to the educated classes deciding cultural taste. More importantly, perhaps, the examples are signs of an increased trust in, and reliance upon, the market as the ultimate arbiter. An ironic American saying is directed towards the bookish: 'If you're so smart, why ain't you rich?' The admiring Norwegian contemporary saying might be: 'If you're so rich, you must be smart!'

The third type of distrust is a more outspoken negative attitude to the authority of science. Alternative medicine and other versions of a 'new age' mentality have become commonplace. So has disappointment with scientific results and scientific achievement, and, with it, the scientists themselves. Is

---

[45] The cases: Anne B. Ragde review by K. I. Skjerdingstad. Debate in *Dagbladet* August–September 2007. Membership: Frid Ingulstad in *Den norske forfatterforening*. Several national newspapers 2007.

it a paradox that a vastly more educated population is seemingly so sceptical of science? One explanation might be that people have learned enough to expect a lot, but not enough to know the limits of science. In any case, the expectation revolution in affluent societies, larded constantly by the media, is an obvious candidate for an explanation. Some claim that secularization has turned to desecularization, making more people turn away from science.

Much of the mistrust of academics from groups with little education stems from the suspicion than academics take a condescending attitude towards them. There has been but scanty systematic research into this, although there is certainly evidence of both condescension and respect. Educating the whole population has doubtless been a major project of the educated classes for the last two centuries. Two studies of the present situation reveal a position of respect from the educated middle classes towards others, and they rarely pass cultural judgements.[46] The popular, in the literal meaning of the word, has a strong position in contemporary Norway. This runs contrary to what the media tells us and what the populist politicians claim. The real issue, it seems, revolves around the judgement of taste. Cultural issues, like taste or religion, demand less from participants in the public sphere. The role of academics as intellectuals in this situation is an important research task.

---

[46] Skarpenes, 'Den "legitime kulturens" moralske forankring; C. Myrvang, 'Forakten for det middelmådige', *Samtiden*, 3, 2007.

Contributors

Martin Eide

is Professor at the Department of Information Science and Media Studies at the University of Bergen. He has worked in the fields of political communication, the sociology of news and the history of journalism and the media. At the moment, Eide is one of the editors of a national project about the history of the press. Among his publications are *Blod, sverte og gledestårer. VG 1945–1995* (Blood, Print and Tears of Joy). The Newspaper *VG 1945–1995*, Oslo 1995), *Medievalgkamp* (Media Election Campaign, Oslo 1991), *Nyhetens interesse. Nyhetsjournalistikk mellom tekst og kontekst* (News Interest. News Journalism between Text and Context, Oslo 1992/1995), *Den redigerende makt. Redaktørrollens norske historie* (The Power of Editing. The Norwegian History of the Editorial Role, Oslo 2000). His latest book, *Saklighetens Lidenskap* (The Passion of Impartiality, Oslo 2006), is a socio-historical biography of a press strategist and newspaper editor.

Brian Harrison

is Emeritus Professor of Modern British History at the University of Oxford. His books on nineteenth- and twentieth-century British social and political history include *Drink and the Victorians* (1971, 2nd ed. 1994) and *The Transformation of British Politics, 1860–1995* (1996). He edited the final (8th) volume of *The History of the University of Oxford* (1994) and *The Oxford Dictionary of National Biography* from 2000 till 2004. *Seeking a Role*, the first of his two volumes contributed to *The New Oxford History of England*, and covering the years 1951–1970, will appear in 2009.

Ben Jackson

is University Lecturer and Tutorial Fellow in Modern History at University College, Oxford. He works on modern British history, and is particularly interested in political thought, labour history and the history of social policy. He is the author of *Equality and the British Left* (2007) and is currently working on the intellectual history of neo-liberalism.

Ragnvald Kalleberg

is Professor of Sociology at the Department of Sociology and Human Geography at the University of Oslo. He has worked mainly in three broad areas: 1) the sociology of science, focusing on the history of sociology and social science, academics as public intellectuals, research ethics and research politics); 2) the sociology of organizations, focusing on universities as knowledge organizations, and on business enterprises (management and power, democratization); and 3) general social theory (the philosophy of social science, theory of modernity). He recently chaired the Norwegian National Committee for Research Ethics in the Social and Cultural Sciences (NESH) for two periods, and here influenced the development of national guidelines for academics as public intellectuals.

Jan Eivind Myhre

has been Professor of Modern History at the University of Oslo since 1996. He was formerly Professor of History at the Norwegian University of Science and Technology and part-time Professor at the University of Tromsø. He has been a visiting professor at Oxford, Cambridge, Berlin, Osnabrück and Leicester. Myhre's main interests comprise social history (migration, urbanization, classes, professions, childhood) and historiography. He is currently working on a social history of higher education as a part of the history of the University of Oslo. His latest books are *Norsk byhistorie. Urbanisering gjennom 1300 år* (Norwegian Urbanization, Oslo 2006, co-author); *The Scandinavian Middle Classes 1840–1940* (Oslo 2004, co-author); *Norsk innvandringshistorie II 1814–1940* (Norwegian immigration, Oslo 2003, co-author); *Nordic Historiography in the 20th Century* (Oslo 2000, co-author).

Glen O'Hara

is a Senior Lecturer in Modern History at Oxford Brookes University. He took his PhD at University College London in 2002 under the supervision of Professor Kathleen Burk, UCL's Professor of Modern History. He took up his current post at Oxford Brookes in January 2005, having previously taught at the University of Bristol and the University of Oxford. Dr O'Hara is primarily interested in British central governments' economic and social policies since 1918, focusing especially on the post-Second World War era. He has recently published *From Dreams to Disillusionment: Economic and Social Planning in 1960s Britain* (Basingstoke, 2007). In 2006 he co-edited a volume of essays about the Labour governments of that period, *The Modernisation of Britain? Harold Wilson and the Labour Governments of 1964–1970* (London, 2006). He is currently writing a history of British views of the sea since 1600, and a volume concerning the history of complexity and decision-making in British government since 1945.